D1267089

Y OF WINNIPEG
BRARY
ortage Avenue
Manitoba R3B 2E9

Central British Columbia : the Fraser Valley

F
1087
.W65

RAVENS
AND PROPHETS

An Account of Journeys in British Columbia,
Alberta and Southern Alaska

by

GEORGE WOODCOCK

LONDON
ALLAN WINGATE
12 *Beauchamp Place, S.W.*3

First published 1952

Made and printed in Great Britain by
William Clowes and Sons, Limited, London and Beccles

CONTENTS

DEDICATION

*To Audrey and David, the companions
on our first journey*

ACKNOWLEDGMENTS

*It would be impossible to thank in detail all the people whose
help, hospitality and friendship were given so freely to us during
our travels in Western Canada, but I should like particularly
to express our gratitude to Mr. Towill of the Canadian
National Railways and Mr. Magor of the Canadian Pacific
Railway, for their assistance in our travelling arrangements,
to Mr. Ross McLean of the Canadian Broadcasting Corporation for his consistent encouragement of our plans and to Dr.
Willard E. Ireland, the Provincial Archivist of British
Columbia, for the very considerable help which he gave us in
tracing points of historical background. I would also express
my thanks to Mr. Towill, Dr. Ireland and the British
Columbia Travel Bureau for the photographs which they have
provided to illustrate this book.*

Map designs by A. L. Savory.

LIST OF
ILLUSTRATIONS AND THEIR SOURCES

Illustrations and their Sources

Introduction

THE aim of this introduction is to summarise briefly, and for the benefit of those who are unfamiliar with it, the history of the area covered by the travels which form the subject of this book. Of necessity, certain facts mentioned in the later chapters also appear here, but I have chosen to retain them, even at the risk of repetition, so that this background picture shall be as complete as I can make it within a relatively brief compass.

Drake, sailing northward from Mexico in 1578, was the first European voyager to catch sight of the misty coastline of what is now British Columbia, and to proclaim the sovereignty of the Virgin Queen over all this vast forested land north of the Spanish possessions. He christened it New Albion. However, he did not touch land any farther north than the present site of San Francisco, and for another two centuries the Indian tribes west of the Rockies and north of California went their own way without ever becoming aware of the existence of the white men who were slowly spreading over the continent from the east and south.

Over this great country—British Columbia is rather larger than the combined area of the British Isles, France and the Benelux countries—was scattered a native population which, at its height, probably numbered little more than a hundred thousand. Yet what the tribes lacked in numbers they made up in cultural diversity, and there were no less than eight different linguistic groups—each as distinct from the other as Greek from Hebrew—and within these groups again there were separate tongues—often spoken only by a few hundred people—as distinct as, say, Spanish and French. Indeed, the variations are so numerous that now, when some of the small bands have died out, it is difficult to estimate just how many tribes existed when the white explorers first appeared. But there was less social than linguistic diversity, and this fact enables one to divide the aboriginal inhabitants into three roughly distinct groups.

In the mountain valleys of the south-east lived the Kootenays, a small prairie tribe who had infiltrated across the Rockies but who retained most of the habits and the relatively egalitarian social

structure of the plains Indians. The plateaus and inland valleys of
the north and centre were for the most part peopled by hunting
and food-gathering bands of the Interior Salish and Athapaskan
groups; some of the latter, like the Sekani and the Carriers, lived
an extremely primitive nomadic existence. But it was on the long,
jagged coastline, among the large islands and up the valleys of the
northern rivers, the Nass and the Skeena, that there flourished the
most highly developed and distinctive native culture north of
Mexico.

The peoples who constituted the Coast Indian culture belonged
to no less than six distinct language groups—Tlinkit, Tsimshian,
Haida, Kwakiutl, Nootka and Coast Salish—but their economic
and cultural life and their social and political organisation displayed a surprising degree of homogeneity, changing its form
according to geographical rather than linguistic patterns, so that
the isolated Salish of Bella Coola were less close in their habits to
the Salish of the Fraser Valley than to their Kwakiutl neighbours
of Bella Bella. The Coast Indian culture, indeed, although it never
passed from the hunting, fishing and food-gathering into the agricultural stage, was endowed with a superabundance of goods
rarely encountered among primitive peoples. The rivers and the
sheltered salt waters teemed with salmon, seal, oolachan (candle
fish) and halibut, the damp forests were full of berries, fungi and
other wild foods, and of gigantic cedars, well adapted to splitting
and carving with primitive tools. This natural bounty not only
saved the Coast Indians from the famines which are the periodic
scourges of most non-agricultural peoples, but also gave them the
means and the leisure to develop a highly complicated social
structure, based on clan, caste and secret society, to evolve elaborate ritualistic forms of dance and drama, song and oratory, and to
perfect a characteristic plastic art, reproducing in carved wooden
"totem" poles, masks and ritual implements, in woven blankets,
in paintings on house-fronts and canoes, and even in coloured
basketwork, their heraldic records, their animistic legends and
their mystical beliefs. It was a luxuriant culture whose very complexity made it ill adapted to withstand the impact of European
invasion.

From 1775 onwards the Spanish navigators began to sail along
the British Columbian coast, more out of curiosity than from any
immediate desire for annexation, since its wet, rocky and forested
shores must have appeared far less hospitable than their own

Mexican and South American possessions. Then, in 1778, Captain Cook landed on the west coast of what is now Vancouver Island and established contact with the Nootka, a proud tribe who, alone among the North American Indians, went out in tiny canoes to hunt and kill the sperm whale. Cook returned with tales of the wealth in furs to be obtained in this unsettled land, and very shortly afterwards the Island was visited by a number of English and American traders, one of whom, Captain John Meares, established in 1788 a temporary trading post at Nootka, the first point of European settlement.

By this time the Spaniards had begun to look interestedly at the potential wealth of the new land, and a series of disputes developed between them and the British captains, which resulted in the Spaniards seizing the post and ships at Nootka and establishing their own fort. The common interest of the two governments against Revolutionary France doubtless induced them to act in moderation, and in 1790 the Spaniards agreed to withdraw. The traces of their presence are still left in many of the coastal place-names—Cortes and Quadra, Texada and Galiano Islands, Malaspina Inlet and Juan de Fuca Strait.

The British now laid official claim to the coast, and George Vancouver began the systematic exploration of its labyrinths of islands, inlets and channels. But there was still more than one rival claimant: as early as 1741, Vitus Bering had annexed Alaska for the Russians, who later demanded the whole coastline down to the 51st parallel. The British disputed this and an agreement was eventually reached defining the line of 54' 40° as the southern end of the Russian littoral, the "panhandle" of modern Alaska.

Finally, the British title was challenged from the south. In the early years of the nineteenth century much of present-day Oregon was in the virtual possession of the Hudson's Bay Company, who had bought the trading rights from the American fur baron, John Jacob Astor, and it was therefore tacitly regarded as British territory. But with the opening of the Oregon Trail this country began to be populated by American settlers, and a series of wrangles over administration led to the claiming of the territory by the United States. The "Oregon Boundary Question" was puffed into a major international crisis by the bellicose demagogy of President Polk, who, not content with Oregon, demanded the whole area west of the Rocky Mountains and as far north as the Russian territory of Alaska, under the slogan of "Fifty-Four Forty or Fight".

Somewhat bathetically he accepted a settlement on the 49th parallel, and in 1846 the British occupation of the British Columbian coast, within its present boundaries, was finally established.

Already the hinterland had been penetrated by the representatives of the fur trading interests. In 1793 Alexander Mackenzie of the Northwest Trading Company performed the first overland journey of exploration through the Rockies and across the centre of British Columbia, passing by the present site of Prince George, descending the Fraser and then crossing the Chilcotin country to reach the coast at Bella Coola. Other major explorations were carried out by Simon Fraser and David Thompson, both, like Mackenzie, officials of the Northwest Trading Company, and in 1805 Fraser established a trading post at Fort McLeod. It was this fur-rich northern area which was first dominated by Europeans—mostly French-Canadian *voyageurs*—and the oldest existing towns and villages in the province are those—like Prince George, Fort Fraser and Fort St. James—which were established by the traders before or round about 1810.

In 1821 the long war, often waged with violence and bloodshed, between the Hudson's Bay Company and the Northwest Trading Company came to an end with the latter's absorption, and for the next thirty years the fur monopoly became the dominant economic and political power. In 1843 the Hudson's Bay Company established its western depot at Victoria, which was developed as a seaport and became the first town in British Columbia. The rule of the Company was consolidated over Vancouver Island and the sections of the mainland where the trade routes ran; its officials were so powerful and so intolerant of outside control that when, in 1849, Vancouver Island was made a Crown colony and Governor Blanshard was sent out from England to administer it, he was rendered powerless by the refusal of the Company, which controlled the whole economy and transport of the area, to give him any co-operation. In 1851 he went home, and the Colonial Office conferred the governorship on the Hudson's Bay Company's chief factor, James Douglas, who ruled the Island and later the mainland as well, as a political and economic dictator.

The domination of the Hudson's Bay Company finally ended with the discovery of gold on the Fraser River in 1858. By this time the Californian mines of the '49 rush had been very largely worked out, and no sooner had the news of the Fraser strike reached San Francisco than nearly 15,000 prospectors swarmed up the coast into British Columbia, to be followed shortly afterwards by other contingents coming by boat from England and Australia and by difficult overland routes from Ontario and the eastern United States. In 1861 the even richer Cariboo goldfield was discovered in the central plateau, and the results of placer mining were so high as to overshadow completely those of California and to start a second stampede which attracted men from every part of the old world. In the ensuing years the prospectors spread far into the unexplored areas, to the Kootenays in 1863, to the Big Bend of the Columbia River in 1865, north to the Finlay River in 1867. But none of their discoveries was ever so profitable as the Cariboo, and these outlying areas were for the most part abandoned after the miners had obtained all the gold they could find by their relatively primitive placer methods.

In order to reach the Cariboo the first road in British Columbia was built through the Fraser Canyon. Victoria grew into a city and towns sprang up on the mainland—New Westminster, Yale and Barkerville. Independent traders came to serve the miners, banks were opened to deal with their gold, and capitalist enterprises soon developed when the surface deposits were worked out and expensive methods were needed to reach the deeper lodes.

Furthermore, agriculture, fishing and lumbering now became actual industries to satisfy the demand of the gold towns. Though land had been cultivated as early as 1811 by a fur trader at Fort St. James in the far north, it was not until 1849 that the first independent farmer, a certain Captain Grant, settled at Sooke on Vancouver Island. Agriculture began to grow in earnest at the end of the 1850's, when settlers started to farm in the Fraser Valley, but cattle raising was predominant in these early days, ranches being established in the Cariboo and the Okanagan.

Salmon was now caught commercially for sale to the miners, and in 1870, after much experimentation, the first cannery was established on the Fraser. At the same time systematic logging began and sawmills were built to deal with the demand for timber in the new towns and the mines. Both fishery and lumber products soon found an additional market abroad, and by the end of the 1860's an export trade was well established.

Thus, within a decade, the discovery of gold had replaced a loosely-knit fur empire by an industrious European society which, though still thinly scattered, was rapidly crushing the Indian culture out of existence. It was a minor social revolution which demanded its appropriate political changes. The new inhabitants of the colony had no intention of remaining under the tutelage of the Hudson's Bay factors, and after the mainland had been formed into a separate colony in 1858, it was united with Vancouver Island in 1866 and a British Columbian Legislature with limited powers and suffrage was formed. The agitation for full parliamentary rights continued. At about the same time the colonies of Eastern Canada had accomplished their confederation, and eventually, after a great deal of acrimonious dispute between the pro-Canadians, the pro-Americans, and those who wished to remain separate, British Columbia entered the Dominion in 1871.

One of the conditions for accepting Confederation was that the Dominion should finance a railway to link the Pacific coast with the rest of the country. After years of delay the Canadian Pacific route was completed in 1885, and its opening changed what was still predominantly a mining colony into a province in which farming, logging and fishing, with a new outlet to the prairies and the east, grew quickly into major industries. At the same time the rich copper, lead and zinc mines of the Kootenays were discovered in the last great mining rush of the 1890's. An urban pattern of life developed rapidly in the south; the number of incorporated cities increased from four in 1890 to thirteen in 1900, while Vancouver, which was not founded until 1886, soon became the third city in Canada and a major Pacific coast port.

New settlers arrived in large numbers over the railways; while in 1881 the non-Indian population was little more than 20,000, by 1891, only six years after the completion of the main Canadian Pacific line, it had risen to 70,000. Today it is more than 1,100,000.

The majority of these settlers were English and Scots, who soon outnumbered by many times the descendants of the early French *voyageurs*. But other nationalities were substantially represented, and often they settled thickly in particular districts. The Swedes, for instance, were inclined to remain in the logging areas, the Italians concentrated most thickly in the smelting town of Trail, the Russian Doukhobors kept to the farming valleys of the Kootenays, the recently arrived German-speaking Mennonites have mostly settled in the Fraser Valley, the Chinese and the Sikhs have tended to gather in and around Victoria and Vancouver (as did the Japanese until their dispersal during the 1939–45 war), while there have been such smaller national concentrations as a Danish colony on the northern tip of Vancouver Island, a

"Cariboo" Cameron (seated), and a Fellow-miner of the 'sixties

Sir James Douglas, Hudson's Bay Factor and first Governor of British Columbia

William Duncan, the founder of Metlakatla

Judge Begbie

Typical Mountain and Forest Scenery of Northern British Columbia, near Hazelton

Norwegian village on the Bella Coola River, a Finnish Utopian community on Malcolm Island and a Swiss settlement in the foothills of the Rockies. The Indians have sunk to a very minor proportion of the population, but, reaching their lowest point at the turn of the century, they are now growing in numbers and represent perhaps 3 per cent. of British Columbians today.

Most of the development during the first half of the present century has been in the southern part of British Columbia, where the climate is warmer and better adapted for the great fruit-growing industry and where the mineral and timber resources are more accessible. Until the last war very little had been done to open up the northern two-thirds of the province, and though the situation has changed a great deal in the past five years, this immense region still retains the character of a wilderness where men and their habitations are few and scattered and where the frontier age is yet uncompleted.

G. W.

San Francisco, 1951.

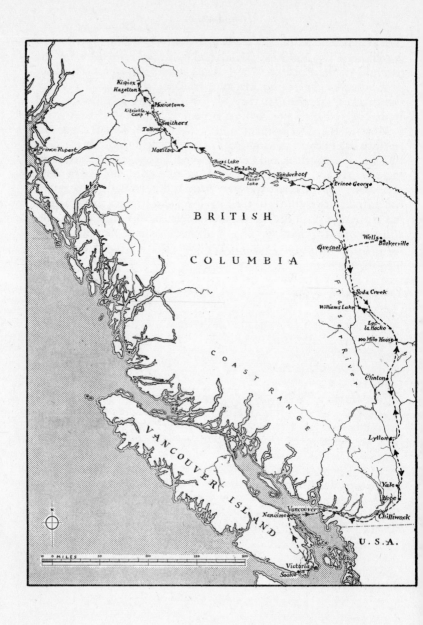

Part One

FOR two years my wife and I lived in a village on Vancouver Island. There was a blue-grey harbour curving in from the Pacific, strewn with wooded islands and looking in calm and sunny hours like an Italian lake, and in the hills behind it a forest of gigantic coastal firs and cedars stretched back into an unbroken inland jungle populated by deer and cougar and bear. Between sea and wilderness the village straggled its four miles of marginal settlement along the highroad, and pushed a tenuous line of farms and homesteads back towards the predatory and ever-returning woodland.

Here I will not attempt to describe Sooke (for this is the village's name) or its people, or our own life among them, since the experiences of such a tethered life, curious though they may sometimes be, do not sort well with the fluid impressions which one records in a book of travel. I merely locate our village as the point of departure for the journeys which form the real subject of this book.

Nevertheless, it is at least necessary to remark that the mounting sense of mental isolation which we both experienced during two years in such a settlement were in a great part responsible for the very existence of this book. Ever since our arrival on Vancouver Island we had looked with almost avaricious eyes upon the map of the mainland of British Columbia, with its incredibly serrated and fjord-bitten coastline, its chains of mountains repeating each other time and again from the Rockies to the sea, its great rivers and multitudinous lakes, and its plateaus and valleys whose broken contours sheltered a variety of ways of human life which we were anxious to explore. Even the names on the map whetted our appetite, for who can fail to be curious about places like Iago and Van Winkle, Jasper and Brilliant, Whisky Creek and Brandywine Falls?

For a while circumstances (which again have no place here) prevented us from starting on the 7,000 miles of travel which our journeys eventually attained. Then the circle of frustration was broken. My publisher agreed to commission a book on British Columbia and to advance part of the costs, the Canadian Broadcasting Corporation asked for a series of travel broadcasts, railway companies offered to assist with transport, and at last, by the end of our second summer, we were ready to leave Sooke upon our travels.

We had anticipated starting in July, but by the time all our arrangements were completed it was already late September. Since we could therefore look forward to little more than a month of snowless weather in the interior of the mainland—and the same period of relatively rainless weather on the coast—we thought it best to strike first for the north and to travel over the more southerly areas after the winter had set in.

This decision was strengthened by coincidence, for while we were making our preparations we received a letter from two San Francisco friends who proposed to spend their vacation driving 1,800 miles to the north of British Columbia, to visit a group of Californians who had started a settlement in the mountains there. They invited us to share their car, and we accepted.

Our friends were due to arrive on the 2nd October. They appeared on the 3rd, late in the afternoon; we had already begun to think of striking up north on our own accord by whatever transport might offer itself, and we were relieved when their battered blue car, with its top piled high with camping equipment, climbed up the hill towards our house, and David and Audrey, stepping out a moment later, overwhelmed us in a flood of greetings in mingled Brooklyn and Bronx. David is a tall, dark, crinkly-haired Jew, with heavy features and dark, sad eyes, from the Brownsville district of Brooklyn, where gangsters and Chassidic enthusiasts were the oddly assorted heroes of his childhood. Audrey, a dumpy girl with finely cut features, is the daughter of an old Polish Jewish anarchist family; the beliefs of Kropotkin were bred in her from childhood. David is an untrained painter of considerable talent; Audrey has the ambition to become a teacher in a free school.

We held a discussion on our immediate plans, and agreed to leave at five o'clock the next morning, so that we could catch the early ferry from Nanaimo, half-way up the east coast of the Island. By this means we should reach Vancouver in time to get well out on the open road to the north by the afternoon. There was some difference of opinion on other aspects of the journey, for David

and Audrey thought that it would be possible to camp out by the
roadside, while Inge and I were doubtful of this, since the clouds
for the past two days had looked very much like a forewarning
that the dry season was coming to an end and the autumn rains
were about to begin. We finally agreed to prepare for every chance
and by the time our suitcases and typewriter, our bags of potatoes
and carrots, our odd cabbages and cauliflowers, had been added
to the existing sleeping bags, tent, stoves and rucksacks, every
inch of storage space in and about the car had been strained to its
furthest capacity.

In the morning, as we had half expected, it was raining with that
ominous persistence which announces the beginning of the wet
season on the coast. As we staggered out of doors into the pitch-
dark early morning, exhausted from scanty sleep and carrying our
remaining belongings over our arms, it seemed a singularly un-
propitious beginning for our journey. Already the sleeping bags
on top of the car were getting wet for lack of a tarpaulin, and we
had to drape the tent over them in such a way as to provide at
least some covering, while inside the car there was so much lug-
gage that we could hardly find room to sit with comfort.

The road was still dark as we started, and almost deserted. Our
way lay first of all along the main road towards Victoria—beside
the palely visible edge of the harbour, through the looming,
wooded rocks of the Sooke hills, along the straight causeway over
Dewdney Flats, where the dawn was just showing up the neat
beds of the Chinese farm. At Glen Lake, where the first outflung
suburb of Victoria begins to appear in clusters of grim little clap-
boarded houses and converted streetcars, we cut over to the Island
Highway, by-passing the city and turning up towards the Malahat.

Here the road rises high on a mountainside that falls almost
sheer for more than a thousand feet into Finlayson Inlet. On a
sunny day the view is a superb pattern of blue sea and green
wooded headlands, with the white mountaintops of the mainland
glittering in the distance; this morning, in the dark dawn of a
cloud-ridden day, the inlet was filled almost to the top with mist,
and only the crests of the hills and capes sailed out like shaggy
whales above its chilly surface. The roadside cafés, with their sham
totem poles, were like dejected lookout stations beside a grey sea.

As we coasted down again into the plain around Duncan the
rain diminished to a thin drizzle. At Koksilah smoke was creeping
out of the chimneys of the decrepit little Indian cabins, a fat

Cowichan squaw, with an orange handkerchief bound tightly round her head and trodden-down shoes, was standing at one of the doors, and on lines in the weed-choked gardens were hanging yards of grey and dull white wool. The Cowichans, who live for the most part at a very low economic level, were never great craftsmen like the pole-carving tribes to the north, but since their enormous decline through the impact of white civilisation they have lost almost every art they had, except for basket making. But they have acquired one rather odd new accomplishment from which many of the women increase their pitifully small livings, and this is the knitting of what are known as Cowichan jackets, woollen garments in a variety of geometrical and stylised animal patterns. When we first saw these garments we were struck by the apparently un-Indian character of their decoration and their similarity to the rough jerseys of the Faroe Islands. Contrary to our first impulsive idea, the resemblance was not an indication that there were similarities between the two cultures; we soon learned that the manufacture of these garments had been introduced by a Scottish woman missionary in imitation of the Faroe Island work, and that the Indians had taken to it as readily as Scotch broom had taken to the island soil, to the great detriment of their native forms of design.

We skirted Duncan on the highroad, and passed into a mainly agricultural landscape, with a few orchards and even, here and there, a small vineyard. There were some woods, occasional knots of houses centring round a store or a filling station, and once another Indian settlement, recognisable immediately by the bare unpainted houses and the general atmosphere of careless poverty which seems to characterise all the settlements of the Coast Salish tribes, a once rich nation of 15,000 people which, because their contact with the whites was closer and earlier than that of other Indians, has sunk to little more than 4,000 of the poorest and most unhealthy Indians in British Columbia. Two adolescent girls were walking along the road as we drove past; they had the usual squat figures and flat unattractive faces of the Salish. Otherwise, with their rather shabby store clothes and bobbed hair, they might have been a couple of working-class girls from the poorer streets of Vancouver.

At intervals we would pass through small towns which, as we went farther north, assumed a progressively cruder appearance. Chemainus, with a vast sawmill stretching its sheds and wood piles all the way down one side of the main street; Ladysmith, whose wide street lined with square-fronted wooden buildings would have looked rather like a boom city from a western film, if it had not been for the salt-water channel beneath it where the logs floated, like rafts of yellow matches in the distance, boom after boom moored out from the bright white beaches.

Twenty miles on we reached Nanaimo—a spreading tetter of wooden and stucco houses, tightening in, with the beer parlours growing more frequent every hundred yards, to a knot of late-Victorian brick streets in the centre. Unlike the southern towns of Vancouver Island, Nanaimo is predominantly a working-man's town, and, except for the Indians squatting round the "comfort station" at the crossroads and the Chinese greengrocery stores, it might easily be a little town in some part of Staffordshire not too far from Birmingham. The resemblance is not accidental, for Nanaimo's masonry buildings are the relics of prosperity which was built on coal. The workings began in 1849 with a typical incident in the colonising methods of the time. A local Indian chief went to Victoria and called in at the Hudson's Bay forge to get his musket repaired. He noticed the heaps of coal there and remarked that he knew where that kind of stone could be found on the island. The factor offered him a bottle of whisky if he would bring some the next time he came. A few months later the chief returned with a canoe full of coal and guided a party of Hudson's Bay men to the outcrops which indicated the Nanaimo measures. He was given his whisky and the Company appropriated the coalfield, using the power of the British Crown, operated by Sir James Douglas in his *alter ego* as Governor of the Island, to crush the scanty Indian resistance.

Today the only relic of this early phase in Nanaimo's history is an octagonal wooden building we saw by the waterfront, a kind of turret which thickens out at the top into a large chamber, standing in the air like a mushroom upheld on its stalk. This is known locally as The Bastion; it is used as a museum, but in the early days it served as a combined storehouse and strongpoint within the stockade of the trading post.

The Company eventually sold its interests in the coalfield to a Scottish mining family called Muir. In the latter part of the nineteenth century both Nanaimo and the Muirs prospered, a Scottish peerage was created, and a host of granite masons were imported from Aberdeen to construct a great castellated mansion outside Victoria. Today the best seams of the coalfield have been worked out and the industry is declining, giving place to timber and tourism, while the business tycoons who made their fortunes here have faded already to little more than a legend in the island's memory, their great sham castle surviving only as a school for naval officers.

2.

The boats which travel between Vancouver and the Island are a mixture of Edwardian and post-1945 styles, and it is very much a matter of luck whether you travel in a streamlined modern ship with extremely comfortable lounges, chrome-steel lunch counters and possibly even a cinema to while away the trip, or in some ante-diluvian monstrosity on which it is impossible to find any kind of comfort. This morning we were unlucky; it was a boat with hard wooden benches and decorations of painted iron acanthus. We tried, unsuccessfully, to gain a little lost sleep; we ate, and drank coffee to pass away the time; we exchanged reminiscences and David told us about a New York poet who was so Bohemian that dirty black streaks would run down from his hair whenever he went out into the rain, and another poet who papered the walls of his room with playing cards.

After nearly two hours' sailing, we began to see, through the hazy morning air, the outlines of the mainland mountains. It had at last stopped raining and we felt a little more optimistic. Soon we ran into Burrard Inlet; northwards the streets of West Vancouver climbed up the hillsides towards the ridges, foreshortened into impossible gradients; around an isolated knoll crowned by remnants of forest the stuccoed villas clustered in imitation of an Italian hill town; the mass of Grouse Mountain soared into a tuft of cloud; mist slunk like a white worm over the trees down the course of the Capilano Canyon, until the river below it flowed into the inlet over a delta covered with dejected and flood-broken trees. To the south, two or three miles away, we could barely discern Point Grey, and the tall blocks of flats around English Bay. Then the beaches thrust up abruptly northwards, and the green shores of Stanley Park nipped in the channel, the Lion's Gate suspension bridge spanned high over our heads, and we sailed into Vancouver Harbour, edging southwards to the wharves and jetties and the low scrappy skyline, broken by a few medium-sized skyscrapers, which Vancouver displays to the sea.

Vancouver is a typical Pacific coast city, differing in little of its atmosphere from towns like Seattle across the border. Its street planning is too regular to allow any immediate charm, and its central area is a jarring combination of dull masonry and concrete blocks of stores, office buildings and hotels, and streets of decaying wooden dwellings and rooming-houses from the end of last century, unpainted, sagging and grimy. Some of the latter are large buildings which, in the early days of Vancouver—the city dates only from the arrival of the Canadian Pacific Railway in the 1880's —were the homes of wealthy merchants. Down the middle part of Georgia Street they still display their turrets and conservatories, their stained-glass doors, their mock-mock-Gothic embellishments of fretted wood, and dim rococo memories in the turned pillars of their porches.

Outside the core of the city there are pleasanter parts—the orderly walkable woods of Stanley Park, the deciduous groves around Point Grey, the experimental modern houses towards Marpole and over in the outskirts of North Vancouver, whose designers have made excellent use of the wealth of varied timber that lies to their hands. But the visitor who just steps from the boat will not find these peripheral attractions for himself, and he is likely to see the centre of Vancouver as drab, clanging and much too crowded, metropolitan in its disadvantages, yet provincial in amenities. There are few really attractive shops—no first-class bookshops—and one looks in vain for the variety of pleasant eating and drinking places one expects in a community of such importance, the only major Canadian city west of the Rockies, the only major Pacific coast city north of Seattle. Vancouver has no permanent professional theatre, it has no hall which is acoustically fit for a good symphony orchestra. Yet at the same time it is a town which is stirring with all kinds of small intellectual impulses and artistic currents: occasionally it throws up a promising writer, a good actress, an original painter, it has the only good poetry magazine in Canada, there are the architectural experiments in the suburbs, and in these ways Vancouver also represents all the genuine creative urges which are trying to break through the materialism and semi-colonial smugness of general Canadian life.

We had planned to buy a few things in Vancouver for our journey—in particular what David called a "tahp" to cover the sleeping bags and the tent on top of the car. I never quite understood—although the subject was raised again on and off for several days—whether he meant top or whether it was an abbreviation of tarpaulin; in either case, we were frustrated, since Vancouver has the exasperating custom of closing its stores for all of every Wednesday. So we decided to find a meal, and set off along East Pender Street into the three or four blocks which constitute the heart of Vancouver's Chinatown.

Here, for half a mile, white faces become the exception, and one has the feeling of being in a rather westernised Oriental city. The shops carry Chinese goods and price tags written in elaborate calligraphy; there are stores where beautiful common household ware —exquisitely shaped bowls in blackbird-egg-green and platters with fine freely drawn fishes and birds—are mingled with ornate rubbish for western eyes. There is a Chinese newspaper, there are Chinese business houses of every kind—indeed, it is a completely self-sufficient community which seems to pay only a token acknowledgment to the outside world in its tourist goods and a few showy restaurants which cater for the western customer. With a population of 10,000 it is the largest Chinese settlement in Canada and second only to that of San Francisco on the whole Pacific coast of North America.

The Chinese have been in British Columbia almost as long as any other settlers; they came first as labourers during the Fraser Valley gold rush of the late 1850's, and, by working patiently on sites which the white prospectors did not think worth their trouble owing to the low yield of gold, they often made enviable fortunes. But the greatest influx of Chinese came a quarter of a century later during the construction of the Canadian Pacific Railway. This was the beginning of a great controversy over "Oriental Labour" which excited the people of British Columbia for many years. The hard core of opposition to the entry of the Chinese—and later of Japanese and Sikhs—consisted of the European working men, who pointed out that the Chinese were engaged for lower wages than the white men, which was correct, and that therefore they should be kept out, which was a blatant *non sequitur*. The Canadian Pacific Railway argued that unless they had Chinese workers they would be unable to find enough labour to complete the railway quickly and thus open a direct connection between British Columbia and the rest of Canada. This again was correct, so far as it went. But neither party hit upon the obvious idea that if the Chinese were paid the same wages as any other labourers the needs of the railway construction work could be met without any danger of the Chinese offering unfair competition. The controversy went on for many years, with the Provincial Government passing anti-Chinese laws which were regularly vetoed by the Dominion Government. Later, when the needs of the railway had been met, certain Dominion laws were in fact passed to restrict the entry of Orientals by means of a head tax, and the Provincial Government was even allowed to make regulations, only repealed during the last two years, forbidding the employment of Chinese workers in certain fields where they might offer competition to white workers.

Today the situation of the Chinese in Canada has changed a great deal since the early years. The first immigrants were mostly anxious to earn plenty of money and then go home to spend the rest of their lives comfortably among their families. Today their successors no longer think of returning, and this is the logical end of a process of assimilation which has been going on for the past thirty years. The Chinese have tended more and more to abandon labouring in favour of agriculture or trading, and now they not only control most of the retail greengrocery stores, but have also a strong hand in the wholesale vegetable and fruit trade of British Columbia. The Chinese in his little truck supplying the community stores is a regular feature of British Columbian life. Chinese proprietors are steadily taking over the small restaurant trade, even in the outlying areas, in many cases displacing the Greeks and Cypriots; they own many small laundries, and are now entering the general store business. Indeed, they are rapidly assuming, though naturally on a smaller scale, that role of traders which their compatriots have pursued so successfully in the Pacific Islands and Malaya.

This change in social status has led to the appearance of a new Canadian type of Chinese. You will, indeed, see many old men who have not changed greatly, except that their pigtails have vanished and any kind of typically Oriental dress has been replaced by the cheapest and most threadbare of store clothes. These are the elderly immigrants who have not had the luck or the initiative to become traders or employers. Often they speak little English and read none at all. From them are recruited the Chinese sawmill hands and the labourers who work for their more prosperous compatriots in farms and warehouses. They are hard, patient toilers, and excellent cultivators. I have seen them start work at five in the morning and finish after seven at night, and this day after day for the whole spring and summer. As they plodded slowly but untiringly over the beds, in their straw sun hats and suits of blue jeans, they would give an impressively Oriental aspect to the scene of fields and woods around them. Between these slow men with their gaunt brown faces over which the skin stretches tightly to give an almost mask-like quality to their patience, and the bustling, round-faced Chinese of the younger generation, there is a world of difference.

The young people are Canadians by birth and rights. They have gone through the schools with the white children, without any of the discrimination that is shown towards the Indians, and they feel a complete equality with their neighbours. They have taken to western clothing and largely to Canadian habits; many of the girls are not only extremely well-dressed but also very beautiful. Since the mass influx of Chinese ended, the popular prejudice against them has largely ebbed away, and the younger people seem to take their places in the community on the same level as any other Canadians, driving expensive cars as soon as they can afford them, and moving into new villas outside Chinatown. Many of them go to the university, and some, like the Jews a generation before, are leaving commerce and entering the professions. But the links with the Chinese community are rarely severed. The younger generation still speak their own language as well as English, there are special classes to which the children go after ordinary school hours to learn their own traditions, there are Buddhist temples and Chinese welfare societies, as well as Freemason lodges which follow a completely different rite from their European counterparts.

In Vancouver you can see plenty of the two generations and their differing ways of life. There are stores as modern and as full of tinned and packeted foods as any Canadian store—with even crisp noodles in tins and deep-frozen chop suey. But there are also dim little shops with all the odd ingredients of traditional Chinese cooking, the sharks' fins, the birds' nests, the peculiar fungi. There are others filled with the disconcerting *materia medica* of the East; Chinese apothecaries, for instance, will go to a great deal of trouble to obtain the internal organs of a bear, which they dry and turn into medicines, and the older people still use many of these traditional specifics which may seem strange to us today, but which were part of the stock in trade of every English physician ten generations ago. There is also a steady underground traffic in drugs, and particularly in opium. Every now and again a Chinese will be prosecuted for growing a patch of poppies or marihuana in a hidden corner of his market garden, and it is said, though such a statement is by the very nature of its subject extremely difficult to check, that many of the older labourers will only work for an employer who guarantees them a daily smoke of opium.

The older Chinese—and many of the younger—are also inveterate gamblers, and fantan games go on in the back alleys of China-town every night of the week. The police have tried unsuccessfully to suppress the practice, they have even attempted to deal with it by allowing licensed gambling clubs with certain limitations to keep them within—but not too strictly within—the letter of the law. Their efforts have been next to useless, and the gamblers have continued in their inconspicuous haunts, perhaps more warily, but with as much patient obstinacy as if a police force had never existed.

A feature of the British Columbian Chinese community which was given a good deal of publicity some years ago was the *tongs*, or secret societies, imported from China by the early immigrants. There are a number of these societies, which are known to perform certain mutual welfare functions, but their secrets are so carefully guarded that little is known outside the Chinese community about their exact constitution, their membership or the way in which their influence has survived outside the older, Chinese-born generation. It has been said that the *tongs* maintain their influence by terror, and that their rivalries often result in bloodshed. But these statements move on the edge of conjecture and are rarely supported by verifiable facts. Some years ago there was a series of unsolved murders among the Chinese in Victoria and Vancouver. The newspapers immediately blossomed with sensational statements that the killings had happened in the course of a war between two rival *tongs*. The only fact of real interest to emerge was that the provincial police (with a long record of unsolved murders to its credit) failed to gain a scrap of significant evidence from any Chinese, a single clue that could point to the murders having anything to do with the *tongs* or, for that matter, with anybody else.

Certainly, if the Chinese *tongs* have ever resorted to violence and death in conducting their affairs, the terror has been entirely within the Oriental community and no non-Chinese has ever been harmed by it. A European can walk at night in the Chinese quarters without the least fear of molestation from the local inhabitants; if he is in danger, it is from hoodlums and hold-up men of his own race who, even at this distance from the violent days immediately after the war, are still active in many parts of Vancouver.

We had lunch in one of the restaurants still patronised by the local Chinese, and ate an excellent and abundant meal. The Chinese cooking in Vancouver is perhaps neither so good nor so varied as that in San Francisco, but it is still among the best food one is likely to find in western Canada.

Afterwards we walked northwards into the lower part of East Hastings Street, one of the seedier ends of Vancouver—small grimy restaurants with empty floral jardinières and dried-up aquaria in the windows, crepuscular and fly-blown junk shops, and news stores carrying an infinitely miscellaneous stock of small papers in minority languages—Greek, Russian, Finnish—and of factional political journals—Communist, Trotskyist, and even Wobbly.

The threadbare, bottle-nosed men who stood in the doorways and clustered at the street corners—each a solitary and misanthropic individual, no matter how he might try in the forced joviality of his kind to dissimulate his essential lack of interest in the world outside—seemed to belong to the same dying age as the Wobbly papers. They were the last representatives of the Great American Bum, the obstinate decaying lingerers from an age when the migratory workers of the west aroused their rebellion against the materialistic and nationalistic standards of the young North American civilisation. Today the majority of these workers have surrendered to the allure of enlightened capitalism, with its high wages and high standards of living. Even the struggles of the 'thirties are forgotten—youths of twenty do not know of such events as the occupation of the Federal Building in Vancouver by the unemployed during their own childhood—and it is now only among a few intellectual rebels and these remaining derelicts who support the skidrow walls from East Hastings Street, Vancouver, down to Mission Street, San Francisco, that you will find some memory of the old days and some lingering loyalty to their more honest and more idealistic values.

Westward, the street changed its character, the bums disappeared, the shops became garish department stores, the crowds

on the pavements were office workers, with here and there a tur-
baned and bearded venerable Sikh or a family of Indians looking
ill at ease as they wandered in the city streets and gaped at the
shops.

3.

It was early afternoon by the time we began the long and exas-
peratingly slow trip through suburban Vancouver, past the used-
car lots that strung out to the edge of town, and through the
built-up connecting roads to New Westminster, a shabby industrial
town which for a brief period was the capital of British Columbia
and has ever since been called, half ironically, the Royal City. Here
we crossed over the wide, muddy tidal waters of the Fraser into a
further belt of suburbs, and then out on to the open road—or as
open a road as you will find in the thickly populated lower end of
the Fraser Valley.

Indeed, from the outskirts of New Westminster as far as Chilliwack, the best part of sixty miles, we were hardly a moment out
of sight of some habitation. Here and there were slight hills, tiny
copses, but for the most part the road ran level across the most
completely cleared and intensely cultivated part of British Columbia. The farms were small, concerned either with dairying or fruit
and vegetable growing; they gave one the impression of being fertile
and well cultivated.

At times the farms gave way to clusters of smallholdings and
little villas in whose gardens their retired owners added to their
pensions by berry-growing or bee-keeping. Outside almost every
front gate there was some attempt to attract the passing motorist
—a little stall with fruit and bunches of autumn flowers stuck in
toffee tins, a showcase with jars of jam or honey, a barrel on a
gaudy stand with CIDER hung in great letters above it. One farm
had a large stall piled with great autumnal orange pumpkins,
another a revolving upright wheel in which pots of honey went
up and down in endless rotation.

At intervals we passed through small towns—Langley Prairie,
Aldergrove, Abbotsford—where the seed and implement stores,
the auctioneers' offices, the warehouses, the crowds of denim-clad
farmers, emphasised the heavily cultivated nature of the district,
and we were reminded, by a green shed with fake pinnacles which
turned out to be a Sikh temple, by a Swedish meeting-house commemorating Gustavus Vasa, by the German names on the gates

for whole stretches of the road, of the extreme mingling of races in this rich area.

Beyond the larger market town of Chilliwack the density of settlement began to ease, the farms became larger, with great barns and wide fields, the hills edged in from either side so that for the first time we became conscious of driving within the confines of a valley. In another twenty miles cultivated land had begun to give way to alder and willow groves in the floodable valley bottom, and at one point, where the road had returned to the river's edge, a great dripping cliff closed in on our right and warned us of the approach of mountainous country.

In the late afternoon we reached Hope, lying in a great sweeping curve of the river just below the Fraser Canyon. Since this was the last place where we could be certain of finding accommodation before the Canyon, which we wished to traverse in daylight, we decided to stay for the night. We turned into a little motel (or auto-court—the names are more or less synonymous) and hired a cabin for four people. In comparison with the urban auto-courts, with their modern facilities, it seemed rather primitive—a single room, with one bed concealed in a kind of alcove, and the other in full view, a shower with a curtain, a toilet with a thin plywood door through which every sound could be heard, a great black stove on which all the cooking must be done with wood fetched in from the pile outside. We felt hesitant—yet a few days farther north we were to remember that apparent primitiveness as something approaching luxury.

We went out to explore the little town and now, free of the car's limitations, we realised fully the impressive beauty of its setting. The one-sided main street ran along the bank of the Fraser which, spreading out after its release from the narrow channels of the Canyon, swept round in a vast curve of grey turbulent water, rushing, even at this dry end of the year, with an almost torrential impetus as it coiled and twisted into numberless interlacing eddies and whirlpools. A single launch was making its slow way upstream; otherwise the whole sweep of the river was empty of craft. This great surging water would itself have been impressive enough, but the scene was given its real splendour by the ring of mountain peaks that surround Hope in an almost complete circle. To the north-west was The Old Settler, then, swinging in a clockwise direction, soared Coquihalla, Tulameen, Outram and Silvertip, the circle closing in Cheam Peak to the south-west.

Hope lies in a deep bowl in the Coast Range, the centre of two passes which cut through to the north (the Fraser Canyon) and the east (the Hope–Princeton route through Allison Pass); the mountains which surround it are not particularly high by British Columbian standards—the highest, Silvertip, is 8,500 feet—but, partly from the completeness of their encirclement and partly from their relative sheerness (for here the valley bottom is little more than 150 feet above sea-level), we found them far more impressive than anything we had seen before or were to see later in the Rockies, where the valleys themselves are often so high as to rob the summits of their real loftiness. Moreover, the peaks around Hope are sharper and more clearly defined than the massive bulks of many mountains farther inland, and, with the snow that was already beginning to tip them in the cold autumn nights, they seemed to belong rather to an Alpine than a Canadian mountain scene.

Here we were once more in a thickly wooded region, the last of the coastal rain forests we should see for some time to come, and from high up the mountainsides dark masses of tall trees crept close down around the town, and towered over the wild and debris-laden shore on the Fraser's far bank. Right in the centre of the river, almost a focal point of this magnificent scene, lay Greenwood Island, covered with a dense thicket of firs and driving a long prow of gravel into the swirling current. The local Indians have a superstitious regard for this islet, where they claim that two murderers were slain by a thunderbolt, through supernatural intervention, and certainly, as we stood with our backs to the town, gazing over the scene of wild river and forest and mountain peaks, it was possible to give sympathy, if not credence, to such a myth. One felt that tragedy belonged by right to such a place.

The town itself had a comfortable air—not too primitive and not too white and efficient. We drank coffee in a deserted bowling alley and afterwards talked to a couple of children who were staring into the window of a general store; they looked a little like Italians, but assured us that they were Indians, from a place called Spuzzum, a few miles up the road. They were probably half-breeds, who are usually classed as Indians in this part of Canada and often remain with the tribe if their Indian blood has been in the maternal line, as is usually the case. They talked about the toys in a corner of the store window, and their minds ran as surely on aeroplanes and automobiles as mine at their age had done on Red

Indians. The boy was rather forward and thought himself a wit, the girl was shy and hardly spoke at all. A few moments later a white woman came out of the shop, bundled the children into a car, and drove away.

4.

Next morning we arose at dawn, to the exasperating sound of rain pattering on the roof of our cabin. Perhaps it was just an early-morning shower, we told ourselves, and would end as soon as the sun began to rise. Hopefully we ate our breakfast, loaded up the car, and set out. We crossed the river and swung northward, where a kind of bench, relatively wide in parts, lies between the Fraser and the mountains, and travelled for some miles through lush green woodland without a sight of the river.

This was the beginning of the country of the Fraser Valley gold rush in 1858, when the "Forty-Niners" left the depleted Californian fields and came north in such numbers that in two months no less than 13,500 men had sailed from San Francisco. It was this gold rush, and its later extension into the even richer Cariboo fields, that marked the decisive turn in the history of British Columbia—indeed, it began the history of British Columbia. Up to this time the whole area west of the Rockies had been little more than a fur-trading reserve, over which, since the start of the century, the Hudson's Bay Company had dotted its forts and outposts and maintained a rough suzerainty. Before the gold rush there was no city, there was not even any place which could be called a town in the real sense of the word, for Victoria was only a glorified company post where a few administrative officers and missionaries lived on sufferance.

In all, there were less than a thousand white men in the future province of British Columbia. There was no industry, almost no agriculture, and, except for the rudimentary beginnings of coal extraction at Nanaimo, no mining, while fishing was still carried on only by the Indians in their old primitive ways. On the mainland there were no roads—only Indian tracks and the packhorse trails connecting the various posts, used two or three times a year when the fur brigades came down from the interior to the main depot at Fort Langley (now Langley Prairie), and returned later with their supply of trade goods. Throughout the interior there was no law but that exercised by the Hudson's Bay factors in protecting their commercial interests; for the rest, tribal usage still

Vancouver

Government Street, Victoria

Nineteenth-Century Missionary Culture: an Indian Band at Metlakatla

A Camel of the Cariboo Gold Rush

persisted over the whole territory, and the life of the Indians was influenced chiefly in a technical manner, by the use of iron tools and firearms, and to a less extent in the moral and physical degeneration caused by the introduction of the habit of drinking (formerly unknown to these Indians) and the spread of white diseases. Hope itself, in its original form of Fort Hope, first appeared during the 1840's as a part of this trading empire.

The Hudson's Bay Company, indeed, hung like a great parasite over the country, draining and corrupting its original life without bringing any fundamental change or any positive development. The gold rush, whatever one may think of the intrinsic folly of men risking their lives in such a gamble, changed all this, and it is to the miners who came in their thousands from the United States, and who later arrived from every part of the earth to swell the numbers who surged up to the Cariboo in the early 'sixties, that British Columbia owes its development.

The arrival of large numbers of white men, many of whom would clearly remain in the country, broke immediately the administrative power of the Company, and forced the foundation of a regular colony, with at least the semblance of a democratic form of government. The Company posts grew into towns; Victoria, where the ships from San Francisco transferred their passengers to smaller craft for sailing up the Fraser, began to assume the proportions of a seaport city; and New Westminster soon arose as a mainland rival. To serve the needs of the miners the old trails proved inadequate, and in the 1860's the Cariboo Road, the road we were travelling, was built from the head of the Fraser navigation at Yale, fourteen miles above Hope, into the heart of the Cariboo at Barkerville, providing the first route by which the interior could be opened to the mass infiltration of western civilisation. The needs of the white miners and settlers brought in private storekeepers, breaking the Hudson's Bay trading monopoly, and nurtured the development of agriculture, for it was disappointed miners of the 1858 rush who first began to till the rich alluvial soil of the Fraser Valley. The fur empire was doomed, for the old Indian hunting grounds were being over-run by the prospectors who began to spread all over the province in search of new goldfields. The traditional Indian society crumbled under the impact of these numerous bodies of white men, particularly as the sporadic Indian resistance was made the excuse for punitive actions like the Chilcotin War and for superseding the tribal law. But the

threat to the Indians was even more fundamental than that provided by the appearance of British law, supported by the rough
methods of the pioneer days. For the arrival of the gold-miners
meant the widespread influx of land-hungry white men, and from
the beginning of the 1860's there started the process by which
the native people were gradually squeezed out of their hunting
and fishing grounds and finally constricted into the reserves where
most of them live confined to the present day.

As we travelled along this road there was little sign of that past
era, and perhaps the Cariboo Road itself, which still follows the
difficult path cut out by the Royal Engineers in the early 1860's, is
its most solid monument. Here in the rush years of the Cariboo
passed a traffic far exceeding in volume anything that is seen nowadays. Tens of thousands of miners, experienced prospectors,
farmers who had abandoned their fields, deserters from the American army, sailors who had run away from their ships, clerks who
had left their desks and shopkeepers who had fled from their
counters, men from every part of America and Europe and China,
tramped on foot towards the diggings. There were stage coaches,
covered wagons and pony expresses, and, during the height of the
rush, between two and three thousand animals worked in the pack
trains—horses, mules and even camels. The camels of the Cariboo,
indeed, have become part of the folk history of British Columbia.
They were a herd of twenty-three beasts from Mongolia that
were brought in via San Francisco. A merchant named Frank
Laumeister calculated that they would be the ideal beasts of burden for the semi-desert country through which much of the road
lay. The camels, however, proved a catastrophic failure; their feet
were unfitted for the rough, stony trails, and an attempt to equip
them with boots was not a great improvement. But the real disadvantage was the rooted antipathy which the horses and the
mules took to these outlandish beasts; at the very smell of a camel
the pack mules would turn and bolt, the horses would wreck their
wagons and buggies. In the end Laumeister became so deeply involved in suits for damages that he decided to abandon what was
popularly called the Dromedary Express, and he turned most of
his animals loose by the Thompson River, where some of them
actually survived, feeding off the rough desert vegetation, into the
1890's. They never, however, took sufficiently well to the alien
conditions to breed and become naturalised.

About half an hour after Hope we passed through Yale. This

was the point at which the goods were transferred from the river steamers for the trip by freight wagon up the Cariboo Road, and throughout the rush it was a large and bustling town, with row after row of log cabins, stores and places of entertainment. At its height it is said to have possessed twenty saloons and dancing halls, and its prosperity continued to some extent even into the 1880's, when it became a glorified construction camp while the Canadian Pacific Railway was being built through the Canyon. We looked in vain, however, for any tangible relics of this past activity. There was a pleasant white-painted church, there were two hotels and a store, a few wooden houses, one or two log cabins which probably dated from a later period than the rush. But all the land running down from the highway to the river, where the old town once stood, was an empty and barren-looking flat, with a little scrub, but no visible sign of the vanished settlement. A prospector, who had passed through this area looking for likely places that might have been missed by his predecessors, once told me that when the old saloons were pulled down some placer miners dug up and panned the surface of the ground beneath their floors and won a fair haul in dust that had fallen through the cracks of the boards during the drunken transactions which had taken place in these buildings. I told the story to my companions; we all felt a little sceptical, but decided that it would be a good tale for anybody who wanted to write a sensational novel of the period.

By the time we passed Yale it was clear that the rain would not stop while we were in the Canyon; worse than that, the clouds were hanging low over the mountains, and we should certainly not enjoy the view we had expected. However, there was nothing to do but travel on and hope for a better day on our return. Before long we saw the first encampment of Interior Indians. A long stretch of meadowland ran beside the road, and dotted all over it were many small log cabins and rough houses of boards, in various stages of decay. Some of them, from the colouring of the timber, seemed to be at least fifty or sixty years old, but even the newer houses looked very ramshackle. There was a minute chapel of boards, with a little wooden spire and empty windows; it looked as though it had been out of use for many years. Only the houses in one corner of the meadow were inhabited; they were grouped about a rough, empty corral, beside which stood the poles of a teepee with the canvas covering half ripped off. Some attempt at cultivation had been made, and the inhabitants were evidently still in the process of lifting potatoes from one patch. We only saw one woman, thinner and taller than the Coast types, hunching in the rain across the bare ground between the houses. In the field a herd of perhaps a dozen horses were grazing, wild-looking creatures with long tails and manes, and untrimmed hair; there were no other domestic animals to be seen. We were to become very familiar with these herds of Indian horses as we proceeded farther into the Interior.

Now the sheer rock walls began to come close in on both sides of the river, and the whole of the Canyon narrowed, so that the road often twisted along the edges of the sheer bluffs and the river below ran turbulently in its constricted channel. As we looked down the almost perpendicular slopes towards it, it had a kind of milky jade colour and, although many hundreds of miles away from its native mountains, looked very much like the water of glacial streams. Just past the little village of Spuzzum, the bed closed in to its narrowest reach. At various points it had already run between precipitous rock walls, with great cubical blocks of rock standing up in midstream and splitting the current into impassable rapids, and we began to appreciate something of the terror which must have been aroused in the hearts of Simon Fraser and his first band of explorers when they came down the Canyon by the narrow Indian and deer tracks, grooved into the sheer sides, which were the only means of getting through until the road was built.

At one place we crossed to the eastern side by a large suspension bridge, and here we were impressed by the extreme vulnerability of the communications in western Canada. For on either side of the river we saw a railway line, and we realised that not only the sole road to the north, but also both the railway lines connecting the Pacific Coast with the prairies and eastern Canada run between the walls of this narrow canyon. Until two years ago, all the road traffic to the east and even to the inner British Columbian valleys came this way; it was the sole way out from Vancouver to anything beyond the mountains. Now the situation has been relieved by the opening of the Hope–Princeton highway, which takes the eastward traffic, but a concentrated air attack might still destroy all the rail outlets and half the road outlets of the most industrial and highly populated part of western Canada. Even a landslide or a heavy fall of snow is sometimes enough to bring about a temporary isolation of Vancouver, and it is difficult to see how, in view of the solidity of the natural barrier presented by the Coast Range, this situation can ever be changed.

On the eastern side the road rose quickly up the sides of the mountain. Soon we were above Hell's Gate, the narrowest spot in the Canyon, where the Fraser forces its way between two great rock buttresses which compress the flow of water to a width of about forty feet. The depth of the river at this point is, on an average, about 280 feet. We experienced an uncomfortably vertiginous feeling as we looked down the precipitous mountainside on to the masses of water struggling tumultuously to make their way between these Cyclopean bulks of granite.

Here, owing to the difficulty which the salmon experienced in passing through the great mass of fast-running water, the Pacific Salmon Commission has recently built two elaborate fish ladders which have added greatly to the number of fish reaching the upper Fraser, and have been the means of increasing the spawning activities of the fish, and also the catch made by the Interior Indians, who are the only people allowed by law to take the salmon on a large scale after they have passed the mouths of the rivers.

A little farther on, the road climbed to a wide bench of level ground, and here we lost sight of the river for a while. There were a few Indian cabins, and then we encountered a couple of children, a girl of about eight and a boy of five, standing by the roadside in the rain, trying to thumb a lift. We pulled up and managed to cram them into the already overloaded car. The boy was intensely shy, but the girl made up for him in talkativeness. They were on the way to school at Boston Bar, four miles away.

Why were they walking? Had they missed the school bus? The girl looked puzzled. They had a school bus, hadn't they? No, there was no bus for their school. They had to walk all the way, unless they were lucky enough to get a lift. We found it hard to believe that this should be the case, since every rural area in British Columbia is normally well served in this respect. However, after we had seen several other children of various ages tramping along in the rain, and had realised that they were all Indians, like our own passengers, we were brought up against the distasteful fact that, while white children everywhere had adequate school transport, if they happened to live in an area where they were required to attend school (some children in isolated places are taught by an elaborate correspondence service), the Indians were left to shift for themselves and forced to walk miles in all weathers in order to reach their schools.

Boston Bar, where we dropped the two children, had been one of the richest spots during the Fraser Valley gold rush. It was operated almost exclusively by Americans, hence the name, for in the Coast vernacular Americans were called Boston men (the first trading vessels came from New England), and in the dying Indian *lingua franca* known as Chinook, America is still referred to as *Boston illalie*, or Boston Land. Now, as at Yale, there is nothing left of the old gold-mining days, and Boston Bar is a village which lives almost completely from being a depot of the Canadian National Railway. On the opposite bank of the Canyon is another village, North Bend, which serves as the depot for the Canadian Pacific. This place has no road connection with the outside, and relies on an enormous aerial automobile ferry which we saw in operation—unique, the local people claim, both in function and in size. The traveller in North America soon learns to stand aloof from these continual claims to superiority—every village has something that is the biggest or the best in some way or another —but I can say at least that none of us had ever seen anything before like this great hanging ferry with its load of cars and human beings.

Beyond Boston Bar the road climbed again in giddy bends far above the level of the river. Sometimes we had to go through echoing tunnels in the precipitous walls. At other places, where the way was hardly wide enough for two cars to pass each other, the difficulty of driving was further complicated by the presence of the road construction gangs, some of whom were working non-chalantly on the sides of sheer precipices, building up and widening the highway.

As we travelled through the Canyon the vegetation had undergone a steady change; in the lower parts it was still the jungle-like forest of the coastal regions, but now it became much more sparse, the giant fir and cedar giving place to scattered and stunted pines as the hills became drier and we approached the arid country of the Interior. On this stretch of the road we first began to meet the hunters coming down from the Cariboo and the north. Most of them had trailers loaded with the carcasses of deer, and here and there a car would carry on its roof the head of a moose, with the great spade-shaped antlers sometimes jutting out on each side to the whole width of the car.

We passed over Jackass Mountain, the high point of the road; afterwards the way became easier and the Canyon widened out into a valley, surrounded by dry hills. Soon we came to the confluence of the Fraser and the Thompson; in the valley below us, its roofs surrounded by deciduous trees which showed the first touches of autumn yellowing, lay the little town of Lytton, named after the celebrated novelist—not from any local literary devotion, but merely because he happened to be Colonial Secretary during the Cariboo rush. On the benches around the town there were fields and gardens more extensive than we had seen since we left the main Fraser Valley, but it was clear, as we looked at the arid uplands around us, that this agricultural activity was confined to the spots where irrigation was easily practicable.

We had left the course of the Fraser a little before Lytton; now we by-passed the town and swung back to the Thompson, a river which ran easily and almost sluggishly in comparison with the wild flow of the Fraser. The country became extremely bare, and as we went along the Thompson we entered a belt, stretching for a good sixty miles, where all except the river bed and a few isolated benches at the sides of the valley displayed something approaching the half-desert condition of such States as New Mexico. The rounded rolling hills—shaped rather like the Cheviots—were grey in colour, owing to the predominance of sage brush among their scanty vegetation. By the river there were occasional groves of willow and aspen, but on the hills themselves, except in a few gullies, there was hardly even a stunted bush.

This landscape was extremely sparsely populated. The only industry was ranching; and the sides of the bare hills had been worn into tiny corrugated ridges by the grazing cattle, but we saw very few animals, for they, as well as the ranch buildings, were evidently far back on the ranges. Once we passed an Indian village—a semi-circle of log cabins radiating around a new whitewashed church. This is a pattern the small mission villages of the Interior seem to follow fairly consistently, for we saw it repeated more than once as we travelled farther north. The present village was cleaner, less decrepit and generally more prosperous-looking in a very frugal way than that we had seen below the Canyon, and this was probably due to the fact that the men could get employment in a ranching country, for the Indians take much more easily to cattle herding than to the more monotonous and exacting labours of arable farming. Elsewhere, on a narrow ledge beside the

Thompson, we saw another sign of Indian activity : a rough open shelter had been erected of poles and thatched with branches, and underneath salmon were hanging to dry, split open, brown in colour, and looking like enormous kippers.

Annoyingly enough, the desert was for once receiving its full ration of rain. At one point we ran into a pool where a drainage channel had become blocked, and a moment later the engine stalled. David, who monopolised our mechanical knowledge, got out and began to fiddle with various parts of the dripping engine and the rest of us stood around in solidarity, useless, but at least bearing him company in getting wet. David's tinkering had no result whatever, so we now had the idea of trying the car on a slope; we pushed it fifty yards to a short hill, and then downwards, but again nothing happened, and we found ourselves at the bottom of a dip, with hills rising up before and behind us. We climbed back into the car and sat glumly waiting for a lorry to push us out. Now and again David would desperately try the starter, and it was actually in this way, after we had waited a quarter of an hour without sighting anything larger than a light English car which did not even stop, that the engine suddenly and inexplicably chugged into action and we were able to resume our journey.

At Cache Creek, a road junction about 130 miles north of Hope, we anticipated shopping and perhaps lunching in the car by the roadside, for the rain had now almost ceased. But this place, which had looked so important on the road map—like so many places in this country—turned out to be a meagre group of wooden buildings at a cross-roads. There was an auto-camp, and a store which looked as though it carried little stock and charged highly for it. Besides, the road was crammed with waiting cars owing to the game wardens having erected a barrier to stop all the traffic from the north to look out for poachers who took more than the regulation number of deer or moose.

So we rode on towards the next settlement, and outside Cache Creek (named after a highwayman's haul of gold which is still said to be hidden somewhere in the neighbourhood) we left the Thompson and drove for a while beside a small river called the Bonaparte. There were wide green meadows in the valley bottom, and we passed a number of ranches, one of which, we were intrigued to see, had been named after Henry George. Very soon afterwards the comparatively good black-topped highway suddenly gave way to the most decrepit kind of gravel road, full of potholes and worn into washboard corrugations which made it impossible to avoid being bumped unmercifully at every yard of the way. We had been told farther south to expect this kind of road, but the fair highway up to the present had made us rashly dubious of this information. However, we now became resigned to the thought of passing the rest of our journey over frontier roads a good deal worse than the average English country lane.

The road was now climbing steadily towards the Cariboo plateau, and the type of landscape began to change once again. The hills receded and diminished, we no longer ran in the bottoms of valleys, but over open country which grew more level from mile to mile, and the typical Cariboo woodland, thin aspens and lodgepole pines and firs, began to appear among the rough grassland. Suddenly, a few miles before Clinton, we drove once again on to an excellent black-topped highway, and were deceived for a while into a renewed optimism about travelling conditions in the north.

5.

Clinton turned out to be a run-down frontier town in the old style. There were ancient, weather-greyed, false-fronted shops and houses, rickety wooden sidewalks raised three feet above the muddy street, even a hotel which had survived from the earliest days of the Cariboo rush, with tying-up posts all along its wide verandah. Nor were the actors lacking in this shabby set, for cowboys in high-heeled half-boots and five-gallon hats strutted along the single street, and a couple of tall, moon-faced, full-blooded Indians lounged arrogantly in a doorway. Clinton had been a big transport centre in the mining era, and we were intrigued to find a place that retained at least something of the look of the old British Columbian gold town. There had been changes, of course—a couple of garages, cold-storage lockers, and so on—but these had been much less destructive of the general impression than we had anticipated.

We entered a store which hid behind the biggest of all the paintless sham façades. The interior was a bare, barn-like room, its floor worn and broken with generations of nailed boots, and dominated by a great horizontal cylindrical stove of sheet iron, above seven feet long and dating from the antediluvian early days of the town. Audrey and Inge went to buy provisions from the grocery counter, while David and I wandered in the other improbable corners of the store. There were stacks of every kind of hat we had ever seen in a western film, from tall ten-galloners to the black pork-pie type with the wide brim which the villains of our childhood so often wore. There were piles of bright shirts and mackinaws, buckskin jackets and waistcoats with long fringes, studded belts, embroidered gauntlets, and a good deal more of the traditional paraphernalia of cowboy splendour. We were a little surprised that such things still existed, since we imagined that real cowboys had long since stepped into jeans and abandoned their old colourful costume to the Hollywood hams. But it was clear that the Cariboo breed had either never abandoned it, or had resumed it under the inspiration of Hopalong Cassidy; we were inclined to think the former more probable.

There was one table devoted to books and magazines where we hoped to turn up a paperback for evening reading, but literary tastes in the Cariboo seemed to have been arrested thirty years ago, and the best we could find was *The Adventures of Sherlock Holmes*. It seemed to complement rather well the atmosphere of western films and mining romances which lingered in the air about us.

Meanwhile, there was a dispute at the grocery counter. Inge was trying to buy bread, and had been offered the usual waxpaper-wrapped product of Canadian general stores. No, she insisted, that was not what she wanted. Had they no home-made, crisp, unwrapped bread? The shopwoman threw back her tight-lipped, tight-bunned head, inflated what dessicated bosom existed beneath her flowered print frock, and declared with haughty indignation: "We have *no* unwrapped bread. Here we believe in doing everything hygienic!" We accepted the rebuke and went away humbly with our germ-free, taste-free, rubbery, but so hygienic loaf.

In the old Clinton Hotel we went through a hall lined with knotty pine, much like the dining-room of a Welsh mountain hotel of the last century, peered at a pathetic little showcase museum of mid-Victorian mining tools and dusty pieces of ore, and found a modern coffee bar at the rear of the house. Later, we walked back to the beginning of the town, where a few thick-skulled Herefordshire bulls, with the tight curled brows and inane expression of the later Roman emperors, gazed at us with animosity from an enclosed field, while a big mongrel gnawed the bloodstained skull of an elk which had been left splayed on the floor of an unattended jeep.

Beside the cold-storage building a kind of gallows had been erected, decorated with the massive hindquarters of a moose. A little lame man in a cowboy's hat was skinning them, and David and I walked over to watch him. He worked quickly, separating the rough-pelted, grey-brown hide from the red, coarse meat with the deftness of long experience. We began to ask him about the beast he was skinning. It had been killed by some Yanks, he explained; they were having it put in cold storage and it would afterwards be sent down to them in the States. The cold storage did a good business of this kind every season.

Had there been many Americans hunting this year? He spat and groaned. More than ever. All week they had been coming down with moose and elk and deer piled up on their trucks. It was a massacre of the big game. Each year the animals were becoming fewer, were being pushed farther back. It was only a matter of time and the moose would go like the bison. He sighed at the thought as he lifted another square inch of moose-skin. "Yep, the bush will soon be finished," he went on. "The Yanks are coming in everywhere. They don't only take our game away—they're digging in as well, buying ranches all round in the Cariboo. They're trying to find oil too—a rig went through this morning on the way to Quesnel. Yes, I tell you, the Yanks are here to stay, and once they're here, the old life will be gone for sure." "You're damned right it will," said David feelingly.

At Clinton one is already on the beginning of the Cariboo plateau, more than 3,000 feet up, but the land goes on rising for another forty miles, until it reaches nearly 4,000 feet, when it begins to fall steadily in a gradual slope towards the north of the province. After the thrills of the Canyon, the road seemed dull in the extreme. There were no sensational cliffs and sheer drops; only the typical rolling upland scenery of plateau country, the thin forests, the stretches of half-barren moorland, the sweeping grass ranges where small herds grazed. Here and there would be a ranch-house by the roadside, with little whitewashed corrals, but it was clear that the cattle-raising operations in this area were on a very small scale, and that the really big ranching lay to the north and west. The country through which we passed had, indeed, a somewhat decayed appearance. All along the road we came across derelict, deserted log cabins, old broken-down barns and large farmhouses whose empty windows and sagging, snow-crushed roofs told that they had been abandoned for some years. Even many of the occupied houses had a worn appearance, but this was partly due to the heavy weathering in this country which turns the old timbers to a peculiarly deep chocolate brown.

From Clinton to Williams Lake, more than a hundred miles, there is not a single town, not even a settlement that deserves the name of a village. Apart from two or three hamlets of Shuswap Indians, there are only occasional small groups of buildings which are usually gathered around the sites of the old post-houses. The original Cariboo Road, before it reached Clinton, went through the town of Lillooet, to the west of its present route, and it was from here that, for some forgotten reason, the miles were numbered. The inns in their turn were named after the nearest mile posts—59 Mile House, 70 Mile House and so on. These became the nuclei of tiny roadside settlements, devoted to the needs of travellers and the few local farmers, and so they have remained. There are usually a garage, a general store which acts as a post office, and a primitive hotel or auto-camp. Sometimes there are a few dwellings clustered around this little knot; occasionally, as at 100 Mile House, there is a big ranch headquarters (in this case serving the 70,000-acre range of Lord Martin Cecil), but this is by no means always the case.

At 100 Mile House we stopped for petrol. The cashier in the garage was selling buckskin jackets and waistcoats which had been made by the Chilcotin Indians, an Athapaskan group whose territory adjoins that of the Salish-speaking Shuswap a few miles west of the main road. The Chilcotins are mostly ranch hands, but the mountains which isolate them from Bella Coola and the coast on the far western side of their country are still relatively full of game, owing to their comparative inaccessibility to white sportsmen, and some of the Chilcotin still earn a living by hunting and by selling garments made from the skins of the animals they kill. The workmanship of the jackets we saw here was very good, but the embroidered designs with which they were decorated were in that formalised and rather debased floral style which was introduced into Canada by the French peasants and which was afterwards imitated by the Indians, displacing their native geometrical and animal patterns. The fashion spread right across the prairies and finally, in the late nineteenth century, reached the hunting tribes of British Columbia. Moreover, owing to the war years, the Chilcotin had been unable to get Czechoslovakian beads, and instead used gaudily coloured artificial silk thread, a very poor substitute.

There were also some moccasins for sale in the garage, of a rather unusual form, extending above the ankle, where they were tied with thongs around the leg. The girl asked two dollars for them, and we bought ourselves a pair each, later finding them clumsy but warm and comfortable substitutes for slippers.

The monotonous landscape changed at last when we came to Lac la Hache and ran for nearly ten miles beside its smooth waters, dense reed beds and green meadows, dotted with clumps of deciduous trees like English parkland. Here we were delighted by a great autumnal flock of several hundred blue-birds, which, when they rose in flight at our approach, revealed a delicacy and intensity of colouring one tends to associate only with tropical species. Half-way along Lac la Hache we ran on to an even more execrably worn and broken gravel road than we had encountered before, and it was over this kind of surface that we travelled for the remaining 500 miles northwards. Yet gradually we became reconciled to this discomfort and the tiredness it involved, and decided that the Cariboo was by no means the depressing country which had been described to us by so many people in Vancouver and Victoria. After the dense forests of the islands and the coast, there was a relaxing quality in the great rolling vistas, the grass ranges and large open fields, and even the relatively flat stretches of open road; it seemed to strike a balance between the monotony of the prairie and the narrow constricted aspects of a country of mountains and tall forests.

We overtook a little horse buggy, full of hay and driven by a short Indian in a cloth cap. On top of the hay sat two fat, swarthy women, with bright print petticoats, and gaudy silk handkerchiefs tied around their heads. The resemblance to a group of gipsies trailing the roads of the English or French countryside was quite remarkable. They all looked at us with a kind of heavy distrust as we drove slowly by, but as soon as we waved they grinned back with the greatest affability. We noticed that in general, after the superficial distrust has been broken down, the Interior Indians are very willing to be on amiable terms with anybody who shows his own friendly intention; among the Coast people, on the other hand, it takes a long time to thaw the Indian's air of rather contemptuous reserve. I think this difference can be explained by the relative simplicity of the hunting tribes, as compared with the elaborate degrees of pride and snobbery which distinguished the social organisation of the Coastal tribes.

The group we had passed were a fair sample of the tribes which inhabit the eastern and northern Cariboo areas. These are Shuswaps and Carriers, the former an Interior Salish group and the latter an Athapaskan tribe related to the westerly Chilcotin. Although Shuswap and Carrier speak mutually incomprehensible languages of quite distinct stocks, their ways of living and even their tribal organisations were closely similar in the days before they had been affected by white civilisation. A common reliance on hunting, a life in the same kind of natural environment, a similar subjection to the diluted influence of the Coast culture, and a mutual inter-course through trade and war had produced a general similarity of life, with inevitable though minor variations. After the arrival of the white men, the two peoples were left with little alternative but to assume once again an essentially similar life based upon sub-sistence farming in the reservations of comparatively poor land which had been left to them, supplemented by a certain amount of work for neighbouring farmers and ranchers. These Indians rarely enjoy anything even remotely approaching prosperity, since they do not take very well to arable farming and are slow to adopt the methods of irrigation, fertilisation and co-operation that might make their land productive. Like the Prairie Indians, they have developed a passionate love for horses, and will keep unneces-sarily large herds to the detriment of their often meagre grazing grounds. If they travel on horseback and by buggy, it is certainly partly by preference, but it is also a question of necessity, for very few of them would be able to buy even a cheap secondhand car in this country of automobile transport. Indeed, many still live in a condition of semi-starvation, and it is the general tendency to-wards malnutrition that still makes them acutely susceptible to such diseases as tuberculosis, even now no less than eight times as prevalent among Indians as among their neighbours of other races.

At the 150 Mile House the road forked; the main highway con-tinued along the top of the plateau and a side road dipped down to make a thirty-mile loop through Williams Lake and then return to the main road at Soda Creek. The afternoon was already grow-ing late and we realised that, with the number of hunters on the road, we should probably have to rely on a fair-sized town for accommodation. It was a question of going through Williams Lake, or travelling straight on to Quesnel, more than eighty miles beyond the road junction. Williams Lake is the largest town on

UNIVERSITY OF WINNIPEG
LIBRARY
DISCARDED
515 Portage Avenue

the 400 miles of road between Hope and Prince George, and it is
the big export centre of the Cariboo and Chilcotin ranching districts. Clearly we should not miss it. Besides, we argued, the road
through there was only five or six miles farther on the map, and
we could not lose very much time even if we had after all to drive
into Quesnel, where we knew there were a number of auto-courts
and hotels.

However, we had bargained without the Cariboo roads. For,
bad as the main road had been, the side way down to Williams
Lake was several degrees worse, despite the relative importance
of the town as a commercial centre. It was worse than any lane I
have ever met in Europe, and at times it was hardly wide enough
for two cars to pass. It fell fairly rapidly towards the lower ground,
and we began to run into a more deciduous woodland; the aspen,
already yellowing with the approach of autumn, became for the
first time a dominant tree in the landscape. Soon we came to the
shores of Williams Lake, by British Columbian standards a relatively small, oval stretch of water, about four miles long, fringed
by wooded hills and bluffs.

There has been some kind of settlement at Williams Lake since
the early days of the gold rush, but the town we entered was rather
raw and modern, with stuccoed banks, stores and hotels, a
modern flat-roofed high school and a hospital, and plenty of new
buildings on the outskirts. A great area of corrals at the railway
depot left no doubt of the leading industry of the town, which
caters for an area stretching nearly 200 miles over the Chilcotin
plateau, and sends out 25,000 cattle every year, but at present the
great pens were all empty. Indeed, we had arrived at a quiet time,
on a quiet day, and there was little evident activity of any kind in
the town. A cowboy rode down the main street in a pair of blue
embossed leather chaps, there was a shop window full of decorated saddles and Mexican spurs, and two or three horses were
tethered to trees on a peripheral vacant lot. Otherwise, with the
parked cars and the characterless modern buildings, it might have
been a town in any agricultural district in Canada. We decided to
go on to Quesnel.

Out of Williams Lake we had to climb a serpentine sandy road
up a high and almost sheer escarpment. We crossed Whisky Creek,
a disappointing torrent bed with a mere trickle of pure water, and
joined the main road at Soda Creek, which had dug a more rugged
and impressive gorge on its way to the Fraser but was almost as

dry after the parched summer. The village of Soda Creek had once been a busy river port in the gold rush days; at first the Cariboo Road ended here, and goods and passengers for the diggings were transferred to paddle-steamers which took them along the upper navigable reaches of the Fraser as far as Quesnel, where they were disembarked again to make the final part of their journey to Barkerville by road. Now, however, there is almost no navigation at all on the upper Fraser, a magnificent potential thoroughfare through the centre of British Columbia, and Soda Creek consists of little more than a couple of primitive stores and a gas station.

The Fraser, so turbulent when we had last seen it more than 150 miles away, was now a wide silvery river flowing swiftly but calmly through woods of aspen and willow. Until Quesnel we followed its course fairly closely, but the diversion through Williams Lake had eaten up more time than we had foreseen, and the sun was setting as we returned to the main road and faced another sixty miles of travel before we could hope to put up for the night. A few miles beyond Soda Creek the light began to fail, and we passed through a gathering nightfall in which the isolated farms and the little settlements—Macalister, Marguerite, Alexandria, Australian—could only be distinguished by their tiny clusters of lights. Once we saw an obelisk in a field and got out to examine it by torchlight. It commemorated the fact that the explorer Alexander Mackenzie had here reached the Fraser on his pioneer journey through western Canada to the coast in 1793. There were cultivated fields around, a ranchhouse near, and one realised that, wild as the Cariboo might now seem, it was a tame landscape compared with that which Mackenzie had seen on the day when he discovered the great river.

After one of those interminable periods of night driving when an hour passes like ten and, peering blindly into the obscurity beyond the headlights, you feel sure your objective must always lie just around the next corner, we finally came into sight of the lights of Quesnel, and a few minutes later crossed a narrow wooden bridge into the town. In the darkness, with inadequate lamps illuminating streets that appeared to be dissolving in liquid mud, Quesnel seemed like an epitome of hick-town history from the 1860's down to the present. Many of the houses, and even some of the shops, were mere log cabins, often with the gaping spaces between the logs stuffed with white cement which gave a curiously streaked and incomplete appearance to the walls. Names

Vancouver in the 1880's

The Gold Town of Barkerville in the 1860's

Barkerville

like The Gold Nugget Hotel reflected early history and the fact
that quite a number of its people still live by placer or dredger
mining. There were grubby little Chinese stores selling cowboy
kit and poolrooms where Indian boys in jeans bent over the tables.
There were also completely modern stores and garages to bring
the picture up to date. It looked a friendly, untidy town, much less
efficient than Williams Lake, but perhaps a good deal more
human.

Our search for accommodation was more difficult than we had
anticipated. On the edge of the town we drove into an auto-court
with a blazing neon sign, built on a shallow bluff like a Celtic encampment. There they had only a cabin for two people, and the
clerk warned us that we might find it difficult to get anything
better. The town was full, not only of hunters, but also of men
who were engaged on the railway extension.

Quesnel, although a town of less than 2,000 people, has been for
many years the terminus of a backwoods railway, the Pacific Great
Eastern, running, as the local wags always claimed, from nowhere
to nowhere, since it began at Quesnel and ended at a minute seaport called Squamish on Howe Sound, about fifty miles north of
Vancouver. The only connection between Vancouver and Squamish is the sea. This railway was started in the wave of activity and
optimism in the north of the province before the first world war,
when the Grand Trunk Pacific was pushed through from the
Rockies to Prince Rupert on the coast. It was intended as a link
between Vancouver and Prince George, but when it became clear
that the anticipated boom in this part of the country had not
matured, the P.G.E. was left as a single line, threading its way
over mountains and plateaus between two tiny termini, with no
industrial centre and no town of more than 3,000 inhabitants on
its whole length of 350 miles. The railway was saved from complete extinction when it was taken over and subsidised by the Provincial Government, but it did not change in any way for the next
twenty years, relying on the cattle of the Cariboo and the lumber
of the coastal mountain area for its income, maintaining its links
with other railroads only by a steamer from Squamish to Vancouver and a bus service from Quesnel to Prince George, and
costing the British Columbian taxpayer almost 120 million dollars
in subsidies to keep the trains running on its line three times every
week.

Since the war the situation in the north has changed: the

4

country beyond Quesnel is in a state of agricultural, mining and lumbering development which is certainly much more than a temporary boom, and the Provincial Government has at last undertaken the extension of the P.G.E. from Quesnel to Prince George, with the prospect of a link from Squamish to Vancouver which, whenever it is complete, will provide the first direct rail link between the northern and southern parts of British Columbia—a significant enough sign of the state of retarded development which has existed in the province up to the present time.

The young woman in the auto-court was indeed right in her warning. Even the most dismal, cheap hotels were crammed from basement to roof peak, and the proprietors of the remaining auto-camps merely shook their heads. We should have started looking at three o'clock, one of them suggested brightly. Another told us of outlying motels—one three miles up the road to Prince George, another at Dragon Lake, miles out to the east. We drove out along the Prince George highway. There was nothing vacant at the camp there, but we were sure to find something if we went another five miles and then turned down a side road and travelled four miles to a lake where there was a very comfortable fishing lodge. We shied a little at this idea, since fishing lodges are either cheap and excessively primitive or comfortable and excessively dear. Audrey enthusiastically suggested camping, but the woods were drenched and the ground was soaking—we gathered that the rain had finished in Quesnel only just before our arrival—and it would have been difficult to make a dry camp in the dark. So we went in search of the fishing lodge. After driving almost eight miles along the main road, without noticing a single turning, we came to the conclusion that it was either a figment of our informant's imagination or much farther away than he had told us, and we turned back to the town, having decided that we would have to take the small cabin in the first auto-court, if it was still available, and make some arrangement with sleeping bags on the floor.

Contrary to all our forebodings, the cabin was vacant, and we were even provided with a camp-bed on which one couple could sleep, while the others occupied the bed. In spite of the freshly painted chalet exterior of the huts, the accommodation was very primitive. There was a large iron stove, but few cooking utensils and no crockery. To wash we had a tiny enamel handbasin, and there was no mirror. The toilets were sixty yards away, in a central building, and it was from here that we had to carry our water in buckets. For such meagre facilities we were charged five dollars —almost two pounds.

In such conditions it was almost impossible to cook, and we went out again into the town, and after a while found a back-street Chinese restaurant which served a surprisingly good chicken chopsuey, over which we discussed our plans.

Inge and I wished to stay on in some of the towns in order to gather information, and we were particularly anxious to visit the centre of the old gold-mining area at Barkerville and also one or two of the Indian villages in the north; David and Audrey were bound by their holiday schedule, and the delays caused by the bad roads would make it necessary for them to cut down their halts. So it was finally agreed that we should make visits together to Barkerville and the Indian villages, while Inge and I, when we had finished our later trip by boat up the coast, would come inland from Prince Rupert and spend more time in the towns we wished to visit.

6.

Accordingly, we rose early the next day, and took the Barker-ville road, which turns east from the main highway about two miles out of Quesnel. We drove almost immediately into a thick forest of spruce and hemlock; soon the road began to climb, and whenever we reached an elevation of any kind we saw the wooded hills stretching before us in unbroken wildness, with not a clearing or a habitation in any direction. For an hour we went on in this way, climbing steadily into the mountains, until we had risen again to a height of more than 3,000 feet. The air that blew in through the open window became sharp and cold, the pools by the road-sides were iced over, here and there we saw a hillside where the trees were dusted white. A little later we ran into fresh snow, covering the narrow dirt road and lying in soft clots on the dark hemlocks, and we realised that in those elevated regions the winter began early.

In a flat piece of valley twenty miles out of Quesnel, where orange-leafed poplars clustered along a shallow river, we came to the first sign of settlement. This was Cottonwood House, a great barn-like log building which had been erected as a calling place for travellers on the way to the mines in the early days of the Cariboo rush. In its day it was a busy and well-frequented place, and the proprietor's journal, preserved at the University of British

Columbia, gives a fascinating record of the times. We had expected to see some tumbling, weather-wrecked ruin; instead there was a well kept and preserved house which was still being used as an inn for passers and a store for the few inhabitants of the surrounding district. It showed that, even in such extreme climates, the log house is a surprisingly durable form of construction if only it is kept in careful repair.

About ten miles beyond Cottonwood there were old broken flumes coming down from the hillsides into the creek beside the road, and then, scattered among tangling vegetation, the black ruins of cabins and houses, collapsing under the strain of eighty years of weathering. This was the deserted ghost of a once busy mining town called Wingdam. Another fifteen miles and we ran into a larger group of ruins—the old town of Stanley, or Van Winkle, where three thousand miners had panned the bars of Lightning Creek, and where a prospector named Ned Campbell once had the phenomenal luck to dig 900 ounces of gold in a day. Little enough was left of that early town of the 1860's, but there was something more fascinating and more depressing, because it was far more complete even in its desertion, about a great quartz mine, with crushing mills, stores, bunk-houses and villas of the managerial staff, which had only recently been abandoned and on which the process of decay had hardly begun. A few miles farther on, at the far end of a dark mountain tarn called Jack o' Clubs Lake, we reached Wells, the only gold-mining town in the Cariboo which is still functioning, based on highly capitalised quartz mining rather than on the individual placer work of the old days.

The two rival mines stood on each side of the valley, driving their galleries for miles into the hillsides. The town sprawled over the flat ground between, a rather ugly modern settlement, founded in the early 1930's, with bad roads and shabby wooden houses which had obviously been run up hastily, as is the custom in mining boom towns, with no idea of lasting or of comfort, and which were already beginning in some parts to lapse into slums.

We continued up the few miles of broad valley to Barkerville. Here, on Williams Creek and its bunch of rich tributaries, tens of millions of dollars' worth of gold were extracted by such figures of Canadian folk history as Dutch William, Cariboo Cameron and Billy Barker, and by the thousands of less celebrated prospectors who followed them during the rush summer of 1862 and the years after. Barkerville was the centre of all this activity, and, remembering the 10,000 people who are said to have lived here, we anticipated something very different from the somnolent snowy village, with its narrow winding street, into which we rode as the valley began to dwindle towards the canyon. We looked for a great ghost town with acres of tumbling houses, and saw a place which still seemed to have a fair amount of life and where there appeared to be very few ruined buildings. Looking down the quiet street, which resembled a little that of a Swiss mountain village, we tried to reconcile it with the wild days when twenty saloons and hotels resounded every night to the noise of the miners and the German hurdy-gurdy girls, whirling in the strenuous dances of the mid-nineteenth century.

David stopped a young woman who was walking on the wooden side-walk and asked her the way to the old town. She told us, with the air of a tidy housewife sweeping rubbish from the front door, that most of the ruined buildings had been pulled down years ago, since everybody thought they were nothing more than an eyesore. But we should find a few of the old places left if we went on down the village street.

We drove through the town and in less than an hour we had traced its surviving vestiges of the gold rush days. Up on the hillside, overlooking Cariboo Cameron's fabulous claim, there was the old cemetery, still dotted with cedar head-boards commemorating the early miners—fortune-hunters from every part of the earth—Russia and Germany, Spain and France, Britain and Mexico and, above all, America. They died young and plentifully: they worked with inadequate protection in wet diggings, often into the winter; their diet of beans and bacon and flour was in no way sufficient to make them withstand the ravages of rheumatism and tuberculosis; while something of the medical methods to which they subjected themselves can be seen from this notice which I once found leafing through a copy of the *Cariboo Sentinel* from those days :

James P. Taylor,
DRUGGIST

Has just received direct from San Francisco Dr. Le Richau's celebrated Golden Balsam, for the complete cure of Secondary Syphilis. Also, a quantity of Dr. Murphy's Mixtures, so well known as a specific cure for the same.

Most of the head-boards were the simple memorials to men who for all their efforts, had died too poor to give them a magnificent funeral. But here and there stood an elaborate stone, and perhaps the most curious in its effusiveness was that erected over an Irish Gold Commissioner called Chartres Brew, something of a figure in the early political history of British Columbia, who died in 1870, and who is described by his epitaph-writer as "A man imperturbable in courage and temper, endowed with a great and varied administrative capacity, a most ready wit, a most pure integrity and a most human heart."

At the cross roads in the village stood the same wooden church which was built after the great fire which burnt Barkerville to the ground in 1868. There were quite a number of old log houses, and a few false-fronted hotels and stores from the past. Beyond these we traced where one or two old streets had been, and began to form some conception of what had formerly existed.

Actually, the idea of Barkerville as a compact town of 10,000 people was quite incorrect. That figure included outlying settlements like Richfield, where there remains only the old court-house, like Maryville and Centreville and Gladstoneville, of which nothing has survived, while all the way up the creeks and gulches stood the cabins and tents of isolated miners. Into Barkerville all these people came to buy their stores when flour was often seventy-five cents a pound, to have their beards trimmed by Moses, the escaped slave, to visit the Theatre Royal, to dance and to drink, to visit the brothels and gamble at 800 dollars a game, and often enough to lose their money to the card-sharping dandies. Like the Klondike, Barkerville even produced its own poets, the anonymous Bard of Lowhee, and one James Anderson, who wrote plays for the Theatre Royal and a book of verse, called *Sawney's Letters*, which had the single virtue that it contained a vast amount of information about Cariboo life. A characteristic poem is that which celebrated the hurdy-gurdy girls, dancing partners employed by the saloons and distinguished by their comparative respectability from the regular prostitutes:

> *They danced at night in dresses light,*
> *Frae late until the early, O,*
> *But Oh, their hearts were hard as flint,*
> *Which vexed the laddies sairly, O!*

> *The dollar was their only love,*
> *And that they lo'ed fu' dearly, O,*
> *They dinna care a flea for men,*
> *Let them court hooe'er sincerely, O!*
>
> *Bonnie are the gurdies, O,*
> *The German hurdy-gurdies, O,*
> *The daftest hours that e'er I spent,*
> *Was dancin' wi' the hurdies, O!*

For what it was worth, this glimmering in a mining boom town was the first literary movement in western Canada.

The Barkerville of history was not without its quota of strange and colourful characters who deserve some place in the story of human eccentricity. Billy Barker himself, from whom the town was named, has left a somewhat dim memory, and his chief title to fame seems to have been that he was the first miner to abandon work on the river bars and sink a shaft down to the rich lode from which most of the Cariboo fortunes were made. But there was Joseph Hough, the dandy, a villain fit for any melodrama, with his slicked hair, stiff white collar, a velvet waistcoat and resplendent watch-chain, mingling in the saloons with the roughly clad miners and fleecing them out of their hard-won dust. There was James Cameron, better known as Cariboo Cameron, the luckiest man in the goldfield, whose haul from his claim below the cemetery has been variously estimated at up to a million dollars. Cameron was one of the few men to bring his wife out to the diggings in the early days; she died there, and the grief-stricken husband decided to take her back to eastern Canada for burial. The journey down to the coast had to be made in the hardest midwinter weather; on arrival the body was pickled in a coffin full of alcohol, and there followed a macabre sea voyage round the Horn, with incredulous customs officials boring holes into the casket to see what strange contraband it contained, until Jessie Cameron finally reached her Nova Scotian resting-place. Cameron systematically lost his wealth in wildcat ventures over the next quarter of a century, and returned to the Cariboo in 1888, a poverty-stricken old man seeking to make a second fortune. His luck did not return, and he died that year and was buried overlooking the scene of his past triumph.

With the name of Cameron is associated that of Twelve-foot Davis. He decided that Cameron's claim was bigger than the legal maximum, paced it out and found that there were twelve feet too much; he filed a claim on this extra piece, thereby gaining the name by which he has since been known and making a modest haul of 12,000 dollars. With this he became a trader in the north country, between Peace River and Slave Lake, and when he died was buried in the mountains with the enviable epitaph: "He was pathfinder, pioneer, miner and trader. He was every man's friend and never locked his door."

But perhaps the strangest of all the Cariboo celebrities was Judge Matthew Baillie Begbie. A lawyer who had been completely unsuccessful at the London Bar, Begbie was sent out by Lytton to become the first judge of the new colony of British Columbia. He rode and tramped about the wild interior with unremitting energy, appearing on the scene of a crime with incredible despatch and acting as policeman, prosecutor and judge in proceedings of dubious legality which won him the fear and detestation of the miners, by whom he was called "The Hanging Judge". His disputes with juries were fantastic; often when men were palpably innocent Begbie would try to bully the jurors into a verdict of guilty, and equally often, out of a desire to pique the judge, the jurors insisted on setting the guilty free. Begbie's comments on such occasions were richly abusive. When a strong-arm man had been acquitted, he shouted: "Prisoner at the bar, the jury have said you are not guilty. You can go, and I devoutly hope the next man you sandbag will be one of the jury." On another occasion, when the jury insisted that a murderer was guilty of manslaughter, Begbie gave sentence thus: "Prisoner, it is far from a pleasant duty for me to have to sentence you only to imprisonment for life. Your crime was unmitigated, diabolical murder. You deserve to be hanged! Had the jury performed their duty I might have the painful satisfaction of condemning you to death; and you, gentlemen of the jury, are a pack of horse thieves, and it would give me great pleasure to see you hanged, each and every one of you, for declaring a murderer guilty only of manslaughter." Begbie was totally lacking in fear, and one night, when he heard a group of men below his window plotting to murder him, he dealt out summary justice by emptying his chamber pot over their heads and returning to bed. Yet this ferocious judge was a much more complex character than he appeared; often, after he had condemned a man to death, he would surreptitiously send an appeal for clemency to the governor of the province, and when he died he left his money to the poor and ordered that the only inscription on his grave should read "Lord, be merciful to me, a sinner".

Now the thousands over whom Begbie and his constables had ruled were reduced to a mere two hundred people, and when we peered into the little wooden houses we saw mostly old men and women. An official in the Gold Commissioner's Office told us that if we wanted to see some real old-fashioned placer mining there were still a few men working in some of the creeks and gulches. In the kind-hearted manner which seemed to characterise most of the people in this vicinity, he even drew us a couple of neat little maps with various coloured pencils, enjoying the job as much as if he were drawing a Government survey. Unfortunately, on crossing the first bridge, we found that the steep road winding along the mountainside was too thickly snowed over for it to be safe to travel without chains, so we were forced to turn back and drive down the open valley again to Wells. Barkerville, we decided as we drove away, was a ghost town which, by adjusting itself to a restricted life, had retained something of its character and even developed—what is rare indeed in the west—a genuine flavour of antiquity. In this it has been helped a great deal by the beauty of its surroundings, the hills which have long since grown over again after the early miners stripped them bare to build their houses and their flumes.

In Wells we decided to visit the quartz mines. At the first a harassed-looking manager agreed to let us see the mill, though it would be impossible to arrange at this time of the day for us to go down into the galleries. We went up some stairs into a great loft where everything was covered with grey dust. The foreman was out, and we waited while a man went to look for him. Pieces of grey rock were going slowly over a conveyor belt into a crusher, with glittering particles showing up among them. On the other side of the room we went out on to a platform over a number of vats which were filled with a kind of dead grey sludge. It all looked very dirty and unimpressive. There were notices warning not to drink the water, which was liable to be poisonous, and there were various production charts hanging on notice boards. But no foreman appeared, and we decided that perhaps gold production was not very exciting, at least in this mechanised form. We seemed to have seen the process of extraction in progress, and a lengthy explanation was unlikely to make it any more edifying. However, we decided to try our luck at the mine across the valley.

This was a larger concern, and the ramp leading up to it was peppered with small glittering lumps of quartz. We scrutinised them anxiously; sure enough, there were small cubical chunks of yellow metal embedded in them. What could it be but gold? We were too excited to doubt that we had hit on a minor El Dorado, and Audrey and Inge stayed behind to fill their pockets with pieces of this clearly auriferous rock, while David and I went on to the low wooden office building on top of the hill.

A grey-haired clerk came out to see us. After some hesitation, he agreed to telephone the various foremen to let us see the plant. But just then a powerful car drove up outside, and a youngish, rather hard-looking man walked into the office. The old clerk winced. "Here's the manager, Mr. ——," he said; "perhaps you would talk to him." Mr. —— came forward and asked our business in a brusque Scots accent. I told him. "You're wasting your time," he answered. "And what's more, you're wasting mine. Visitors aren't wanted here. They're just a nuisance. So good day, gentlemen. And don't stay around."

It was, I must say, the only time—except for one later incident —on which we encountered such downright rudeness in the whole of our travels. We all felt intensely annoyed at the time, yet in retrospect I wonder if there is not perhaps more reason for surprise at the forbearance of all the other people on whom we descended for information than at the suspicious hostility which our demands aroused in this devotee of bluntness.

A mile or two beyond Wells we noticed a large and apparently deserted flume which carried water across the road to a sluice-box running down, among piles of dirt, towards the creek. We got out and began searching among the silt that lay between the baffleboards. Suddenly David pulled out a glistening lump as big as a sparrow's egg. A moment later I found a pocket which held a dozen little glistening cubic particles. We all became very excited at these discoveries, and in a quarter of an hour we had collected a good handful of what, to our eyes, looked convincingly like small nuggets. We questioned for a moment why anybody should have left a sluice-box full of gold, but this was immediately replaced by a thought that perhaps the box had not really been abandoned, and we decided to make a hasty departure with what we had found. Besides, snow was beginning to fall, and we thought it would be better to reach the lower ground before we were caught in a blizzard. We returned to the main road without any further incident, making chimerical plans as we went of what we should do if we really had lit upon a rich and abandoned claim.

Here and there the main road to Prince George passed through some quite spectacular scenery. There was the deep canyon into which we descended when the Cottonwood River cut down between some sheer and impressive bluffs to join the Fraser. Here we passed through a minute settlement called Cinema, one of those inexplicably capricious names one so often encounters in the North American back-country. At another spot we drove by a group of impressive basaltic columns which resembled, though on a much smaller scale, the Giant's Causeway at Ulster. For the last forty miles to Prince George the land was much more intensively farmed than it had been in the real Cariboo, with frequent homesteads beside the road and much land under the plough. The settlements once again became fairly frequent, and at one of them, called Woodpecker, we stopped for petrol. As he paid the proprietor of the gas station, David asked him quietly, "Do you know anything about gold?"

"I guess I do," the man answered slowly. "When I was diggin' a well in back of my place I found three nuggets big as pigeons' eggs."

"Is there much gold round here, then?" David fenced.

"Fair bit, I reckon. When they were workin' on the railway cutting this year the men were always pickin' up nuggets. Had a bit of trouble about it, you know. The railroad claimed the nuggets were theirs, being found on their property, you know, but plenty of men just kept 'em and said nothin'."

"What do you think of this?" David flashed his big piece of yellow metal and a handful of smaller pieces.

The man looked dubious. "I sure wouldn't know about that. Mine looked different, but then, they weren't pure gold. Gold don't run very pure up here, you know, like it does over in Barkerville. You want to take those to an assayer. He'll tell you sure enough." He handed the big nugget back with a tactful air. It was the first of a whole series of encounters in which we exhibited our treasure to people who invariably cried off an expert knowledge and passed the metal back with ambiguous smiles. At last even we began to lose faith—all except Inge, who seemed to have been afflicted with a mild touch of gold fever and stood firmly to the conviction that we had literally hit on a bonanza. She would have been ready at any time during the ensuing days to hasten back to Barkerville on the first bus if she had received the slightest support from the rest of us.

Eventually, on our return to Vancouver some days later, we strode into the Government Mines Office and, after looking in vain for anything like our own metal among the samples on show, we went up to the counter and poured out our wealth before the attendant. He looked at it and laughed. "That, ma'm," he explained to Inge, "is what we call fool's gold. It's iron pyrites. This is what a real nugget looks like." He waved a ring on which was set a great soft-coloured yellow piece of metal whose edges had been worked smooth in an age of rubbings in the beds of streams before it had finally been panned out by some prospector, or perhaps, since he wore it, by the man himself. We crept out in humiliation; it seemed for the moment almost as devastating as losing a fortune one already possessed.

7.

But all this took place later, and for the moment we drove on with a fluctuating confidence in our good fortune and with Inge whiling away the moments of boring countryside by counting our nuggets and weighing them in her hand to decide just how much wealth we already had. A few miles farther, on a piece of straight and unusually smooth piece of dirt road between some dense groves of thin lodgepole pines, our dreams of good fortune were interrupted by a sudden loud explosion at the back of the car and an ominous flapping sound as the front wheels swerved towards the ditch. An almost new tyre had burst into shreds. We hurriedly unloaded the intricately dovetailed miscellany of goods in the baggage compartment and unearthed the spare wheel from its place at the back; by the time the replacement had been completed and everything repacked, we had wasted the best part of half an hour.

A large airport and a Dominion Experimental Farm, with elegantly painted buildings, large flocks of white chickens and plenty of invitations to enter and look around, indicated that we were near Prince George, and a little while afterwards we began to descend a long wooded hill towards the Fraser. We could see the city lying on the farther bank, in the angle formed by the large river and one of its major tributaries, the Nechako. We had an immediate view of large railway sidings and timber yards, and a spreading prospect of town roofs, dominated by large hotel signs. It was evident that we were entering a much larger centre of industry and population than anything we had seen since the middle of the Fraser Valley.

As Inge and I spent a longer and more informative time in Prince George in a later part of our journeys, I will content myself now with giving the impression we gained on a first brief encounter. We ran into a town with long, wide streets of shops and stores, restaurants and hotels; it was clear from the first sight that this was the centre of British Columbia's north country. Indeed, after nearly 500 miles of three-house settlements masquerading as villages and villages masquerading as towns, Prince George with its paved roads and concrete sidewalks, its new public buildings and clinics and cinemas, seemed in comparison almost metropolitan.

It was Friday night, pay night, and the streets were crowded, but people in town clothes were in the minority among the outdoor men, the miners and loggers and cowboys in their mackinaws, buckskin jackets and Cowichan sweaters, who had come drifting in from the surrounding territory to fill the cheap hotels and the beer parlours and roam noisily through the town. There were many Indians; they had more clearly cut features and neater figures than those we had met farther south—indeed, throughout our journey we were impressed by the variations in native physical types from one locality to another. For the first time we noticed some Indians who seemed to have lost their air of town-shyness and even to have gained a certain appearance of well-dressed prosperity. There was one girl among them who was very beautiful in the flat-faced expressionless manner of women in classic Japanese paintings. But by no means all were of this sophisticated type, and many had come in from the villages of the surrounding reservations to stare at the enjoyments of the white men, to peddle some of their leather and bead work, and to get drunk illegally if they possibly could.

There was a remarkable atmosphere of raw life and movement in the city and this, I am sure, was due not merely to the hundreds of men who crowded the sidewalks with money burning holes in their pockets. It was the atmosphere of a town in the nervous process of growth, the centre of an expanding territory, of growing industries. There were the big sawmills down towards the river, with their tall conical drying kilns, their great sheds and

their piles of yellow sawn wood; there were the new buildings
rising at the end of every street, the long expensive cars which
made parking difficult, the fashionably dressed girls we would
occasionally see pushing their way among the visiting rough-
necks, the shops full of clothes and food and sports goods which
it would be impossible to buy anywhere else nearer than Vancouver. The atmosphere of awakening at the end of a long sleep
which characterised Clinton and Quesnel was quite absent here.
There was the feeling of a full impetus of expansion, and it became clear, even before we knew a great deal about what was
happening in the north, that there must be a vast amount of new
activity to nurture a town of this kind.

We bought food and a new tyre, and then went in search of an
auto-court. There were some of these on top of the hill going out
of town to the west. The edge of the escarpment was crested by
a whole colony of churches clustering on a single large green-
swarded area, evidently the result of an interesting theory of town
planning which intended to keep the smoke of incense as well as
that of industry well out of the city centre.

Beyond the churches lay the auto-courts. In the first we visited
a large and rowdy party was going on in the office, men and girls
sitting round with full tumblers of rye, singing and shouting with
the rather artificial gaiety of the first hour. Eventually we made
our presence known and, after numerous voices had yelled invitations to join in, the young proprietress emerged, stared a little
glassily, giggled and hiccuped, and then told us that she was right
full up. We had better luck at the next motel, a group of pseudo-
rustic log huts kept by some sour, elderly Scots. These cabins
were certainly more spacious than that in which we had spent the
previous night, but once again conditions were almost eccentri-
cally primitive, and we even had to creep furtively into the women's
toilet building to get drinking water. That evening we had a long
discussion on slang; I taught David some of the rhyming talk of
the Cockneys, while he related the argot of the San Francisco half-
world; a drunk, I remember, was a lush, a marihuana addict a tea-
head, a pansy a fruit or gay.

8.

Next morning we took the road to the west; for a couple of
hours we drove through the singularly dull countryside of an
almost flat plain; at times we would go for miles through mono-

tonous second-growth forest, consisting largely of thin, over-grown saplings of fir or aspen, or pine on the stonier ground, often crowded so thickly that one wondered how they could possibly survive. Some agricultural activity was going on, and here and there whole areas had been cleared by bulldozer and the trees pushed into ragged piles for burning before the land was ploughed for seeding the following year. There was no settlement of any kind for seventy miles west of Prince George, and we hoped that in all these deserted leagues we should see some of the game, the moose and elk and deer, with which this country is said to abound. But, though we strained our eyes for any possible sign of wild life, we saw nothing bigger than a couple of black squirrels.

Eventually we reached Vanderhoof, an ugly flat town with two mud streets at right angles. We wanted to buy milk, and went searching unavailingly through the few shops. There was even a dairy, but still no milk. We protested that we had heard Vanderhoof was in the middle of a dairying area. "It sure is, but that don't mean we get the milk. It's all sent down to Prince, you know, and we get the leavings."

A leathery-faced man in a skiing cap and a mackinaw jacket came up and condoled with us. Why didn't we try the first farm on the left going out of town? They might have a pint to spare, if they hadn't already sent it away. "Folks round here don't worry much about cow's milk," he cracked. "They prefer moose's milk." We looked blank, thinking, and immediately rejecting the thought, that perhaps some enterprising northerners had taken to keeping herds of moose as the Laplanders kept reindeer. "What," we asked cautiously, "what is moose's milk?" He beamed with the happiness of superior knowledge and explained that it was a home-brewed spirit made out of fermented wheat which was commonly regarded as having as much punch as the headlong charge of a bull moose.

That brought us to the question of the big game. Why had we not seen any moose on the way? He shook his head. "You won't see any moose down here. There are too many hunters round, and by now all the moose and elk have high-tailed up into the north, way off the roads."

He went on to tell us that the moose were common enough around Vanderhoof during the closed seasons, and in the deep winter, when the wolves would drive them down into inhabited areas. Then, escaping from their pursuers, the bulls would go through the hard crust on the snow, cutting their shins in the process, and enraged with pain they had more than once attacked cars on the roads, particularly at night. You had to look out at that time of the year. A moose might not be able to smash up a car by direct impact, but he could cause a nasty spill on a slippery road.

The man looked down at the registration plate on the car. "It sure is good to see folks from home!" he remarked nostalgically.

"Why, do you come from San Francisco?"

"Yes—just outside it, Oakland. I came here twenty years ago, when the bush was a good deal wilder than it is today."

He had not found life harsh or irksome. In some ways backwoods existence was certainly primitive, but it was interesting and satisfying. He'd done about every outdoor job you could think of, and he hadn't regretted a day of the whole twenty years, and had never wanted to go back to the city life. But it was sure good to see some folks from home again!

A couple of tall, angular Indian women walked along the plank sidewalk and into the post office. They wore rusty black satin dresses, antique cheap tweed overcoats and thick white woollen stockings rolled below the knees.

"They're Babines," our informant went on. "They do those stockings by crochet work. Some of the Indians round here are real primitive. Only last month they went into the bush to pick up a woman way out beyond Fort St. James and bring her down here to the hospital. She'd never seen a car before in all her life. The funny thing was, though, that she knew all about planes— she'd seen the bush pilots landing up in that north country where there's not a road for donkey's miles."

Inge and Audrey returned from their shopping, and we said goodbye to the man from Oakland; after having called at the Liquor Store and bought a gallon crock labelled "Canadian White Wine" for the reunion, we set out on the road once more. At the first farm on the left we asked for milk; needless to say, they had none left—it had all gone off to Prince George! But we might get some in Burns Lake. That was eighty-two miles on.

As soon as we left Vanderhoof the countryside became much more satisfying. The whole of central British Columbia, north and west of Prince George, is dotted with lakes of all sizes, varying from Babine Lake, more than 120 miles in length, down to sheets of water which are little more than pools. The alternation of lake and hills, woodland and river, gives a great variety to the landscape, and I imagine that this territory is in many ways similar to Finland, though on a much vaster scale. The largest lakes are situated in the bush, well away from the highway, but even those we passed—Fraser Lake, Burns Lake, Decker Lake—with their wooded shores and islands and their numerous populations of wild duck, were sufficiently impressive. In this broken country the settlements again became more frequent—there was a village with a store and a hotel almost every twenty miles, and the land was much more widely cultivated.

The first of these places was Fort Fraser, one of the oldest settlements in British Columbia, antedating Victoria by nearly forty and Vancouver by seventy years, for it was originally founded in 1807 as one of the posts of the old Northwest Trading Company, later absorbed by the Hudson's Bay Company. But these trading forts were never more than isolated posts in the wilderness, and the mining and agricultural interests which turned the settlements of the south into cities and towns and villages have not operated in these areas until comparatively recent years. Thus Fort Fraser is still a tiny settlement, and there is little except an indefinable kind of English village atmosphere and a still functioning Hudson's Bay store to indicate its special antiquity or its important role in the early settlement of the far west of Canada.

A little way beyond Fort Fraser we passed a red-brick collegiate building standing on the shore of Fraser Lake. In a field beside the road potatoes were being dug by machinery, and a swarm of little Indian boys were gathering them up and putting them into sacks. This was the Lejac residential school for Indian children, operated by the Oblate Fathers, who for the last century have held a virtual monopoly of educational and missionary work among the Carriers. At least one of the Oblate Fathers, Morice, was a notable pioneer in the study of the Carrier customs and languages (the tribal name came from the obligation imposed on a widow to carry her husband's charred bones on her back for a period after his death), and his writings provide a mass of important information on the early days of settlement in the north country, and particularly on the rough treatment of the Indians by the Hudson's Bay Company's representatives—details which might otherwise have been unavailable to historical students anxious to make an objective study of British colonisation in western Canada.

However, these contributions to knowledge by one of the Oblate Fathers did not save the order from some bitter criticism

5

on the part of Audrey and Inge, who interpreted the scene we had just witnessed as the exploitation of child labour, which they regarded as all of a piece with the Roman Catholics' attempt to gain converts through their privileged positions as educators. David and I disputed this contention, at least in part, having carefully pointed out that we were not in any way partisans of the Catholic Church and did not excuse the situation in which the priests were allowed to supervise the education of Indian children. We admitted that, being fanatical devotees of their own way of thought, they could not be expected to do anything other than attempt to transmit it to the children under their care. On the other hand, we suggested that the priests might individually be very just and humble men, who acted, not from a desire to dominate, but out of a genuine love for the people among whom they worked, that they might indeed be men whose sincerity and goodness should inspire our respect for them, however we might disagree with their creed and detest some of their church's social manifestations. As for the employment of the children, we had no proof that this was really exploitation. It would be a logical part of vocational training, and the children themselves had not looked unhappy, nor, indeed, had they been working very hard.

The conflict ended in stalemate when our attention was diverted by a herd of horses which ran away before us into the woods, after having galloped magnificently down the road before us for nearly a mile. This sight illustrated admirably what we had already noticed on our journey—the relative abundance of horses in this area as compared with their almost complete elimination, due greater mechanisation of farming, in southern British Columbia and in the northern United States. Here we saw horses used frequently for draught work as well as riding, and the pleasure we gained from watching them made us realise how much has indeed been lost in agricultural landscapes where horses have now disappeared.

Beyond Fraser Lake the small towns strung out along the road —Burns Lake, Decker Lake, Houston—showed every sign of raw and rapid growth. These settlements arose originally as railway halts when the Grand Trunk Pacific was built through the northern wilderness just before the first world war. But it was not until the early 1940's that, at the insistence of the American Army, the road on which we were travelling was built from Prince George to Prince Rupert, and it was this that gave all these railroad villages a second link with the outer world and conferred a certain flexibility on their exploitation of agricultural and timber resources. Since then they have grown quickly, their dirt side-lanes are developing into streets of houses, new sawmills deal with the products of the woods, new warehouses canalise the increasing field crops, new stores serve the growing population, and new hotels and auto-camps cater for the tourists and transient workers. In Burns Lake we at last obtained our pint of milk, but it was only because the customer who would normally have bought it had not appeared that morning. Such fresh commodities are still so scarce in these mushrooming towns that an unofficial rationing is imposed to make them go round.

At a tiny hamlet called Rose Lake I remembered suddenly that the last day had arrived on which I could post an application for a Guggenheim Fellowship I wished to obtain in order to write a book on Proudhon. There was a pile of railway ties beside the road, and I set my typewriter on these and, squatting before it, composed and typed the application impromptu, with the wind almost blowing the paper away from me as I worked. The scene— the dirt road, the copses of thin trees, the distance from any centre of culture (even Vancouver was 700 miles away)—the fact that when Proudhon himself lived this country had been a total and unbroken wilderness, gave irony to the situation, and I could not believe seriously that my application would succeed. Perhaps the crowning irony was that it did.

Soon we entered the valley of the Bulkley, the largest tributary of the Skeena, in its turn the most important river in northwestern British Columbia. We crossed the Bulkley itself at Houston, a town largely inhabited by Dutch immigrants who arrived during the 1930's. The decking of the bridge was being renewed, and for some inexplicable reason a beam at least eight inches thick had been laid, and apparently secured, right across the highway. We had no alternative but to drive straight for it; to our relief, the wheels mounted over it with no worse trouble than a great shaking up of the whole car which pulverised the dried mud that had collected underneath it during the last few days. The interior was filled with a cloud of white dust which gritted the teeth and set us all sneezing.

Beyond the bridge lay a long level stretch of moderately good highway and, since we wished to reach Smithers, another forty-four miles on, before the post office closed, David hoped to make

up a little lost time here. He was frustrated, however, by an
ancient two-seater which either kept to the centre of the road or
weaved from side to side, going all the time at a crawl of no more
than ten miles an hour. Sometimes the driver would go far to the
right-hand side, but whenever David tried to pass, he would
waver over and swing into the left. This went on for nearly four
miles, until, in one of the right-hand swings, David took his
courage into his hands and drove ahead at top speed. Providen-
tially, he was too quick for the other man to make his customary
swing. We all looked round in passing, and a lolling, pie-eyed
face drooled back a vacant grin; it was a drunken homesteader
making his Saturday afternoon way home.

We crossed the Bulkley again and the road began to climb. We
were leaving the lake-strewn and relatively flat interior plateau,
and at the end of a long, steep hill we finally came to a kind of
elevated bench land, over which we travelled for more than
twenty miles. The views here were panoramic and magnificent,
falling away to the left in wooded hills and deep valleys, with
thick forests of hemlock and spruce and aspens, which in this
northerly region, with the earlier onset of autumn, were already
assuming the final orange tint that comes just before the fall of
the leaves. The combination of this vivid colour with the sombre
green of the hemlocks and the silvery, slightly frosted green of
the spruce, stretching over mile after mile of hillsides, gave a
variety of texture to the landscape which one rarely sees in the
forests of the Pacific regions. Soon we came into sight of mountains, the first peaks of the 200-mile belt of chains that make up
the great aggregate of the Coast Range, which we were now re-
crossing after having penetrated it at Hope, more than 600 miles
farther south. Over the valley we could see the Telkwa mountains,
and to our right and somewhat ahead were the Babines, heavily
capped with snow and dividing the end of the great Babine Lake
from the mountain country of small tarns into which we were
advancing. Farther on, we began to see the distant ridges and
peaks of other groups and ranges rising on the horizon, all now
wearing their white caps of autumn.

The road finally descended in another long hill into a belt of
well-tilled farming country. The Bulkley Valley has a fertile alluvial soil and, despite the hard winters and the short growing
season, it is one of the best arable regions in British Columbia.
It has been farmed ever since the coming of the railway, but the

last few years, since the building of the road, have brought a great impetus to its development, and it was evident that most of the farms we passed were better equipped, more prosperous and more productive than any we had seen since we left the lower Fraser Valley. The Bulkley Valley, indeed, may well become a northern equivalent of that fertile region; its climate is too severe for fruit to be grown on a commercial scale, but it is excellent for dairying and vegetable growing, while the farmers have already become expert at the raising of seed, to such an extent that in Telkwa we found a producer's co-operative which dealt exclusively in the marketing of seed crops.

We ran into Telkwa along the banks of the river, which for a mile or so before were fringed with heavy woodland. This little town seemed the most pleasant of all the settlements we had seen that day. The main street skirted the Bulkley and was edged with a line of tall poplars. The side streets were sloping and consisted largely of old log cabins and well-established gardens. There was more of an air of settled existence than in the boom towns along the road.

This is due to the fact that Telkwa's main industry—the coal mines whose wheels and shafts rise up on the other side of the river—was in existence long before the building of the highroad. Coal, like most other important minerals, is found in many spots throughout the north of British Columbia, sometimes in very considerable reserves, but, except for the fields near Peace River, on the other side of the Great Divide, Telkwa is the only place where it has so far been exploited. The main difficulty in these northern regions is the lack of transport. Many of the really good measures lie literally hundreds of miles from railways or from the kind of roads which would support heavy freight traffic, and the mine of Telkwa owes its existence entirely to the accident that the Grand Trunk Pacific Railway happened to be built forty years ago right beside its location.

There was even something of the European mining town atmosphere about Telkwa—the men looked much more toil-scarred than the ordinary northerners, and there was an air of grime and poverty about the smaller streets; the older cabins had a neglected look, there were down-at-heel, sluttish women in the doorways, and one bedraggled girl in particular, who looked no more than a child herself, was pregnant and led a tiny boy by the hand.

9

Another ten miles along the valley we finally reached Smithers, where we had to enquire about the exact location of the settlement we intended to visit. Smithers, with about 1,500 inhabitants, is the largest town between Prince George and Prince Rupert, a railway, farming, lumbering and mining centre. A wide, dusty main street runs down at right angles from the highway, and as one turns into the town one's view is immediately dominated by the mass of the Hudson's Bay Mountains looming up beyond the railway station and the river, with their snow crests and the glacier hanging low in their folds. The square-fronted stores and hotels of the main street peter out into a withered park and some waste lots towards the railway. On each side a few dirt roads run off, sparsely studded with dwellings and barn-like lodging houses, and down on the low-lying land beside the tracks lie the crowded and cramped shacks of Indiantown, where some of the local tribesmen migrated years ago when they were starving on their reservations.

As it was Saturday night, all the outlying people from twenty miles around had come in to enjoy themselves. There were more drunkards even than in Prince George, and a stream of men went in and out of the liquor store, hurrying to lay in a stock before closing time.

Here I think it is worth while to make a small deviation to explain the eccentric liquor laws of British Columbia. Public drinking can only be done in the beer parlours, which sell a single yellow, highly gaseous and highly chemical brew, to be drunk under ludicrous conditions. In these houses it is forbidden to drink standing up, to sing, to play cards or dominoes or darts, or to indulge in any of those activities which give drinking a social value and raise it above mere guzzling; moreover, unattached men are segregated from the women as strictly as the goats from the sheep on the day of judgment, and to the Indians of either sex the doors of the beer parlour are firmly closed.

All other drinks, spirits, wine and so forth, must in the letter of the law be bought in liquor stores which are the monopoly of the Provincial Government. As these establishments exist only in moderately large settlements, and as they are never open in the thirsty evening hours, illegal liquor peddlers flourish and many policemen are afflicted by a kind of collective myopia whose virus is carried on fifty-dollar bills. The drinking public in general consumes more liquor than it wants, for no other reason than the difficulty involved in getting it, and the racketeers who profit by this situation join in a solid and most unholy alliance with temperance advocates and political job-holders to oppose any referendum that attempts to establish a more rational system.

Around the door to the liquor store in Smithers that night stood a semicircle of expectant-looking Indians; as each white man came out a couple of them would follow him round the corner and bargain for some of his liquor, which they usually obtained at 50 to 100 per cent. more than he had paid for it. This kind of individual bootlegging, we gathered, was a regular procedure in this area, with its large Indian population.

In the post office we asked where we could find David's friends. They moved out into the hills a month back, we were told; the postmaster couldn't be sure how we should reach them, but we'd best ask at the next store down the street. The storekeeper was equally vague, but the very man to tell us, a Swede and a neighbour of the Americans, was right in town. He'd last been seen making his way from the beer parlour to the coffee shop down by the railroad. If we were quick we'd catch him before he went back into the beer parlour, and he'd be sure to tell us where to go.

So we went off towards the station. It was a hilariously elated town through which we passed and, though it was barely six o'clock, every other person, whether white or Indian, seemed well on the way to intoxication. Outside the taxi stand a little crowd of Indians were passing bottles from hand to hand, with no attempt at concealment, despite the penalties to which they were theoretically subject for illicit drinking. There were both men and women among them, and a jovial man in a bright red jacket seemed the centre of the group, clowning to his friends with a complete lack of inhibition. They laughed and talked in one of their own languages; whether it was Babine or Gitksan we could not be sure, since the two tribes mingle in this area. They seemed a very light-hearted and amiable crowd, and it looked as if the days when Indians went berserk over a dram of spirits were long past.

We found the Swede, sprawling tipsily across the bar of the coffee shop. Sure he could tell us where our friends were living, and he stumbled out and stood gesticulating and shouting in thick Scandinavian accents beside the car. We must go northward on the main road for about fifteen miles until we came to a curved trestle bridge. We must not go over the bridge, but back up a

hundred yards and then follow a side lane, at the end of which
we should find the Californians encamped in an open field.
"Don't forget the curved bridge," he kept shouting as we drove
away.

We had hardly left him, and were still in the middle of Smithers
—dusk had fallen in the meantime—when the headlights suddenly
flickered out. We tried to determine the trouble by the light of a
street lamp. A little fiddling, and the lights seemed to work again.
But no sooner had we reached the highway and turned north than
they began to flash on and off erratically, and a pungent smell of
burning rubber filled the inside of the car. It was clear that some
kind of faulty contact was occurring which might easily cause a
fire, but try as we might with our weak flashlight, we were quite
unable to locate it, though we had little doubt that it was somehow
the result of the drastic shaking to which the car had been subjected during the last few days. There was nothing else, if we
wished to avoid abandoning our car by the roadside, but to take
the risk of driving as best we could without lights. Fortunately
the night was not completely black, and it was possible, over most
of the way, to discern at least roughly where the road ran. I hung
out of one window, flashing our torch to give at least some warning of our presence, and David occasionally turned the headlights
quickly on and off, to make sure of his position on the road. In
this way it took us more than an hour to travel our fifteen miles,
but fortunately there was absolutely no traffic, and we did not
have the ill luck to fall in with a police patrol.

Between the fourteenth and sixteenth mileposts we crossed no
less than three creeks with their wooden trestled bridges, all of
which were perceptibly curved. At each of the first two we halted
and backed up in search of a lane, but unsuccessfully, and then,
finally, we came upon one bridge which was bent almost in a long
semicircle; we had no doubt now that this was what the Swedish
homesteader had meant, and when we searched with the flashlight,
there was the black entrance to a lane on the left-hand side of the
road. We turned into it, bumped over a level crossing, and then
continued interminably up a slimy way with overhanging bushes
on either side. Once the whole car seemed to fall bodily into a
muddy hollow, where it churned a moment and then contrived
to clamber out. Then the lane began to rise gradually, and finally
the car became stuck in the ruts and would not make the rest of
the steepening grade.

At this moment, however, we heard a dog barking. David blew his horn loudly and a moment or so later a storm lantern began to gig down the lane towards us. We had ended within hailing distance of the camp, and David got out and began walking towards the light. An old man's quavering voice addressed him, and he replied by greeting somebody called Pop. The two of them came down to the car and, in the light of the lantern, we saw that Pop was a little old man with sharp, wrinkled, pink features, penetrating dark eyes, and a mass of white waving hair which stuck out in all directions; he looked like a cross between Bertrand Russell and the more sober moments of Harpo Marx.

Under his guidance we unloaded whatever goods we might need for the night, and set off in Indian file towards the camp. A large dog came snuffling and leaping round us, invisible but unpredictably active in the darkness. Then a vague black cube, laced with little streaks of light, loomed up beside us, and Pop opened the flap of a large square tent. We followed him inside, bumping our heads with dismal unanimity on a hot stove-pipe that stretched across the entrance about five feet from the floor. The stove itself, a great black iron cylinder, dominated the centre of the tent; a large mattress, a table, two rickety chairs and a litter of boxes filled the rest of the floor, and in the midst of it all a tall, elderly woman, with the remnants of beauty, wrapped a shawl about her and stood up to greet us with the manner of a great tragic actress. This was Mrs. K., Pop's wife; they, we learnt immediately, were the only members of the community left on this spot. The rest had gone days before to form a camp in the mountains, two hours' climb away, and nothing had been seen of them since; they had even, we were told in aggrieved tones, left their rearguard without adequate provisions. We had better stay the night in another tent that was still standing and then in the morning we could all make an expedition up the mountain to see what had happened to the main body of the community.

So we made a meal, to which the K.'s contributed a great saucepan of boiled wheat grains, on whose alimentary virtues they expatiated at great length, and then, in the course of the conversation, we pieced together the adventures of the community so far as it had gone. It was by no means an easy process, since Pop had the habit of interlarding his conversation with obscure philosophical divagations, while Mrs. K. could not be restrained from declaiming eloquently on the beauties of the mountains we should see around us when we awoke and emerged from our tent in the morning.

The substance of the story, as we learnt it during that and the subsequent day, was that John, the great-grandson of a noted American radical, had been troubled for many years with the problem of a moral and libertarian reformation of contemporary social life. From an undefined radical pacifism, he had moved towards anarchism, and had come to the position when he felt that the solution would be reached, not by any romantic revolutionary uprising, but by the patient building up of new forms of society within the old. It was this that had brought him to seek a way out through that old hope of radicals disillusioned with mass movements, the small community as a school and a laboratory of living. Thus far John's ideas and actions did not depart very far from those of many small English and American community groups since the collapse of Stalinist visions at the end of the 1930's. He tried, with qualified success, to form a community on the outskirts of San Francisco, but the lesson he gathered from this was that an incomplete community, dependent on urban standards and urban means of earning a livelihood, is vulnerable both economically and morally. The greatest self-sufficiency must be the aim, the maximum cutting of links with a diseased metropolitan civilisation, and if these things were achieved, the moral independence, the impetus to create a new communal form based equally on freedom and mutual aid, would follow naturally. A place must be found, as far as possible away from the centres of American civilisation, where these theories could be lived out to the full. John was not ill-equipped for such a venture, since, as well as an intellectual, he was an outdoor man who had been brought up on a farm in Wyoming and had acted as a forest and mountain guide in the Rockies. Nor did he shrink from the logical consequences of his conclusions, but set off with a couple of his associates to find some place in the Canadian backwoods where the experiment could be started. He discovered eight hundred acres of land in the hills just above where we were sitting, bought it for a little more than 2,000 dollars, and then, travelling by lorry the tedious miles from San Francisco up to Smithers, transported his family and his belongings into this isolated region, surely wild and detached enough to provide all the economic and moral isolation one could desire from the pernicious influences of metropolitan America.

He had secured the site for his community, but what of the community itself, the people without whom the experiment could not exist? Friends had come and gone, Pop explained sadly, but none had lasted very long. Indeed, what existed seemed, as we listened between the words, to be a tribute to John's own determination and to family loyalty rather than to the power of a really vigorous social philosophy to draw and to hold people despite the hardships that might be involved. For now the eight people that remained were all members of the family, John, his wife, their three children, his mother and her parents—Pop and Mrs. K. The thought occurred to us that perhaps, even though family loyalty was the cement that held this remnant of the community together, it might also repel the outsider as much as actual physical hardships. For the strongly united family group, in the very act of drawing itself together, seems to present an impenetrable surface to the outer world, and it needs a certain moral courage to become the first man or woman to join such a group from the outside. After we had left our hosts, we discussed the problem far into the night as we lay uncomfortably in our sleeping bags on the floor of the spare tent, surrounded by chests of drawers, trunks, carpets, broken chairs, a folding chess table, the impedimenta of an American life brought up to brave the last frontier, as John's ancestors had braved every frontier in the long development of the continent. But we came to no conclusion that even seemed to approach a solution.

10.

In the morning we stepped out on to the rime-whitened ground and saw that we were situated on a hillside which looked down on the broad Bulkley Valley. Immediately around us was the rich turf of cleared ground, fenced on all sides by aspen woods whose golden leaves were now, in the slight morning breeze, beginning to drift and eddy to the ground. Behind us a wooded mountain rose, dark but slightly dusted by the frost, and before us on all three sides we could see more mountains, for the most part new aspects of the same snow-covered ranges we had already seen on yesterday's journey. Almost immediately Mrs. K. was among us, declaiming and describing and enthusing with the elaborate gestures of a miraculously surviving Ellen Terry.

We went into the woods to get water from a spring where the dead leaves lay thickly and a large frog flopped into the depths as we lowered our cans. We found a homesteader's meagre summer hut, and learnt that the ground on which we had camped, forty acres of excellent potato-growing soil, was for sale at a tempting 200 dollars (£70).

Eventually we were ready to start off, having draped ourselves fantastically in every piece of red material that could be found, in order to placate Mrs. K.'s fears that we might be mistaken for moose and shot by big game hunters as we climbed through the forest. The way was very easy, a wide path sloping not too abruptly up the hillside, with no precipitous cliffs or any other frightening feature. We went through a woodland of spruce mingled with various deciduous trees, and undergrown by whortleberry and blueberry plants, which had already been stripped by the birds, bears and Indians, who regard berry-picking grounds as important tribal properties to be exploited as thoroughly as a piece of tillage. A few straggling wild columbines were still blooming, and now and again some unidentifiable but intensely sweet smell would float across the path. It was the typical mixed woodland of northern British Columbia. Occasionally a rill crossed our way and turned it into mire. Twice, at such muddy spots, we saw the big splay-hoofed spoor of moose, but encountered no other sign of these formidable animals. Indeed, the only creatures we did see on our ascent were a number of ruffed grouse; one of them, a handsome bluish cock, paraded and danced with ruff extended for some time before he realised that we were watching him and flew away.

The top camp consisted of one very large oblong tent, whose roof we saw a few minutes before we entered the clearing in which it stood, at the base of a long smooth hill of brown bracken. Three children, a boy and two girls, were playing with a pair of goats in front of the camp, and set up a series of yells as we approached, which brought the remaining members of the community out into the open to peer at us and then welcome us.

John was a tall, thin-faced, slow-spoken, bespectacled American, a difficult-to-place mixture of the ancestral man of action (the family myth and model) and the personally developed and superimposed intellectual. His wife Sally was a handsome, bouncing kind of girl, with a way of making even the rough clothes of the outdoor life, the trousers and small-size army windcheater, take on an almost urban chicness. The first impression, despite the robust good health of her appearance, was that she would feel happier in San Francisco than in the wilds—a suggestion, needless to say, she would have rejected with indignation. Mrs. B., John's mother, was a wiry, grey-haired little woman of the pioneer generation, the kind who would adapt herself to any situation without losing a grain of her own peculiar kind of gnarled femininity. She, indeed, apart from the children, who quite evidently enjoyed the whole affair thoroughly, seemed least of all out of place. After we had talked for a while, we had to go and see the great tent. It was a much more comfortable place than we had at first thought, a 32-ft. by 16-ft. relic of the Alaskan army, made especially for hard weather conditions and erected by John with a real woodman's expertness. Inside, Sally had divided it, with hangings of brilliant Mexican blankets, into two bedrooms and a large kitchen and sitting-room. There was even a kind of passage which served also as an office and in which a typewriter and a great metal filing cabinet were installed, as if in preparation for any sudden influx of adherents from the still unregenerate capitalist world.

The complaints of the deserted elders were satisfied, and a meal was scratched together of toasted cheese sandwiches and dried apricots. This kind of meal, indeed, seemed to be in accordance with the general plan on which the settlers lived; imitating the pioneers, they gathered sacks of all kinds of foods which could be stored in bulk—dried fruits, beans, wheat grains, flour, potatoes and so forth. There appeared to be little variation in their diet— no fresh fruit or vegetables whatever, and I sensed immediately the old community malady of a Spartanism which is partly forced by necessity but partly also by a desire to live in a half-puritanical way (it gives a feeling of virtue, it adds another to the sacrifices one is ready to make for one's principles). This point of view, indeed, became explicit in the way in which John explained that, all else failing, they would never want, since there were always potatoes to be had from the farmer down below and they could see the winter through on a diet of these and moose-meat. We all felt uneasy about the ultimate effects of such feeding, but before John's idealistic enthusiasm it needed an almost churlish frankness to put forward such a matter-of-fact contention.

But that was not all, for the water supply at this higher camp was of the most dubious kind, coming from a shallow rain pool, full of leaves, behind the tent. The water had a yellowish look, and this seemed to be due to decaying vegetation rather than mineral colouring, while in one glass there floated three translucent pond animals, each almost half an inch long. Everybody, except the visitors, drank it unboiled with a blithe disregard of any possible danger; pioneers could not be squeamish.

As the conversation grew more general, it became evident that, though there was a great deal of unanimity among all these people, the attitudes they adopted towards their life and the satisfactions they gained or expected to gain from it were very different indeed —so different that we might almost say they had at least six individual intellectual viewpoints and were only drawn together by feeling.

Pop, as befitted a philosopher, was loyal but cynical. Mrs. K. watched all the activity with the detachment of a great lady who cannot possibly be really concerned with anything but what is going on in her own mind. Mrs. B. saw the fulfilment of the great family tradition into which she had become incorporated by marriage so many years before; she stood beside the only one of her sons who was fulfilling in his own way the promise of the great ancestral B. Sally's attitude was doubtless most truly expressed in the remark with which she had greeted us: "It's all a great adventure." And the eldest girl was perhaps the spokeswoman for unadmitted thoughts of the elders as well as for the candid feelings of the children when she said confidentially: "It's safe, you know, and there are no nasty schools." (They were among the beneficiaries of the excellent system of education by correspondence which had been established for isolated children in British Columbia, Sally herself acting as their teacher.)

John spoke mostly of practical issues. He had to cut a road through to the creek beside which they intended to build their permanent settlement, and then the cabins must be built. They would have to spend the winter in tents, but that need be no particular hardship, for a tent could be made as snug as a house. In the spring, they could move to their permanent homes, plough some of the natural pastures for growing potatoes and grain, start their herd of cattle and their poultry flock, and the economic foundation of the community would be assured. I had heard the story told before and just as confidently by community experts who later failed in their efforts. On the other hand, it had been done occasionally, and John looked the man with the kind of combined enthusiasm and practical sense which might actually succeed.

He had just discovered, when we arrived, that the horses had strayed away. Perhaps we would like to join them in search. It would be a way of seeing the land. So David and I set out with

him and Sally, and after stumbling through woods and tramping
over open slopes of meadowland, we eventually found the animals
in a spot where the wild pea vines grew particularly lushly. There
were three, a white gelding, a brown mare and her colt. We stood
for a while looking at the view of mountains, more of which had
appeared from this high vantage point, and discussed the possibilities of the land. There was no doubt that the soil in this high
valley was unusually fertile, there seemed plenty of pasture to provide feed for a fair-sized herd even without clearing, and the woods
contained many acres of good spruce for building, fuel and also
for sale, if this were necessary in order to subsidise the more purely
agricultural work. Even as a straight farming and lumbering proposition it looked a good chance, and it seemed unlikely that the
community, if it came into existence, need fear disaster for purely
economic reasons. Beyond that, of course, it would be a question
of personal relationships, the most difficult and unpredictable of
all elements, particularly in a small and relatively closed social
microcosm such as community experiments always produce.

We started for home, with Sally leading the procession mounted
on the white horse, and returned with no incident except the
occasional friskiness of the colt, which would suddenly race from
one end of the column to the other, shouldering everyone off the
path in its wild progress. Later in the day we all went down to
the lower camp. The two horses were attached to a heavy buggy,
and John and Sally, Inge and I mounted on this to drive down to
the bottom of the hill. It seemed a pleasant way of saving our
legs, until the horses started to gallop down the steeper slopes.
Then we had to squat low to avoid the branches that swept close
overhead, and at the same time to hold on tightly to prevent ourselves being thrown about. Eventually our career came to an
abrupt halt when the buggy was stuck in a mud-hole at the
bottom of a sharp upward slope, and Inge and I gladly took the
opportunity to walk the rest of the way.

At the camp we chopped wood, built an enormous fire, and
then sat down to sup and to drink our gallon of wine. Over it we
discussed with John his relations with his neighbours, on which
seemed to us the success of any community would largely depend.
On the whole, he said, they had been good; most of the farmers
with whom he had any contact were old homesteaders, men who
had come in the days when land was given away in the wilderness
just in order to get people to cultivate it. They had cut their

farms out with their own hands, had learnt in these early days the vital need for mutual aid among the few settlers, and, now that they had succeeded, were always ready to help anybody who was starting anew. Of course, John pointed out, he did not exhibit his ideas too openly. That would certainly lead to antagonism, whereas if the community were a practical success it would do far more good among people of that kind than any amount of theoretical preaching.

How did he get on with the Indians? John became enthusiastic on this subject. He had seen a good deal of one of the Gitksan bands which had formerly inhabited this valley and whose people still occasionally came through to hunt or pick berries. He had found them excellent folk, but it depended a great deal on one's own attitude. Naturally enough, they were reserved on first encounter with white people, and it took a little time to get beyond this protective shell. But once they realised that you were willing to treat them as equals, then the distrust vanished and they would do anything for you. Just after his arrival, he had helped some Indians with his lorry, and this had not only brought him a great gift of salmon but also the friendship of the band, who had given him much friendly advice and helped in innumerable small ways. The white farmers and lumbermen in the locality employed Indians and complained that they were unreliable, but this was due partly to the Indians' more natural outlook on work (if he does not feel like it he just stays at home or goes to lie in the sun), and partly to the attitude of the white men themselves, who treat the Indians as a lower race, and towards whom the latter, quick to sense such things, do not feel any obligation to act conscientiously as they would do towards people whom they accepted as friends.

The wine we were drinking, though it was an innocently pale liquid which did not even taste particularly strong, turned out to be unexpectedly potent. Later, indeed, we learnt that this drink, made locally from imported grapes, is well laced with alcohol, and is even favoured by some of the loggers because they can get drunk more cheaply on this than they can on whisky. I remember we all had great difficulty in finding the openings to our sleeping bags that night.

11.

On the following day we intended to complete the last stage of our first journey, to the Indian village of Kispiox, and then to begin our swift return trip to Vancouver. The two horses dragged the car off the muddy bank where it had been stuck two nights before. Mrs. K. appeared, in pyjamas which were tucked into thick socks like plus-fours, and, spreading appealing hands towards the south, looked over the frosted fields and declaimed in her most tragic voice: "Oh, my Hudson Bays! The clouds have taken them away from me!" We said goodbye all round, and Inge and I promised to look in again on our way back from the coast. Then we drove slowly down the lane and took the road once again towards the north.

Beyond Smithers lies one of the most predominantly Indian areas of British Columbia, with large Gitksan and Babine reservations interlacing over many miles. Most of the villages are Indian, and the white trading centre of Hazelton, thirty miles away, is a small outpost in this territory, surrounded by a native population of about 3,000 who live by hunting, fishing and casual logging work.

The first Indian village we reached was Moricetown—named after the anthropological Father Morice I have already mentioned. Here we saw very clearly the difference in the ways of living between the northern Coast Indian tribes and the southern Interior Indians of British Columbia. The Gitksans of Moricetown, although their settlement is nearly two hundred miles inland, belong to the same cultural and linguistic group as the Tsimshians of the coast, the whole nation having, according to native legend, originated in an earthly paradise near Hazelton and spread down the Skeena to the coast. While the Interior Indians inhabit small, low cabins, the houses in Moricetown were mostly large, two-storied, clap-boarded buildings, built in a style reminiscent of the older dwellings of Vancouver. This type of individual family house was adopted after the missionaries had persuaded the tribe to abandon the great communal buildings, in which each clan used to live under its own chief. It seems as though the memory of the clan dwellings and the Coast Indian tradition of displaying family wealth combined to make the Gitksans and the related Tsimshian and Niskan groups favour big houses in preference to the small huts of the other tribes, who in their primitive existence were used to scanty and often temporary shelters. However, once their pretentious homes were built the Indians evidently had taken very little care to keep them in good repair, for hardly any of the houses in Moricetown had been painted, and most of them looked

6

extremely weather-beaten owing to the warping and decay of their outer boards.

But to us the really interesting fact about Moricetown was that there were two memorial poles planted in little fenced enclosures along the highway; both of them were very recent, having been erected during the past ten years. The Gitksan poles have always been more primitive and less impressive than those of the real Coastal tribes. They have not the large cedars out of which the Haida and the Kwakiutl made their massive carvings, and their poles, while often thirty or forty feet high, are comparatively thin —rarely more than two feet in thickness and usually a great deal less. This lack of bulk is probably the reason for the relative scarcity of the kind of three-dimensional sculpture which you will see in the poles from the Queen Charlotte Islands or from Bella Bella or Bella Coola on the coast. Where the Haida took the solid mass of the tree and carved his motifs in relation thereto, the Gitksan took its surface, paring it back so that in most cases the figures stood out in relief from the cylindrical ground. Consequently, their work in this respect was never quite so impressive as that of the Haida, and the craftsmanship of these newer poles, in its turn, was of a clearly degenerate type, marred by haste and carelessness. The more interesting—the date 1942 was carved on its tip—bore a highly conventionalised human face at the base, above that the rampant figure of what appeared to be a wolf, above that again two beavers proceeding head downwards, their feet splayed out on either side of the pole. These animals were at once the heraldic symbols and the supernatural guardians of the man for whom the pole had been erected.

Contrary to popular belief, the Indians of the north-west Pacific coastal areas were never totemists in the strict sense of claiming that their clan or phratry had descended from a certain animal, and it is thus incorrect to call any of their carved poles "totem" poles. They actually believed that certain ancestors had been given the protection of spiritual beings who assumed the form of animals, which became the phratric or clan emblems. So-called "totem" poles may actually have been erected for different purposes, according to the tribe and the occasion. Sometimes a pole is part of a house front and serves the same purpose as an heraldic escutcheon over a European mansion, declaring the chief's ancestry and pretensions. Sometimes it is erected to celebrate some event in his life. Sometimes it is a mortuary pole, with a recess in the top where the ashes of the dead chief can rest. But perhaps most numerous of all are the memorial poles, and this was the type we found still in use among the Gitksan. The later and less interesting of the two actually bore the legend—"Agnes Dennis, died May 8, 1946."

We decided to photograph the better pole, and Audrey stepped out of the car for this purpose. While she was taking the photograph an old woman came out of one of the gardens carrying an axe, and began shouting violently and gesticulating with her free hand. For a moment we thought she intended an attack, but she crossed to the other side of the road, still shouting in a tone which undoubtedly conveyed hostility, though her Gitksan insults were quite incomprehensible to us. David asked her politely what was the matter, but she could not or would not understand us. Her attitude may have been due to the fact that the Gitksan, and the Niskan to the north, were the last Indians in British Columbia to put up any serious resistance to the Canadian authorities, and the tradition of resenting the white men is still strong among the older people, whose own fathers took part in the risings of the last century.

We drove on for a little way, very much intrigued by what we had seen. Until recently the custom of erecting poles has been regarded as moribund, and among such great craftsmen as the Haida it is certainly dead. But here, if it had ever died, were evident signs of a renaissance. What could be their significance? We dismissed immediately a flippant thought that the poles were possibly intended as tourist bait. But if they were erected for their traditional purposes, it was clear that the tribal customs were still taken seriously, even in a world of automobiles and tractors. For the erection of a pole is an expensive process; not only has the craftsman who makes it to be paid handsomely, but the person who raises it would lose greatly in the prestige which is so important to the Indian mind if he did not attend the process with great feasts and the giving of many and expensive presents.

We soon had some further enlightenment on this subject of surviving Indian customs. Outside Moricetown we stopped at a wayside store, kept by a French-Canadian, one of the many descendants in northern British Columbia of the trappers and *voyageurs* who first penetrated the country 150 years ago. He had little to sell us, and explained that the Indians had held a potlatch over the weekend and had bought up almost everything in his shop. In these remote parts it took some time to renew one's stock. He was out of change too: the Indians had been in and out all last evening, breaking up twenty-dollar bills into smaller values to give away.

The potlatch, I should explain, was—or is—a kind of feast among the Pacific Coast tribes (it has also been imitated by some of the Interior bands), in which the giving or destruction of property is the central feature. Potlatches have various forms and celebrate many different occasions, from the assumption of a name or a title, or of the right to dance a certain dance or sing a song, to the erection of a pole or a house. More than that, in their primitive society the potlatches were a vital part of the economic life of the Coastal tribes, owing to the importance laid on the giving of large and numerous presents to the guests. A chief would often impoverish himself in this process, but at the same time gain the all-important prestige he desired. But the distribution of gifts was by no means altruistic; it was, indeed, a highly capitalistic institution, a kind of insurance or gilt-edged security, for the recipients were bound at their own potlatches to make restitution to the givers with substantial interest (at least 100 per cent.).

In this way the relationships of the various chiefs and villages were tangled in a network of obligations which were often the causes of bitter feuds, while many of the wars between villages were caused by insults or by differences over matters of right or prestige which had arisen during these potlatches. The demands of their potlatch obligations also caused the chiefs to exploit the energies of their followers and largely offset the relative abundance in which these people normally lived. Yet potlatches, despite the evils attached to them, nevertheless played such a part in the economic and ritualistic life of the tribes that many anthropologists now consider that nothing has been more harmful to the native social order than the unthinking attempt to suppress these feasts on moral and religious grounds.

I have heard rumours of secret potlatches among the Songhees near Victoria, but this was the first really credible piece of information we had received of the survival of this custom. "I thought potlatches were illegal," remarked David. "They don't seem to be illegal here," the shopkeeper said. "Everybody knows they go on."

At this moment a light truck drew up; a young pale-skinned Indian climbed out and entered the store. He smiled politely but

An Indian Woman at Moricetown

Gitksan Pole Carving

A Gitksan Chief in Ceremonial Regalia

The Poles at Kispiox

with a suggestion of rather sly mockery. "That's right, isn't it, John?" the shopkeeper shouted. "You folks held a potlatch last night." The young Indian continued to smile. "Maybe someone had a party. I don't know." "That's always how they are," the shopkeeper whispered. "They won't tell a thing about themselves."

We went away, pondering the question of how indeed we might find out something more about what was going on among the Indians. The shopkeeper's hint about their reticence in this part of the country I knew to be substantially true, since an anthropologist had told me just before we left that he had visited one Gitksan village in which he had learnt hardly a single fact from the Indians directly and had to base his conclusions on their present life almost entirely on conjectures he drew from his own direct observations. He admitted that it was not a satisfactory process. But what could he do, short of living among the Indians all his life? And even then there was no guarantee that he would be able to understand the mental processes which prompted their customs and which derived from preconceptions basically so different from those of a white man.

If an anthropologist, with at least some extensive prior knowledge of the mentality of primitive people, had found it so difficult to establish trust, how could we expect to do anything better? However, we resolved to go on and see what we could find in the other villages along the route. We drove down the Bulkley Valley, and came eventually to Hagwilget, inhabited, owing to the extreme complexity of the racial boundaries in this area, by Babines, a Carrier sub-tribe. This village was more substantial than those of the Carriers farther inland, and there was a large white wooden church, built in a pseudo-gothic style, with an elaborate pinnacled belfry. Standing on an elevation this building completely dominated Hagwilget, and gave it, as we approached from a distance, an illusory resemblance to an English village. The Carriers rarely erected poles of any kind, and there was only one standing here, a thick, very weather-beaten specimen which at one time had carried a long-since detached sun mask on its crest. It may actually have been a Gitksan pole, but it was more probably a result of the imitation which goes on where tribal frontiers run together.

Just out of Hagwilget we crossed a modern suspension bridge over the deep Bulkley Canyon. It was a very ordinary erection, and not nearly so spectacular as the celebrated bridge which the Indians themselves erected at a narrower point of the canyon in the early 1870's, and whose history is certainly worth recording.

Round about 1860 an American promoter, Perry McDonough Collins, conceived the idea of an overland telegraph line, running through Canada and Alaska, across the narrow Bering Straits and, through Siberia to Europe. The scheme of Collins' Overland Telegraph seemed to prosper, the blessings of all the interested governments were obtained, capital was raised, and the work on the line was begun. It was planned to run through northern British Columbia, by way of Hazelton, and in the preparatory survey work much of the early exploration of this part of Canada and also of southern Alaska was carried out. The scheme was certainly a grandiose one, particularly considering the wildness of the country at that period, but it was carried out by men of great energy and resourcefulness, like Colonel Bulkley after whom the river was named, and the work advanced so quickly that it became a race between the Overland Telegraph and the Atlantic Cable which many people at that time believed could not possibly succeed. A trail was cut right into the uninhabited wilderness of northern British Columbia, and the line was actually taken about forty miles beyond Hazelton when the unexpected news came through in 1867 that the Atlantic Cable had been laid and had in fact proved satisfactory.

Its success automatically involved the failure of the Overland Telegraph. Work was immediately abandoned and, while the lines in the southern part of the province were later acquired by the British Columbian government, those in the virtual jungle north of Quesnel were left to the elements and the Indians. The latter turned the insulators into drinking cups and made nails out of the iron wire, but their most ambitious undertaking was to construct from the cables their own primitive suspension bridge over the Bulkley Canyon at Hagwilget. Having built it, the men forced the women of the tribe to test its safety by walking across first, and afterwards for many years it was used as a short cut to their salmon-fishing points on the Bulkley. This strange Indian bridge, for whose relics we now looked in vain, and the old trail into the north, which was later used by the "Ninety-Eighters" on their overland trek to the Klondike, were the only long-standing relics of the Overland Telegraph, apart from a few place-names, like Telegraph Creek. (In a new country like British Columbia the place-names, studied carefully, hide a wealth of historical allusion beneath their apparent eccentricity.)

Beyond Hagwilget we came into full view of the great squared hulk of the Rocher du Boule, which dominates the landscape around Hazelton. A little farther, on the outskirts of the town, there was a baseball park by the highway, and lined along its far side, a series of half a dozen memorial poles. Again there was one undoubtedly recent specimen, erected to the memory of a certain Tom Campbell who had died in 1930. Some of the others were rather older, and showed considerable virtuosity of execution, particularly one on which three bears sat on each other's heads—this showed a sense of three-dimensional solidity rare among the Gitksan. On another pole the dominant motif was that of frogs clambering upwards, and a touch of the bizarre was given by a third whose base was a squatting female figure, with breasts represented by wide-eyed reptilian heads. Similar heads peeped out of her eye sockets and further pairs of open ophidian eyes were set in her wrists. Certainly, in view of their state of preservation in the open air, the oldest of these poles could hardly have been much more than forty years old, and it suggested the superficiality of missionary influence in this area that such a rich pagan fantasy should have survived over the years of nominal conversion.

Hazelton itself was a dingy village of mean cafés and poky shops, dominated by a hotel and a large Hudson's Bay trading post. David and I were still suffering from our introduction to Canadian wine, and we went into the hotel to drink some beer as a pick-me-up. We asked some drinkers the way to Kispiox; as they told us, one of them added ironically: "You'll find the Indians up there a very friendly bunch." The others laughed. "I can remember the time," a second said, "when they used to stop the hunters going up the Kispiox River and refuse to let them go any farther." "Ah, but that's years ago," the hotel proprietor answered. "They won't worry you. But they won't exactly welcome you either."

With this promising forecast we left the hotel and found Audrey and Inge, once again renewing our stocks of food in one of the shops. In the dusty window there was a pile of assorted bric-à-brac, tourist goods from Japan mingled with a few genuine pieces of Indian workmanship. Little was of any interest—some plain alderwood rattles and a shaman's headdress of grizzly bear claws. The shopkeeper asked five dollars for the headdress, and we would have bought it, had she not aroused our distrust by remarking that she had to write out her price tickets in code, otherwise the Indians would ask too much for their goods to allow her a fair profit. Inge immediately took the point of view that she must be exploiting either the Indians or ourselves, and the crown went unbought; later we learnt that we had missed a relatively rare specimen.

Out of Hazelton the road led right into the bush, unbroken for about twelve miles by any sign of cultivation or habitation. Then we drove into a sprawling settlement which proved to be Kispiox, our destination. It seemed a large place, but what had actually happened was that the people had merely moved out of the old village and built a new street behind, so that there seemed to be two villages, one inhabited and alive, and the other abandoned and dead.

It was to the latter that we drove. A long row of two-storied barn-like houses, their balconies garnished with ornate fretwork, looked out from empty windows on to a green meadow, grazing cattle and a shallow river. In front of them, standing and leaning at all angles along a narrow dirt road, was a group of almost twenty poles, weathered silvery grey against the leaden sky. They were carved in a bizarre variety of heraldic patterns, each telling something of the mythical history of the chief's family and the supernatural beings who patronised it. But, like the houses, most of them were decaying fast under the impacts of age and weather. Some had already fallen to the ground, and in the long grass beside them we found two magnificently carved grave figures, one of a killer whale and the other of a beaver with exaggerated teeth and enormous eyes, and these, like an old dugout canoe lying beside them, were in such a condition that two or three winters would destroy them entirely.

The space behind the houses was also full of indications of the past of Kispiox. We discovered the rectangular patterns of earth banks which marked where the walls of large communal dwellings had stood in the days before the Indians adopted European houses. And on a slope beyond these we saw what looked rather like a little town of garden sheds. We walked up to them and found ourselves in the midst of a derelict burial ground. The little sheds were grave houses which the Indians had erected over their dead in order to provide shelter for their spirits. There were also decaying wooden pyramids and a few more orthodox tombstones surrounded by elaborate wooden fences, tottering at all angles.

On some of the graves were lambs carved out of marble and sitting upright like begging dogs, an interesting indication of the way in which the Indians had retained the fundamental elements of their own beliefs while superimposing Christian imagery, for the lamb had clearly replaced the older phratric animals in their function of guardians over the destinies of the families involved.

Nothing has been done to preserve any of these relics at Kispiox, and it seems clear that in a few years this large collection of primitive craftsmanship will have decayed beyond salvation. Yet the problem of preservation is by no means straightforward, since the Indian families maintain very strict proprietary rights over their monuments and would probably not allow anthropologists to interfere. Anything that is done must be by the relatives of the dead people. On the other hand, the Indians themselves usually think that prestige is fulfilled once the pole or the grave house has been erected; there is no obligation to keep it in preservation, and any renewal or alteration would have to be attended by expensive feasts, the money for which they usually consider might be better spent on some ceremony of more spectacular importance. For here, again, we noticed that some of the poles had been erected not very long ago—one, indeed, the crudest of all, as recently as the preceding year.

In this part of Kispiox only one dwelling, a small wooden hut in a much poorer style than the other houses, seemed to be inhabited. For a while, as we examined and photographed some of the poles, a woman looked at us coldly from one of the windows. A little boy pushed a wheelbarrow with a tub on it down to the river for water, and on his return stood and stared at us solemnly for a long time. But otherwise the Indians left us severely alone, no one came near us, and the village might have been uninhabited for all the signs of activity we could see among its people. Clearly the days of open hostility were past and the villagers had adopted a policy of boycotting the unwelcome stranger. We could not help feeling sympathetic, and we realised that nothing would be gained by any direct attempt to intrude on their privacy. Yet Inge and I decided that we would try by whatever other means we might to learn about the apparent resurgence of Indian culture in these areas.

Kispiox was the most northerly point we intended to touch on this part of our travels—it is more than 750 miles beyond Vancouver and level with the southern parts of Alaska. There were other Indian villages in the district, with equally rich collections of poles, but we realised that there would be little to gain by visiting them, particularly as David and Audrey had scanty time for their return journey. But the ancestral spirits of Kispiox had evidently no intention of letting us depart so lightly, for when we returned to the car, we found that one of the back tyres had subsided, gently this time. We extracted a two-inch nail, wondering whether its presence was entirely due to accident. The laborious ritual of unloading our goods and changing the wheel once again was watched with great interest and satisfaction by the small Indian boy, Kispiox's sole evident witness of our plight. Then we drew out and began our long and hurried journey southward.

12.

Now we were going over familiar ground, and we had little time to halt, at least voluntarily. Yet even in this passage we gained some new impressions and had certain experiences thrust upon us. The most striking impression, indeed, was that of the onset of winter in the brief few days since our journey began. Woods that had been covered with yellow and orange leaves when we had driven up were now becoming bare and spindly in the high winds that blew, and the roads were scudded and patterned over with their coloured cast-offs, while a northern rigour, unperceived before, began to emerge in the denuded landscape.

We decided that the repair of our tyre was essential if we were to face the Cariboo roads without the risk of being stranded, but we had forgotten that the day was a public holiday, and not until the edge of Telkwa, sixty miles on, did we find a garage that was open; even here we had to take our turn in the queue with hunters preparing themselves for journeys into the northern bush. As we waited a car stopped on the road ahead, a woman got out, pointed a gun into the sky, fired, drove on a little way, picked up a fine cock grouse that had fallen to her shot, and proceeded on her journey in the most casual manner imaginable.

Beyond Houston dusk began to fall, but we decided to continue for the next fifty miles in the dark, in order to make up for some of the time we had lost during the day. Finally, about eight o'clock, we began to look for accommodation. We stopped at two autocamps near Burns Lake. Both were full, so we drove on to a settlement called Tintagel. There a quavering, persecuted-looking woman came up to the car. Yes, she had cabins free. The tourist

commissioner had said they were the best on the road. There was
no water laid on yet, but the commissioner had said they were the
best on the road. No, there wouldn't be any electric light either.
The plant wasn't working, and her husband was away, but the
commissioner had said that her cabins were the best on the road.
We didn't doubt that at all, and we weren't fussy people—we
could probably get along with a bucket of water and a candle. But
how much did she charge? Nine dollars. Nine dollars! Why, we
had paid four dollars for a cabin with water, electricity and a
shower. Yes, that might be so—but what kind of cabin was that?
The commissioner had said that her cabins were the best on the
road. Doubtless they were the best in North America, we agreed,
but we did not intend to pay nine dollars for the privilege of carrying buckets and going to bed in the dark. Even as we drove away
we heard her shouting after us that the commissioner had said her
cabins were the best on the road.

Eventually, another forty miles on, and at ten o'clock, we
reached Endako. The only building of any importance was a big
wooden hotel, and there we managed to get rooms. The building
dated from the railway construction days, and there was a vague
atmosphere of an English small-town inn about its papered
walls and corridors. We had to be content with oil lamps, but
there was piping hot water in the baths.

A deep frost next morning not only warned us more emphati-
cally than ever of approaching winter but also incapacitated the car
until the morning was well advanced. Once we did get started,
however, we made good time down the road to Prince George.
This time we did not linger, but went straight on through Quesnel,
going by the main road and avoiding Williams Lake. The country
we had previously missed by leaving the highway was rich farming
plateau land, full of cattle and pleasing to the eye with its silvery
grey snake fences and rolling pastures, already becoming a little
greener from the autumn rains. It was here, just before dusk, that
a second tyre blew out with a loud ripping explosion. By this time
we had developed a routine of work and it was not long before we
had the replacement fixed and were running down towards the
south. Once again it was hard to find a place to sleep. There were
even more hunters about than before, and at last we had to accept
a bare and dusty log cabin at one of the post houses—the most
primitive accommodation we had yet discovered. Its sole merit
was that it was also the cheapest—only three dollars.

Next morning, as we were leaving, a Canadian hunter told us bitterly that no less than 463 moose had already been taken out of the north that season, mostly by Americans. Once again the complaint was raised—why do they come here when they have killed off all their own big game? The only answer I could suggest was that the Canadian Government, in its wild search for American credit, did everything in its power to tempt people from the United States to kill off Canadian game. This did not seem to satisfy the hunter. The Government knew its own business, but still, if something weren't done the moose would soon be finished.

Towards the end of the thin Cariboo woodlands we saw our biggest game of the journey, a beaver swimming sedately over a pool in a piece of moorland country. And then we were back in the semi-desert landscape below Clinton. In our absence the autumn had given it an unanticipated splendour. The dwarf sumach bushes, hitherto unnoticed in their dull green obscurity, had turned a brilliant vermilion, the stunted aspens in the gullies were richly orange, and along the roadside the seed heads of wild clematis and milkweed lay like innumerable puffs of white feathery smoke.

Our third tyre burst, very conveniently, just as we drove along the string of garages and cafés which comprises Spence's Bridge. This time we had no replacement, and a garage proprietor sold us a reconditioned tyre which he assured us would see the car home to San Francisco. As it was fitted we drank coffee in a snack-bar where a waitress with a Mexican accent complained that their trade was being killed because the Government had a habit every now and then of closing the road and diverting the traffic through Lillooet, to the great benefit of the latter place and the great disadvantage of Spence's Bridge. Perhaps sometimes they stopped the Lillooet road, we suggested. That wasn't necessary, she sniffed, nobody would go that road if they could help it. She ignored us when we suggested that in that case it seemed almost an equitable arrangement to give Lillooet a chance to make a little money now and again,

The tyre which was to last until San Francisco blew out less than ten miles beyond Spence's Bridge, on a steep downward hill where the road passed along the edge of a precipice of crumbling rock falling almost perpendicularly to the railway lines many hundreds of feet below. David managed to pull up without mishap, and hitched a lift back to Spence's Bridge with the tyre, leaving the

Hazelton and the Rocher du Boule

Seton Lake in Central British Columbia

A Doukhobor Woman and Child

rest of us sitting beside a car standing on three wheels and a jack, on a steep hill in almost deserted country. There was not even any-where to wander, for the bank above was as steep as that below. We occupied ourselves with gathering sticks and building a fire by the roadside, and so we spent two hours, gradually resigning ourselves to the idea that our plan of reaching Vancouver that night would almost certainly be frustrated. David at last returned, the wheel was refixed, and we resumed our journey. But even this was not our last delay, for when we got down into the Canyon beyond Boston Bar, we found that there had been a great mountain slide and the road gangs were working to clear it away. There was only single-line traffic, and even then we had to drive through a terrifying minimum of space which brought us at times within half a foot of the edge, with a vertiginous cliff and a wild river beneath. We were impressed with the uncanny judgment of the lorry drivers who were employed dumping the debris and who would back their lorries until the rear wheels were within two or three inches of the edge before releasing their loads. We experi-enced a vicarious but terrible agony of apprehension every time we saw them, but they seemed to take the same pride in their risky task as a craftsman in a piece of work which is exact to the fraction of an inch.

Eventually we reached the bottom of the Canyon, and came on to the clear, broad road beyond Yale. Then we realised that one of the springs in the rear of the car was broken, a final memento of the Cariboo road.

That night we reached an auto-court on the outskirts of Chilli-wack, kept by an old Englishwoman of the Brighton landlady type. Her cabin seemed the height of luxury after our recent experi-ences. There was a great complicated oil stove which none of us could master, there was a shower, there were two separate bed-rooms as well as a sitting-room. We did not stop to criticise the cheap, uncomfortable furniture or the inadequate, badly washed crockery. Instead we gratefully swilled the dust of the Cariboo from our bodies and enjoyed our longest and most comfortable sleep since the journey began.

The next morning we ran through the Fraser Valley, which now looked incredibly civilised and over-populated, and reached Van-couver in time to eat fried oysters for lunch. As we all hated pro-tracted farewells, we got over them as quickly as possible and parted outside the restaurant, agreeing to meet in San Francisco in the spring. After David and Audrey had departed, Inge and I gaped at shop windows like visiting Indians and saw a film in which Bob Hope impersonated a fox-hunting English gentleman. For once, after the north, Vancouver appeared genuinely metropolitan, and our return seemed to emphasise the roughness of the country we had left. It was not until the next evening, when we went to a meeting of young authors, listened uncomfortably to contorted prose and sheer bad poetry read by perfectly sincere people under the influence of passing literary fashions, and were expected to put forward constructive criticism of material only fit for the wastepaper basket, that we began to realise that even the isolation of the Cariboo might have its merits, might produce, as well as the material riches of an unexploited land, a climate of the mind not wholly dominated by the effete and secondhand influences which, in the cities at least, seem to hover always over the culture of a colonial country. Why, I thought, should not the Cariboo produce its Mark Twain or give sanctuary to its Thoreau? Or was all that we could expect a new flowering, in modern guise, on the level of *Sawney's Letters*, a rustic capering in place of an urban inanity?

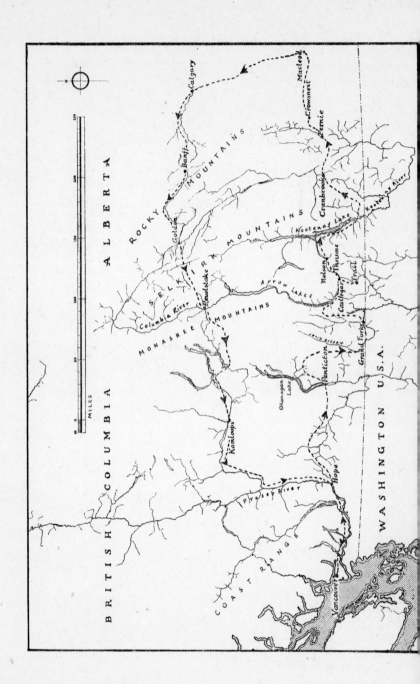

Part Two

AFTER two days in Vancouver had more than satisfied our taste for its limited amenities, we started out through the southern valleys and mountain ranges towards the Rockies and Calgary. The Canadian Pacific Railway runs two lines in this direction—the main north-easterly route through Banff and a lesser-known but in many ways more interesting route which is called the Kettle Valley line. We decided to go on the latter and to return by the main line, interrupting our journey wherever it seemed worth while.

The train left in the evening; this would mean that we should travel by night through the Fraser and Similkameen Valleys, and across the mountains between, but there was no alternative, since only one train travels each day on this line (there are some, as we were to find later, where the scattered population and the long distances make the trains even more infrequent, while even on the main lines in the west of Canada there are rarely more than two trains a day—the traveller, unless he has some alternative means of transport, must arrange his journey accordingly). That evening we reconciled ourselves to the thought that we had already seen the Fraser Valley and that we should doubtless be able to visit the Similkameen on one of our later tours.

We travelled in the day coach, since we should be alighting at our first stop, Penticton in the Okanagan Valley, in the early dawn hours, and it seemed hardly worth the trouble of taking a sleeper. Canadian day coaches are fitted with comfortable fauteuils; the backs can be let down at night to a fairly flat angle, and it is possible to hire pillows from the newsman. Usually, taking into account the disturbances caused by stops and by people walking up and down the carriage to the smoking saloon (in the older carriages this is graced with leather-covered benches and big brass spittoons), it is possible to get three or four hours' sleep of a night. The train was crowded when we boarded it, and we looked forward to a rather uncomfortable night. But one by one the commuters alighted at the little stops along the north side of the Fraser

Valley, and when we reached Hope the coach had emptied to a comfortable few people, so that we could stretch our legs on the opposite seats and rest in relative comfort.

Now the train began to groan and shriek on the grades into the mountains, and stopped every three or four miles on some tiny halt. For a while we lay awake, entertaining ourselves by reading the names on the station boards. Out of the first eight, seven were those of Shakespearian characters—Othello, Lear, Jessica, Portia, Iago, Romeo; chastely separated by a halt named after Mount Coquihalla, Juliet made up the list. Canadian place-names have often an oddity which is at times amusing as well as perplexing. In this case the halts were originally spaced out at fairly regular intervals, when the railway lines were driven through the mountains, to serve any loggers, miners or cowhands who might be working in their locality. As there were no established settlements, names had to be invented; sometimes the engineers commemorated the natural features of the land; sometimes they immortalised themselves; as often as not they were guided by some personal crochet or pet interest. That the engineer who constructed this part of the line had been a Shakespearian enthusiast was evident enough; what intrigued us more was the reason for his choices and his omissions. For the list was an odd jumble of characters, some pleasant, some unpleasant, of heroes, heroines, villains and mere nonentities. If Othello and Lear were included, why not Hamlet? If Portia and Juliet—and even Jessica—why not Desdemona and Cordelia? If Iago, why not Macbeth? Above all, in this wild and unknown country, why not Ariel and Miranda?

The newsman made his last tours for the night: a trip with periodicals and comic books; another with a great metal pot, a stack of paper cups and a tray of sandwiches, crying, "Any of you folks want any more cawfee?"; a third with pillows; and a last with cokes and orange crush and pop.

We slept fitfully, and at five o'clock limped stiffly out of the train at Penticton, rubbing our eyes in the pale light of the first dawn. We spent nearly half an hour finding a clerk who would take charge of our suitcases, and drank a wakening cup of coffee in an Italian café outside the station. Then we walked off in the direction of the town. We intended to visit a German fruit-grower down the valley to whom our new friends at Smithers had given us an introduction, but we felt that it would hardly be considerate to call unannounced at such an early hour, so we decided to explore the town first.

Penticton is an extremely prosperous little community, one of the centres of the great Okanagan Valley fruit industry, but the trouble with most successful modern towns in western Canada is that they have very little individuality to distinguish them from other successful towns, and this feeling of rather dismal familiarity is only accentuated when, as in Penticton, they lie on an almost completely level site, with no internal hills to interrupt their monotony. We walked down a long main street of stuccoed buildings, clean-looking and by no means always badly designed, but presenting a low flat skyline and a general lack of eccentricity which made our walk between them an extremely tedious experience, particularly as, at this early Sunday hour, there were few people about to distract our attention. The only real variety was in the churches, of which there seemed an incredible number, of many denominations and every style from Pugin Gothic to Bedford Park Modern. We ended at Okanagan Lake, which here begins its eighty-mile course up the valley. The waters were greyish blue in the early morning light, and on the opposite shore the grey, arid mountains rose up above the pine groves and the lush vegetation on the lakeside. It was not difficult to imagine what a Swiss city would have made of this situation, and any moderately intelligent planner would have laid out walks and parks on the lake shore to mitigate the general dullness of the town. But the people of Penticton, intent on commercial rather than æsthetic interests, have allowed this shore to be occupied by an ugly jumble of wharves, mills and mountainous piles of raw yellow sawdust, wholly destroying the effect of the natural environmental gifts.

We walked back into the town, more depressed, had breakfast at a restaurant with filthy toilets, and found our way out towards Skaha Lake, near which Mr. P., the man we were seeking, had his orchards. Once outside the town, at the beginning of our southward walk, we began to get a better conception of the general character of the valley. Originally it was a dry trough of desert, fit only for cattle ranching, until one of the early missionaries, a Father Pandosy, experimented with fruit-growing during the 1860's. He found the climate ideal, but it was only thirty years afterwards that the farmers began to use irrigation to grow fruit and vegetables extensively in the hot valley. A single experimental car-load of fruit sent out in 1903 was the beginning of a great export industry, and since then 50,000 acres have been brought under irrigation, nearly 20,000 truckloads of fruit are sent away each season, and the Okanagan has become the biggest centre of apple, pear, peach, cherry and grape production in the whole of Canada, besides developing a great industry in such luxury vegetables as asparagus.

As we walked down the broad road towards the end of the valley and the United States border, we soon realised the magnitude of the improvements which human ingenuity had made on the valley's natural state. The hills on each side were grey and parched, scurfed, like those of the southern Cariboo, with sage brush and bunch grass, dotted here and there with scrubby dark thickets of stunted trees. Even on the floor of the valley there were still patches of dry waste ground covered with bunches of ugly little cacti like squat green thumbs.

Yet the whole valley was populated thickly, the road was lined on each side with orchards, most of them relatively small in size, and on the benches of higher land under the hills there were other orchards as far down the valley as we could see. Along the roadside and among the trees ran the wooden and metal irrigation flumes, most of them dry now that the year's watering had done its work. The low, compact apple trees were heavy with the red, painted-looking fruit which is grown for export in western Canada, and the pickers were at work in many places, rapidly filling their large satchels, while piles of filled boxes stood at every gateway, waiting for the co-operative lorries to take them away to the packing warehouses.

There were also frequent hillocks of apples which had been thrown aside for some slight defect; unused to waste on such a scale, we would pick out delicious fruit, marred by some very slight bruise, and eat them as we walked. Remembering the fruit-starved existence of many people in Europe, we could not help feeling indignant at so much being thrown away. We even spoke about it to a farmer who was standing at his gate; he laughed, and said that this was only the beginning of the process. At the packing depot many more would be rejected because they were under or over size. Only perfect and regular-sized apples were sent out, so that the standard of the industry could be upheld and consistently good prices maintained. Some of the rejected apples were pulped for juice, but most of them were just ploughed back into the ground.

At certain points the orchards alternated with lush green meadows, and the roadside ditches were filled with the white floss of milkweed and the plumed foliage of wild asparagus. Down towards Skaha Lake we could see the hillsides splashed red with autumnal sumach and maple, mingling with the sombre grey and black backgrounds. In this almost harshly coloured landscape it was clear that the inhabitants lived in considerable prosperity. The houses were large, big American cars often stood outside them, there were many luxurious auto-courts. Once we passed that epitome of automobile-conscious North America, a drive-in cinema, with its great white screen towering over the roadside orchards, and once a string of beautifully kept horses from a dude ranch was led past by a couple of halfbreed grooms.

Eventually, after reaching the shore of Skaha Lake, making several fruitless enquiries, and then retracing our steps for a mile or so, we found a wayside shopkeeper who could direct us. Then, after climbing up a long sandy hill and through a dry scrubby canyon on to one of the benches, we reached Mr. P.'s orchard. There was a stage by the roadside, and here a lean man in a blue French-Canadian woollen cap was loading empty boxes on to a trolley attached to a tractor. We introduced ourselves, and when we said that we had just come from Smithers he invited us in a strong North German accent to jump on the trolley and ride home with him. We bumped through orchards whose fruit had already been largely picked, and then came out on to a crag where a new white house had been built; below, the lake was intensely blue and bordered by trees in every shade of autumnal transition, and down to the States and up towards Penticton we could see the valley receding into the grey-blue haze of a sunny autumn day.

Our host led us into his house and introduced us to his German wife and mother-in-law, his three blonde, handsome children. They treated our arrival, unexpected and unknown strangers as we were, with that wide and generous hospitality which immediately set us at our ease and made it seem the most natural thing in the world that they should insist on our not only joining them at lunch but also staying the whole day to talk about the many ideas we must hold in common, and spending the night in their house— the idea that we should go to a hotel in Penticton they swept aside as an unreasonable suggestion from people whose arrival constituted such a pleasant variation in their own existence.

We sat down to a large and excellent vegetarian meal, and then, while the children went off to pick fruit in a neighbouring orchard, where they were earning pocket money at the rate of ten dollars a day (some really expert pickers can make twice as much), Mr. P. announced that he would devote the rest of the day to showing us over the property, and to discussing with us anything we might wish to know. The conversation ranged over some very wide fields, from the prevalence of rattlesnakes in the Okanagan to the methods of fruit-growers' co-operation, from the bootlegging of gin in the high schools to the improvement in irrigation owing to the activity of the beavers, whose dams in the mountains had greatly increased the available water supply.

But perhaps most interesting of all were the family's history and the picture of their present life which Mr. P. sketched for us. It was a life in some ways typical of many immigrants who have become prosperous in this part of Canada, but also peculiar to the man himself in its enviable appearance of equilibrium.

He was a Hamburg man who had originally made the beginning of a successful banking career. During the 1920's he became converted to pacifist and vegetarian opinions, and, seeing the futility of his own life in Germany, he joined a party of idealists who emigrated to Canada about 1930, with the intention of founding a Utopian community. The community bought land and began its activities in the Okanagan Valley, but very soon the prosperity of the area corroded the ideals of the members in a way the social stresses of their native land had been unable to do, and they parted company and began to seek their own fortunes as individual farmers. Most of them were still in the district, they kept contact with each other, and retained their humanitarian beliefs, but they had completely lost their communal ideals in gaining individual wealth and security. It was the repeated history of many similar endeavours in North America.

When P. and his wife started on their orchard twenty years ago, they set themselves two main aims: to become as self-sufficient as they could, and to attain as near as possible a balanced life. The first year had been difficult indeed, breaking the unsympathetic ground, planting the trees, building up the orchard to its full productivity. But now they seemed to have gained as much of both of their objectives as any man could hope to do.

It would have been hard to imagine a man more protected economically against the storms of the outer world. In his orchard he had been careful not to specialise, but had planted every species of fruit tree that would grow well on this soil, and in some cases two or three varieties of each. In this way his farming economy was resilient; in the great frosts of the previous winter he had lost nearly 5,000 dollars worth of peach trees, but thanks to his other more hardy fruit he had hardly felt in his income the effect of this capital loss, and now he could console himself with the thought that in a couple of years the trees would in any case have been past their period of economic bearing.

But our host was not content with commercial adaptability. He and his family had also striven for the utmost self-sufficiency in their daily lives. They kept a cow, and made their own butter and cheese, they had bees for honey, they grew all their vegetables, made their own bread, bottled and preserved everything that was suitable, and so, being vegetarians, they provided themselves with most of the food they needed. Now they even considered putting a spare acre under wheat and buying an electric grinder.

With all this industry, the family's organisation of work and utilisation of machinery had been so wise that their activities still left them free to follow other interests of their own. Right from the beginning Mr. P. had set out with the aim of diminishing the work on his farm to a reasonable minimum. He had replaced irrigation trenches with sprayers, and these he could also connect with an insecticide tank in his basement and so eliminate the need for treating each tree individually by hand. By these and other similar means he had contrived to cut his daily working time, except at the peak periods of thinning and picking the fruit, down to four hours.

In the time thus gained he followed a variety of occupations. He had built his own house and was still in the process of completing it, while he was also building a smaller dwelling where he could accommodate friends who were temporarily homeless. When he grew tired of building, he would go down into his basement and turn wooden bowls and platters on his lathe. He took great care to work according to the nature of each particular piece of wood, to follow its peculiar grain and other qualities so as to enhance the formal value of the object he was making. He showed us several pieces of his work, and it certainly exhibited a very high degree of craftsmanship and of formal sensitivity.

With all this he managed to read a great deal, he had collected a large library of English and German books, and his conversation showed him to be one of the few really well-read men I have encountered outside university circles in western Canada.

In the evening we talked about the fruit-growers' co-operatives. He described the terrible days of the 1930's, when the prices of fruit fell steadily until growers, at the mercy of a hundred private selling agencies, were expected to sell their fruit at derisory prices, half a cent a pound and even less, which did not even repay them for their expenses. They finally reached the situation where combination and direct action seemed the only way out. A campaign of refusing to accept cheap prices was started, and, to the slogan of "a cent a pound or on the ground" the growers started their war against the middle-men. The result of the struggle was that they finally decided to undertake their own marketing, and founded the Fruit-growers Co-operative, which, buttressed by Government support, now virtually controls the marketing of fruit in the southern valleys of British Columbia and makes it almost impossible for any private fruit-selling to exist. The old private packing houses continue, but as employees of the co-operative, and the twenty-five million dollars which come in each year are paid out to the farmers without any profit being taken by the organisation, after the expenses of packing, storing and transport have been deducted. The organisation also acts as a buying agency for equipment, fertilisers and other supplies which are needed by the growers.

One could not help being impressed with this example of mutual aid, yet it was evident that the growers had acted in some ways against the interests of the general public. Mr. P. agreed with us, but he argued that this was inevitable in a society where co-operation was limited. In such conditions those who had become conscious of the need for co-operation must make their own positions good, and then, when co-operation had extended into wider fields and the old competitive spirit had disappeared, it would be possible to make the adjustments which would assure everybody a fair living and eliminate the wastefulness we criticised.

The next morning he insisted on driving us into Penticton so that we could join the single daily train at six o'clock, and the whole family rose to see us off, a last gesture which we found most moving after all the hospitality they had already shown us. We went away with the feeling that, on the whole, they were the happiest and most fortunate family we had yet encountered in North America.

14

Out of Penticton the train climbed almost immediately into the mountains on the western side of Okanagan Lake, rising and re-turning on serpentine curves until at last we could see the whole southern end of the valley, with its orchards and dry hillsides, with its blue lake and the outspread streets of Penticton lying be-neath us to the south and then, as the line reached the farthest loop of its ascent, at over 4,000 feet, the map-like pattern of Kelowna, the valley's largest town, away to the north.

As we climbed, we entered first the region of parched slopes and the copses of undernourished pines on which we had already looked from the valley road. But the vegetation began to change quickly as we drew near the watershed, and then we ran through woods of thick spruce and fir, with a tangled undergrowth of berry bushes and ferns. This thick coniferous woodland extended right over the top of the mountains and down on to the farther descending slopes. It was an almost completely deserted region, where a little logging was the only industry, yet here again, as in the mountains outside Hope, the little halts by the side of the line appeared every few miles; here the engineer had been concerned with family affairs rather than literary tastes, and we passed the stations of Lorna, Ruth and Myra, named, so one of the train crew told us, after the constructor's own daughters.

The train crew, indeed, we found extremely friendly; they were anxious not only to impart information, but also to find out as much as they could, in the usual Canadian way, about our lives. North American trains are remarkably heavily staffed in compari-son with their European counterparts. Apart from the enginemen, there is a conductor, usually with two assistants, who deal with the general running of the train and examine the passengers' tickets, as well as a sleeping-car conductor, and a porter, usually a Negro, to each sleeping car. There are a baggage-car attendant, a newsman, a carriage cleaner, and finally the dining-car staff, often consisting of as many as five men. Thus an average long-distance train will carry between fifteen and eighteen men; this great staff is due in part to the extra functions which are inevitably involved in long cross-country journeys of several days' duration, but it is also due in a large degree to the power of the unions, which specify the staffs on each train and lay down carefully what each man may do, as a safeguard against under-employment. As a result, although the trainmen often serve long shifts, they have equally long rest intervals and do not work very hard while they are on the train, so that they have always plenty of leisure to talk to the passengers.

The conductor evidently considered such gossiping beneath the dignity of his gold-braided office, but his two assistants and the newsman took turns in chatting with us for practically the whole of our day's journey into Castlegar, in the Kootenays, which we reached late in the afternoon. The trainman who attached himself particularly to us was a slight, Celtic-looking young man, who had fought and been taken prisoner in the Canadian army. The Germans, he said, had treated them reasonably well; indeed, he had kept his eyes open, and it seemed to him that the prisoners who received Red Cross parcels were often living on a better level than their guards or the civilian German population. He said that the Nazis had directed much propaganda to the Canadian prisoners, to try and convince them that the war was none of their business. But he had not needed any of that kind of talk to teach him its general futility. He had gone into the army full of patriotic feelings; next time they would have to find him where they could, and he knew enough of the British Columbian mountains to make that a very difficult task.

He was typical of a certain section of the Canadian left, more numerous, I think, than in any other country, who are themselves sincere devotees of freedom and equality, and who cannot yet reject the vision of Russia as a perfect state which their fellow-socialists elsewhere, nearer to the centre of attention, have been forced to abandon years before. This is due to a number of special causes, of which the first is undoubtedly the widespread Canadian contempt for American neuroticism; they are so anxious to avoid the witch-hunting mentality that they develop an obstinate loyalty to discredited idols which is just as unrealistic and subjective. But there is a second reason for the survival of sentimental fellow-travelling in Canada, and that is the rudimentary state of an informed left-wing press in this country. There has, in fact, been little effective presentation of evidence against Communism except in the daily press, which is regarded—not without justice—as tainted and venial. It is only during the last year or two that the books of writers like Orwell and Koestler have attained any currency in Canada.

When the trainmen left us to go about their light duties, the newsman would come and sit beside us. He was a quiet elderly man who had been in British Columbia before the first world war. He spoke nostalgically of the days when the stern-wheelers had run up and down Okanagan Lake and one could buy a seven-course meal for seventy cents. During the last war he had gone to England and worked as a War Agricultural Committee official. He had returned to Canada and had found himself at a loose end, waiting for a job which never turned up, and at last he had taken a chance to become a railway newsman. He was paid by commission, and a man who was a good salesman could make a fair living, particularly if, as some of them did, he introduced a sideline of his own. But he himself had no enthusiasm for that kind of work, and confessed that he made a very poor income out of it. Two months later I met him by chance in Vancouver; he had abandoned the railway and become a gardener, which he found a more congenial way of waiting for the job which still had not materialised.

We had descended from the mountain crests towards a broad and singularly beautiful valley, with wide coniferous forests on its sweeping sides, and clear shallow streams running down in its depths between thick, autumn-bright deciduous woods. This was the Kettle Valley; we travelled through it for two hours during the morning, descending into the lower levels where quiet homestead farms occasionally bit into the woodland. This is a part of British Columbia which has received very little publicity, but, like other sections of this secondary Canadian Pacific line, it offers beauties of scenery which, if perhaps no greater than those on the more publicised main line, are all the more pleasing for being unknown and unexpected. One day, we promised ourselves, we would return to the area and try to explore its woods and hills at leisure and perhaps on foot.

After Rock Creek we reached the more level part of the valley, and passed the old copper town of Greenwood, through which we travelled some weeks later on another journey, of which I shall have more to say. Some time afterwards, as the valley began to broaden out towards Grand Forks—another mining town which has become an agricultural centre—we saw the first Doukhobor dwellings, large square brick houses dotted over the cleared and cultivated slopes of the valley. In the fields beside them we could see the Doukhobors working, the women wearing the full skirts and head shawls of Russian peasants which, like many of their customs and ideas, still distinguish them from their Canadian neighbours.

15.

The Doukhobors are a Russian dissenting sect which arose some time in the seventeenth century, at the time when the Great Schism within the Orthodox Church caused a vast proliferation of sects among the peasantry. One Doukhobor legend claims their descent from Shedrach, Meschach and Abednego, another asserts that the sect was founded by a brother of the Tsar who renounced his position to live and work among the poor. A third story, told me by a Doukhobor leader, brings in a Quaker who was somehow taken prisoner in a war (which war and how a Quaker happened to be fighting in it is not specified) and transported to Russia, where he became the first of the Doukhobor prophets. This sounds as absurd as the other tales, yet there is in fact a remarkable similarity between Doukhobor beliefs, even in the present day, and those which the early Quakers and the other radical sects of the Reformation professed.

The central idea of the Doukhobor faith is that of a direct communion with God within, which has made them opponents of any kind of organised religion. Since they hold that all men are directly in touch with God, they condemn man-made laws and institutions, and in its purest form the Doukhobor faith also condemns such material trammels as the owning of private property. For these reasons there has always been a tendency—fluctuating according to individuals and periods—towards social anarchism and a form of religious communism. Add to this a literal interpretation of the commandment, "Thou shalt not kill" as an injunction both against meat eating and the bearing of arms, and you will readily see why the Doukhobors found it impossible to make their peace with the militaristic autocracy of Tsarist Russia, and were forced to emigrate to Canada. You will also see that these beliefs, though they were rarely followed with total consistency, must inevitably make the Doukhobors a difficult element to assimilate in any society, however democratic, where even a slight measure of compulsory uniformity is exacted by the governmental structure.

After their first appearance in Russia the Doukhobors were at times persecuted and at times patronised by the rulers, according to whether their radical beliefs or their excellence as farmers received the most attention. For a while they lived in the Crimea, and later they were exiled to the Caucasus. It was here, during the 1890's, that the ruthless methods of Alexander III came up against a fanatical resistance which had been inspired by a reformation and revivification of the sect under a new leader, Peter Verigin. The Tsar tried to enforce conscription on the Doukhobors, the faithful replied with a campaign of obstinate passive resistance, and a cruel series of persecutions were inflicted on them, until at last, through the intervention of Tolstoy, Kropotkin, the Quakers and other sympathisers, they were allowed to emigrate to Canada.

Here again they soon began to experience the difficulty of reconciling their radicalism with the demands made upon them by governmental authorities. Chiliastic enthusiasts set off on pilgrimages to find a promised land below the American border, let their horses and cows go free as a gesture of complete brotherhood, and began the custom of parading nude as a sign of Adamite simplicity and Christian renunciation of vanity. All these activities involved the Doukhobors, and particularly the new faction of zealots who called themselves Sons of Freedom, in considerable trouble with the rather unimaginative Canadian authorities of the time, and finally, because they refused to take an oath of allegiance to any earthly ruler, even Queen Victoria, the sect was deprived of most of the lands which had originally been granted in Saskatchewan— an act of crass folly on the part of the authorities which bred an enduring resentment between Doukhobors and their fellow-Canadians.

The most devoted of the believers, about half the sect, migrated over the mountains to the inner valleys of British Columbia, where this time they bought their land. There Peter Verigin attempted to found a great communal colony, the Christian Community of Universal Brotherhood. For a time it was very successful; the land was cleared, orchards were planted, sawmills, brickworks and a jam factory were built. Then Verigin died in an unsolved railway explosion in 1924, disputes over leadership wracked the community, and it began to decline; it finally broke up at the end of the 1930's, owing largely to the intervention of creditors. The recent Doukhobor "troubles" have been in great part due to an attempt by the more radical elements to bring the movement back to what they consider its true and God-given purpose.

One of the reasons for our trip into this southern part of British Columbia had been to find out what we could from the Doukhobors themselves about those recent events in their history, and also to try to discover how far the majority of them, outside the more extreme groups, had in fact compromised with Canadian society. During the previous year we had visited a small community of Doukhobors on Vancouver Island who were attempting to put into operation a purely communal economy, involving even the abolition of marriage, but these were a few individuals who by no means represented the Doukhobors in general. Now we were anxious to meet some of the more typical members of the sect, both among the so-called orthodox faction and also among the Sons of Freedom, and to gain a more comprehensive view of their attitude towards their own position and towards the world in general.

The houses we saw in the valley near Grand Forks were part of the old Christian Community of Universal Brotherhood, but the larger settlements—and the headquarters of the community— were farther east, at Brilliant in the Kootenay Valley, and it was here that we intended to start our investigations. I had been in correspondence for some years with a Doukhobor writer and historian who lived in that area, and I was sure that through him I could gain the information and introductions we desired—a highly necessary precaution in dealing with Doukhobors, since, after years of hostility from the ordinary Canadian press and of prying on the part of policemen and officials, they are naturally cautious and uncommunicative to strangers. But before we paid this visit to the exponents of a radical Christianity, we intended to turn aside for a very different trip—to the great metallurgical plant at Trail, the most important and most monolithic centre of modern industry in British Columbia.

At Grand Forks a number of Doukhobors boarded the train— gnarled men who might have been peasants of almost any European country, and broad-bottomed women in bright skirts and shawls who might have come that very day out of Tolstoy's Russia, though all but the oldest of them had probably spent their whole lives in Canada. We ran out of Grand Forks along the Kettle River, and about five or six miles farther on we saw, on the opposite bank, a small village of about fifty low, single-storied wooden houses, each in its own garden.

"That's Gilpin," the trainman explained. "One of the Sons of Freedom villages. If you look out carefully, you may see some of 'em walking about naked in their gardens—though it's a bit cold now for that kind of thing." We saw no naked Doukhobors, and began to suspect that our acquaintance, despite his tolerance for Communists and his great regard for Negroes, had at least one blind spot of prejudice. We probed him gently, and he admitted that he did not really like Doukhobors. It was their spontaneity, their complete unpredictability that frightened him. One day, he complained, a farmer might be a good, solid, law-abiding citizen, condemning extremism and respected by his neighbours, and the next day he might be standing with a crowd of Sons of Freedom, stripped to the buff and lustily singing hymns while his own house or somebody's else's was being burnt to the ground. What could you do with people like that? They weren't even reasonable.

He voiced the more sober type of criticisms one hears against the Doukhobors, and we could see his dilemma, that of a man who believed in a rational, materialistic, ordered society, faced by the anarchic impulse, the Dionysiac religious force breaking out spontaneously in its flash of insight and turning the sober citizen into the God-intoxicated enthusiast. Yet we also realised, and tried to point out, that it was only possible to emerge from such a situation when the rational and irrational tried to come to terms, to comprehend each other in both senses of the word—a process which, in any case, might be beneficial for both sides. He did not agree, and seemed to regard our attitude as a little suspect, as though we too might at any moment begin to divest ourselves in the middle of the day coach.

After Gilpin the railway swerved away from the Kettle Valley and began to climb again, this time across Cascade Mountain, a long pull of nearly three hours, in which the track rose at the head of the pass to almost 4,000 feet. Once again the scenery was very impressive. We skirted the long, oval Christina Lake, rising steadily until our last sight of its waters was taken from more than a thousand feet above. Beyond it the full magnificence of the mountains was rather marred, for the slopes had been heavily logged off and in parts were just bare areas of stumps with rejected trees lying scattered over them—looking in the distance like matches fallen higgledy-piggledy out of a box.

The train stopped for a while at the entrance to a long tunnel on the downward slope, until its westbound counterpart from Medicine Hat came crawling out of the dark mouth. The two trains lay panting side by side for a while, the crews stood on the track and talked together, and in the middle of this highland wilderness the newsman suddenly came along the coach with copies of the morning paper from Nelson, the last big town to the east.

When our train emerged from the opposite end of the tunnel, we found ourselves travelling precipitously along the almost sheer cliffs that tower over the yellow beaches and intensely blue waters of the Lower Arrow Lake. The Arrow Lakes are really parts of the Columbia River which have been dammed naturally in their narrow valleys into two long sheets of water. In all they are about a hundred miles long, but very rarely more than a couple of miles wide. The Canadian Pacific travels for about twenty miles at the bottom of the lower lake's western shore, and a dirt road runs up the Slocan Valley from Nelson to the narrow connecting river between the lower and upper lakes, but otherwise the only transport is the old paddle-steamer *Minto*, which has sailed up and down the whole hundred miles of waterway since the gold-mining days.

The few lacustrine settlements lead an exceptionally isolated and self-sufficient existence, so much out of the present that they still grow varieties of fruits and vegetables which were brought by the earliest pioneers but which have long since been abandoned elsewhere in the province. The old custom of communal working— the working bees—and other mutual aid institutions of the frontier days still persist among them, and they offer the traditional homestead hospitality to the very rare travellers who visit them. As we ran along this shore we could see several farms on the scattered flats and benchlands which are hemmed in by the steep mountains on the far side of the water. One of the trainmen told us that they would shortly have to be abandoned, since it was proposed to dam and deepen the lake in order to create a head of water for providing power.

One cannot help wishing that this scheme will never come to fruition, for the beauty of the Arrow Lakes as it exists now is literally unique. The strong current has caused the yellow beaches to thrust out into the water sharply pointed triangular bars, which the early settlers likened to arrow-heads. Off these strange golden tongues the water assumes a very delicate green colour, and this merges through turquoise into deep blue and thence into shades of violet as the waters deepen. All along the shore these combinations of colouring vary—because of the altering configuration of the lake bottom, because of the changes in the light, because of the difference of the angle from which one looks down into the depths. This view—certainly one of the most pleasing and rewarding of a journey through southern British Columbia, cannot fail to lose all its peculiar grace when the beaches are finally submerged deep under the dammed waters of technological progress.

Eventually the lake narrowed into the normal greyish flow of the Columbia, and then, at a small station called Castlegar, we had to hurry out of the train and climb on board the bus down to Trail, which has no passenger train connection with the outside world, although it is served by a goods line along which many trains of coal and ore concentrates go every day to the smelter and corresponding trains of metals and of fertilisers go out to the customers of the vast Cominco plant.

16.

The highway ran for nearly twenty miles down the Columbia Valley, sometimes over flat, cultivated benchland, at other times through places where the hills edged to the river and the road crawled precariously around their bulging faces. At last we came in sight of the great bowl in which Trail lies, with scrubby, barren-looking slopes rising on three of its sides, warmed by the autumn red and gold of the stunted trees and bushes. The smelter and its subsidiary plants lie on the hillsides which descend into the city from the north, but they seem to dominate it completely from whichever way one enters. For a mile we drove past the bewildering conglomeration of smoke-stacks and great buildings and power-stations, clustering and spreading over the double hill into the town. From below, as we stepped out of the bus and looked upward, the plant hung like a smoky and most monstrous citadel, and later, when we had found ourselves a room in a grimy, noisy residential hotel and emerged into the town after dark had fallen, it was still almost tangibly present, a black mass studded with myriad lights, an inescapable mechanical version of Kafka's Castle. I have never, indeed, encountered any other industrial town in which one felt so strongly, so immediately and so almost physically overborne and dominated by a single factory. It seemed, even at this first sight, a kind of imaginary cinematic symbolisation of the power of great industry, an improbable simplification on reality. Trail people, significantly, call it just The Hill.

The centre of Trail, which was all we had the enterprise to explore by lamplight, was a dull rectangular conglomeration of

8

offices, stores and hotels. We ate in a Chinese restaurant where they served us a surprisingly good escalope of veal, and then we decided that there was nothing to do until we visited the plant next morning.

Accordingly, having risen early, we climbed the laborious hill and eventually reached a gate where a security guard looked us over and asked our business. We explained that we wanted to learn whatever we could about the plant. There was a conducted tour at eleven, he said gruffly. That wasn't exactly what we wanted, we explained. We were much more interested to learn about the effect of the plant on the life of the people. He looked at us suspiciously. In that case we had better go up to the office building. He pointed out a broad walk, sending us on our way with injunctions not to leave the prescribed route. However, as the whole area around it presented an unfamiliar and therefore terrifying tangle of hideous metal erections, among which trolleys of all kinds darted to and fro with insect-like quickness, we had no desire to stray far away, and soon we walked into a big white administration building, the keep of the citadel, where a second guard received us. Once again we told our business. He'd find out what could be done, but his voice seemed intended to convey that we need hope for very little. Soon afterwards he said that if we cared to wait, the Public Relations Officer would be very pleased to see us. In due course we were ushered into the office of a very genial official who immediately made us feel so much at ease that we began to lose the impression of a Kafka-like bureaucracy which our first experience had given us.

The Public Relations Officer gave us first a potted history of the Consolidated Mining Company and its plant, which would help us to put what we had seen and were to see and hear into perspective. The real beginning was in 1890, when the rich gold and copper lodes up the hill at Rossland were first discovered. The ore was then shipped down the Columbia to Montana, and Trail was the landing at which it was transferred to the barges. Five years later a smelter was built at Trail itself, and three years afterwards this was acquired by the Canadian Pacific Railway. Lead-processing plants were added, and in 1906 the C.P.R. amalgamated its smelter interests with the mining companies of Rossland and founded Cominco, or The Consolidated Mining and Smelting Company of Canada, Limited. The Canadian Pacific, though our informant did not stress the fact, has since that time remained the dominant interest in this greatest of Canadian metal and chemical producing combines.

The most important event in the history of Cominco was the acquisition of the fabulous Sullivan mine at Kimberley, in the East Kootenays, situated on a mountain so rich with metallic ores that since the first shaft opened no less than 45 million tons have been removed from it without the lodes showing any sign of exhaustion. As the Rossland mines became uneconomical, the mining activities of Cominco were concentrated at Kimberley. To provide the cheap power which would make it virtually self-sufficient, the company bought up the West Kootenay Power and Light Company, and thus—quite apart from its metallurgical activities—it controls the electricity supplies of a network of valleys from Princeton in the west to Nelson in the east, a distance across country of nearly 120 miles, including almost all the principal towns of the southern interior of British Columbia. The expansion which followed during the latter part of the first world war enabled Cominco to render uneconomical the working of small independent smelters in such places as Greenwood and Grand Forks and Nelson, causing the decline of their respective towns (this again was not mentioned by our informant), and so all the smelting in southern British Columbia was concentrated at Trail and the remaining metalliferous mines were made dependent on the great combine.

Today the ore mined at Kimberley, which constitutes very much the major proportion of Trail's raw material, is subjected to a selective flotation process, by means of which 8,500 tons a day are separated into lead and zinc concentrates, which are then sent to Trail for smelting. Altogether, about 350,000 tons of lead and zinc—10 per cent. of the world's production—and about six million ounces of silver are extracted every year at Trail, as well as substantial quantities of cadmium, bismuth, antimony and tin. This makes the town easily the most important industrial centre in British Columbia and the leading non-ferrous metallurgical centre in Canada.

At first the by-products were unused and the fumes were allowed to float over the valley and to kill off the vegetation on the hillsides. Even towns over the American border were affected, and the plant became a centre of diplomatic acrimonies. In 1930, however, the manufacture of chemical fertilisers began, and a total of about half a million tons of ammonium phosphate, sulphate and nitrate are made every year from the smelter waste. Once they could be turned to commercial purposes, the fumes ceased to poison the air, and the stunted vegetation was able to grow again.

As we were discussing these subjects, the telephone rang, and a conversation ensued about a lecture which it was proposed to deliver to the technical workers of the plant and how far it was affected by Security. The P.R.O. looked at us a little uneasily, and then gave the pronouncement that as no members of the Press would be invited the talk might be held not to impinge on Security. I rather think he expected us to make some reference to this incident, and for a moment he hesitated anxiously. We, in our turn, knew that a carefully shielded section of the Trail plant was working on some project in connection with Canadian atomic development, but we realised that, as journalists, we were hardly likely to be told or shown much more than we already knew, and in any case we were not really interested in technical processes on their own account.

So we let the matter rest and turned the conversation to the subjects which interested us more. The Cominco plant was the biggest employer of labour in Trail; its own employees totalled 5,200 out of a population of 17,000, and although some of these workers lived actually outside the city in dormitory communities, it still remained true that the smelter was directly or indirectly the only important provider of work in Trail, for all the other businesses in town were connected with distribution or with services which would not exist if the smelter did not give the excuse for an urban community. There was, in fact, no other productive industry, and therefore Trail must in some measure be considered a representative of that wide Canadian genus—the company town. How far, we wanted to know, did the Company wield a direct and deliberate influence on local affairs outside its position as chief employer? And what, in general, was its attitude towards its employees?

The P.R.O. was anxious to point out that Trail was not one of the towns in which the Company owned everything, shops, houses, etc., and interfered directly in public life. On the contrary, Cominco followed a deliberate policy of minimum direct interference outside the factory gates. They preferred that people should take their own initiatives, should show that they genuinely desired some social amenity and were ready to do something about it themselves. Then the Company would make gifts and grants, but always in such a way that the direction of the project, whatever it might be, remained in the hands of the municipality or of some voluntary association. No doubt we had seen the big new recreation centre which had just been built down in the town? That had started as an initiative among the people, and then, when it was well under way from voluntary efforts, the Company stepped in with money which enabled it to be completed on an adequate scale. But was not that in its way a form of influence, we suggested, since if the people knew the Company would give, then they would start schemes which might not otherwise exist? Certainly, said the P.R.O., but that was hardly a bad thing—to make people feel that they could take initiatives which had some chance of being nurtured to success. In other circumstances many good ideas remained unheard because there seemed no chance of the benevolent intervention that makes all the difference between failure and success. It seemed a good point—if you accepted the situation in which it was made.

But did the Company do anything in the way of providing facilities for its own employees, such as housing and stores? Here, as well, the P.R.O. explained, Cominco had followed, with some exceptions, the policy of eschewing direct intervention. They had built a couple of small housing schemes, but they found that people were much happier in their own homes than in large uniform estates, and now they much preferred to lend the workers money and encourage them to build for themselves. They also operated one of Trail's department stores, but they put no pressure on employees to use it, and in general did not try to work against the normal retailers. At this point we remarked that we had looked into some shop windows and had noticed that prices were rather higher than in Vancouver. The P.R.O. immediately became interested. Was that the case? He must make a note and look into it. For one of the reasons why they operated the store was to provide a means of keeping local prices from rising unreasonably high; if the Company's store maintained a competitive level, then there would be no chance of private traders ganging up to make too much profit.

What about the conditions of work, we asked? On the whole, he suggested, they would compare favourably with those in other industries. There was a minimum of $1.10 an hour, but most of the workers, particularly if they had been there a number of years, earned considerably more. All employees were paid pensions on retirement, according to salary and length of service, the whole cost of this being borne by the Company. In addition, there were accident insurance and medical aid schemes. These features of the employment policy, the P.R.O. went on, would not seem very strange to us; they represented the policy followed by most enlightened employers today. But there was one feature of work at Trail which was rather unusual and which we might find interesting. During the depression Cominco was faced with the problem of cutting costs; they did not want to burden the district with unemployment, so they suggested that the misfortune should be shared out equally by all the employees going on three-quarter time, working twelve days and having four days to themselves. The men agreed and, after thinking for a while that they were just making the best of a bad job, they actually began to like the arrangement. They had enough money to live, and found that the periodical lay-off allowed them to develop new interests. They could build, go on fishing expeditions, do a little farming and fruit-growing on the side. Indeed, so much did they like the leisure that had been imposed on them by adverse circumstances that, after having worked full time all through the war, they asked that the old arrangement should be resumed in peacetime, and now the regular four-day break is a feature of Trail life.

This experience taught the management that increased leisure among the workmen, far from lowering production, tends to raise it, and since then they have applied the policy in other ways. In certain branches of the plant, for instance, a modified piece-work arrangement exists, by which a certain number of operations, well within the ability of a normal worker, is set as the quota for the shift. If a man can do his work in less time, he is free to go, and in this way some of the men work shifts as short as five hours. In general, the experiment which the managers have carried out in this field seemed to have proved to their satisfaction that increased leisure is really a great incentive to production—a fact which European employers and government officials might be very well advised to consider in their recent tendency to reverse the pre-war trend towards the progressive shortening of hours.

The P.R.O. offered to loan us a car to see the plant, supplied us with Security permits, and sent us off with one of the younger publicity officials. We went into the plants for refining lead and zinc, into the fertiliser factories, we gaped at the smelters, and it was only the secret sections that remained unshown and undis-

cussed. It was a bewildering experience which, as I know very
little of the technical meaning of the processes that were described
and demonstrated, is now represented mostly by a few impression-
istic mental pictures—of dazzling white streams of molten metal
being poured out of crucibles, of the rasping atmosphere in the
rooms where men were stripping sheets of zinc from the cathodes
on which they are precipitated, of the great green unattended and
almost silent machines in the fertiliser plant and the vast steel
globes of ammonia, covered with rime and icicles, standing in the
yards outside. The fertiliser processes perhaps impressed us most
of all, particularly when we remembered how much we ourselves
had paid for a bag of nitrates. Water, air and the waste products
of the smelter are the main constituents, and all that must be
brought from outside is the phosphate rock, imported from a mine
operated by a subsidiary company in Montana. We questioned our
guide as to why a material which evidently cost so little to make
should be relatively more expensive than animal manure by the
time it reached the grower. All he could reply was that the distribution charges and the profits of middlemen and retailers had
to be taken into account before the material actually reached the
ground.

Afterwards we returned into the hollow and wandered about
the town. The configuration of the land, with its broken hills and
ravines, does a great deal to save Trail from the monotonous uniformity of most industrial communities. The centre, as we had
seen last night, was very much in the familiar pattern, but across
the river and in the hilly residential sections there were a surprising
number of little individual quarters, often out of view of the
centre and sometimes even given a certain grace by the efforts of
the inhabitants to decorate them with trees and flower gardens.
One quarter was occupied by the Italians, who came to Trail in
the railroad-building days and remained to work in the smelters—
they still make up about a sixth of the town's population. There
we saw Italian fraternal organisations, and shops full of European-
looking sausages and cheeses. There were dark-skinned and dark-
eyed women going about their shopping who might have come
straight from Naples; they still spoke Italian among themselves,
and some of the older people had hardly any English. The younger
generation, we gathered, were tending to move out into the peripheral suburbs and, like many of their fellow-countrymen in the
United States, to become absorbed into the anonymous life of the

country around them. Another quarter was inhabited by the technical and managerial staffs—this, naturally, was the most flowery and wooded of all—and there was an almost fascinatingly vulgar housing estate in a kind of Port Merrion New Art style, with steep fairy-tale roofs and candy-coloured walls; its local name was Micky Mouse Town.

When one remembers so many industrial towns, there is in comparison a rather relaxed atmosphere about Trail; the monstrous iron citadel is inhabited by a despot who has realised that it is wise to be benevolent. There is even room for at least some genuine manifestations of free co-operation. We were interested in a transport arrangement which the employees who live in the outlying settlements have worked out. A man from Rossland told us that it started some years ago when a group in his town clubbed together to buy an old jalopy to take them to work. Soon others realised that they were making economies, both in cash and time, and the idea spread, until a whole worker-controlled transport service has arisen and operates buses and limousines.

All these circumstances have combined to give Trail, despite its inevitable physical ugliness, a less concentrated feeling of restriction than more regimented company towns. The people can get away into a wide countryside or take trips across the nearby border, they have periods of leisure when they can forget their work environment for a time, and they have the illusion, and even at times the reality, of doing things for themselves. Finally, there is not the same superlatively frustrating feeling that the company is not only one's boss, but also one's landlord, one's grocer, one's butcher, baker and candlestick-maker all combined.

Yet this relatively greater freedom is, in fact, conditional and therefore illusory. In one way I suppose it is possible to argue that none of us is free, however much he may feel so, in a society where his life is very largely ruled by economic and political forces which are beyond his immediate control. And if one takes this view, then a town like Trail is only an extreme example of our condition. These people are at the mercy of one particular factory; if its mills cease to clank, not only will Trail as a town cease to have any reason to exist, but the whole mining area of southern British Columbia will be left without an outlet. In such an event the people involved will find themselves forced to starve or to uproot their lives and move away.

The problem of Trail is the problem of centralisation. In the short run it may have proved economically more feasible for a couple of dozen small smelters, scattered over the south of the province, to be closed down and their work concentrated in one spot. But in the large run one begins to doubt whether it is socially healthy. The centralised and specialised industry, like the overgrown metropolitan city and the monolithic political state, is a symptom of the tendencies in contemporary society which inevitably weaken the freedom of individual development.

17.

Later in the day, after being hunted out at the bus depot by a breathless clerk who wanted to retrieve our Security passes, we returned to Castlegar. It was a white, antiseptic little dormitory town; the rain began to fall heavily as soon as we arrived and it drove us down to the station to wait for our train to the north-east. This journey was very short—a mere six miles up the Kootenay Valley, with the meadows and orchards and some of the square brick houses of the old Doukhobor Community at Brilliant lying out by the river to our right.

Thrums, our destination, was not a village in the real sense, but a tiny railroad halt beside the main road in a narrow valley with the Kootenay River rushing on the other side of the track. We were the only people to step down from the train. Outside, on the road, a car full of workmen had stopped. I asked them if they knew where Pete M. lived. "Sure, more than a mile down the road," one of them replied in a thick Russian accent. "Too far to carry a suitcase in the rain. Crowd in, and we'll take you." So we managed to squeeze ourselves in among the six people who already occupied the car and set off down the road, past frequent plank houses lying in large gardens filled with fruit trees. In the porches there were women in Doukhobor costume; for Thrums, despite its name, is almost exclusively Russian, populated mostly by orthodox Doukhobors who had formerly belonged to the Christian Community of Universal Brotherhood, and now lived and worked on their individual garden plots, following the methods of intensive culture which their sect had perfected years ago in the Crimea and the Caucasus.

We stopped outside a large house with Virginia creeper hanging brightly red over its front wall. Around it were fruit trees, much cultivated ground, and a number of cabins, some of which appeared to be inhabited. This was Pete M.'s place, the driver told us. We went up to the front door of the large house. A young girl of eighteen or so answered the door. She was fair complexioned and slender and had abandoned the customary Doukhobor dress and wore denim trousers and a tartan shirt. But she had the slight South Russian accent which survives even into the second and third generation of these people who cling so obstinately to their own identity and their own language.

Pete, her father, was away. "He's gone into another valley to buy apples, and he might be back tonight or tomorrow morning. Mother is with him too, but you must come in and stay the night!"

Though we knew the Doukhobor reputation for hospitality, and had already experienced it on Vancouver Island, we were nevertheless surprised at such a spontaneous offer to two complete strangers. Why, that was nothing. They were always having people in to stay—her father had so many friends, at some time or another everybody came to stay. Besides, he liked to meet people whom he knew by letter, and he would certainly be very disappointed if he thought we had gone away without seeing him.

So we stayed, and Nadia led us into the kitchen and immediately prepared an enormous Russian meal—borscht, and vegetables cooked in oil, and pirogi, and casha, and Russian tea. Pirogi are a kind of patties filled with fruit or cheese or vegetables which are usually eaten with sour cream. Casha is a thick, delicious porridge made of millet and butter. All the dishes were vegetarian, for most of the Doukhobors eschew the eating of meat, as well as the use of alcohol and tobacco. Their food—the best we encountered in our whole trip through British Columbia—is vastly superior to the kind of denaturised and indigestible substances normally eaten by English vegetarians, and the latter might do a great deal worse than send a mission of food reform cooks to learn a few lessons from the hospitable Doukhobors.

There was a tiny child in the house, a nephew of Nadia, who spoke to us in Russian baby language, and we realised that still, even for the youngest Doukhobors, English is learnt only as a foreign language, after they grow up and mix with the outside world. Even those who know English still use Russian exclusively among themselves, as we soon learnt when two young men appeared and Nadia explained to them who we were. One was our host's son, the other one of his sons-in-law, and both of them worked as carpenters in Trail. We talked to them generally about the Doukhobor movement, and they described their own experiences in prison, when they had been arrested during the war for taking part in pacifist demonstrations. They complained bitterly of the prejudice which many ordinary Canadians showed towards them, and one of them said that even his workmates, who in general were not a bad set of companions, would sometimes turn mean and abuse him as a "dirty Douk".

After a while a car stopped outside and a moment later a tall thin man with a lurching peasant gait and a slim woman in Doukhobor clothes (she had a thin, dark, Italian-looking face) came peering in out of the darkness. They were our host and his wife. He immediately made us welcome, and began a flood of questions about England, the English radical movements, and people like Fenner Brockway and Runham Brown whom he had admired in the past. He was an impulsive, awkward man, given to quick, clumsy movements, to hesitant insights and sudden fits of enthusiasm. He spoke in a flowery kind of English, packed with slightly outmoded superfluities and literary clichés, which one often encounters among people who have learnt English as a foreign tongue and have become familiar with it largely through reading poetry and the writings of idealists. It was, indeed, a little like a spoken version of the English which men like Kropotkin wrote.

During that evening and the following morning we talked with Pete about his own life and ideals. He classed himself as an Independent Doukhobor. At one time, during his boyhood, his parents had left the movement and lived in the United States, and this had taken him away from the narrow environment of the community and enabled him to learn a great deal he would otherwise have lost. He had come to appreciate literature and, while never discarding the main Doukhobor philosophy, he had learnt that there were other men who had similar conceptions and expressed them in new ways which broadened his own insight into social and religious problems.

After a time he had returned to the Doukhobors, had been an active Son of Freedom, but always he had fought against the narrowness which often afflicted his fellows. He had found their anti-literary prejudices a particular source of annoyance. Some of the orthodox, as well as many of the radicals, believed that books were useless, almost a diabolical device, and that all knowledge should come to a man from within. He thought that this was an idealistic belief which might have some relevance if men were really free, but that at present books were a way of conserving human wisdom, of transmitting useful thoughts, of developing the mind and helping it to shed the prejudices which were a bar to spiritual and moral development. He thought the same of education. He agreed with the other members of his sect that education by the state should be resisted, since it instilled militaristic and slavish thoughts. But he did not agree that children should be brought up as illiterates, and he had been careful to educate all his own sons and daughters, so that they would have access to books as well as being able to earn their living in a practical manner.

In recent years he had tended to stand aside from the Doukhobors because he felt that none of their factions—Orthodox, Independents, Sons of Freedom—was adhering to the true and radical Doukhobor teachings. He had made it his task to write the history of the Doukhobors, and had tried to analyse the events of the past in such a way as to show the errors which had led to the relative decline of the movement as a moral force. He had paid for the publication of the book out of his own earnings as a truck gardener, but very few Doukhobors had bought it, and many of them, particularly among the orthodox, had subjected him to insults and even to threats of legal action for the criticisms he had made of the errors of the past.

He would like to talk to us more about the movement, but there was much to be said, and he thought we should see others beside himself. It might take time to arrange, and it would be better if we could return for two or three days a little later on. Then he would try to put us in touch with some of the Sons of Freedom, and we should be able to see for ourselves the kind of people they were—certainly not, despite his differences of opinion from them, anything like the monsters whom the popular press loved to portray. We agreed to this, since we had already decided that later on we should have to make a further trip into the southern interior to visit the Similkameen and the northern Okanagan valleys and also to fill in the gaps on some other places to which we had not been able to pay sufficient attention owing to the deficiencies of the railway timetables. Then it would be relatively easy to return into the Kootenays; we certainly felt that the chance to spend more time with these people and particularly to make the acquaintance of their radical faction was not to be neglected.

18.

It was still raining hard next day when we caught a Greyhound bus to Nelson, burdened now not only with our heavy suitcase, but also with about twenty pounds of apples and pears which our Doukhobor friends had thrust into our arms as we left them. The road followed the Kootenay River which, from Brilliant almost as far as Nelson, had been dammed into a series of lakes to provide the power for the whole of southern British Columbia, as well as for the metallurgical plant at Trail. The highest of these dams were at Bonnington Falls, and here they had been built around and between the original rocks in such a way as to allow at least some of the wildness of the original cascades to remain even in the midst of mechanical improvements.

Nelson is probably the most attractive of the larger interior towns of southern British Columbia, but its pleasantness lies not so much in its architecture (that of the era of its prosperity as a mining centre, which ended before the 1920's) as in its situation, for it rises in parallel streets from the edge of the Kootenay Lake up a moderately steep and wooded hill. In itself, the town is rather dull and lifeless. It began, like most of the Kootenay towns, during the gold and copper rush at the end of the 1880's. But the mines around it were never phenomenally rich, and it was as an administrative, railway, steamboat and fruit-growing centre that Nelson survived. It is still all of these, a few small mines produce in the area, occasional prospectors and hunters make it a centre for expeditions, and a steady trickle of tourists passes through. But its life has settled down to such a low pulse that the leisurely atmosphere is more like that of a very ordinary English market town than an average North American city.

The rain continued, with varying intensity, all the afternoon. We intended to catch the daily train, which left here in the late afternoon, and to travel to a place called Yahk, on the American border, nearly a hundred miles south-east, where we had heard that we could stay the night and catch a train next morning which would take us through the Rockies in daylight.

We tried to discover a Nelson Quaker who had been investigating the Doukhobor problem, but neither of the addresses we had been given was correct. The shops were closed, the cinemas opened only in the evenings and we looked vainly for readable books in the newsagents' stalls. To while away the damp afternoon we went down to the flat piece of low land near the lake where the original mining town had been built in the 1880's. There were many buildings left from these early days—an assay office, a Chinese laundry, a whole cluster of junkmen and old-clothes dealers inhabiting the false-fronted shops of the original city. A couple of tall-stacked stern-wheelers were moored close into the shore and the usual sawmills and lumber yards completed the lakeside scene. Here, as in Penticton, the townspeople have done almost nothing to bring out the beauty which a town acquires gratis from a waterfront situation.

Later we ate ice cream at a lunch counter and talked to a man who started bemoaning the decline of Nelson. "Way back it used to be a good little town," he complained, "plenty of money, plenty of life, plenty of work, a really prosperous place. But now it's nothing, quiet as a grave. And do you know what caused all that?"

"The failure of the mines," we suggested brightly.

"Not a bit of it. It was those God-damned Doukhobors."

"Oh . . .?"

"Yep, the Douks frightened people and trade away with their antics. Who's going to open a business if he's likely to have it burnt over his ears by a pack of Russian nuts?"

I protested that we had heard the Doukhobors only burnt schools, and did not destroy non-Doukhobor private property.

"Well, burning schools—that's bad enough, ain't it? Who wants to pay for schools and then have them burnt down? It don't make sense. Anyways, you've got to live near the Douks to know what they are like. They live just like pigs, the men make the women do all the work, and when the old 'uns are past working, why, they just lock 'em away in an outhouse and let 'em starve to death."

I expressed incredulity and asked him if he had any facts to prove his statements. For instance, had any actual case of Doukhobor ill-treatment of old people ever been brought to public notice?

"Holy Cow, they're too clever to be found out. You can't ever prove anything about a Douk, and you can't believe a word they say. But you won't live near 'em for long without knowing what goes on. Ask anybody in Nelson, they'll tell you the same. Ship the whole lot back to Russia, and give ordinary folks a chance to live."

We gave him up in despair. But what he said had been repeated to us so often, in slightly varying forms, that there seems no doubt that it does represent the attitude of many people in British Columbia. It reflects the kind of paranoiac mentality, in perpetual need of some whipping boy to blame for everything that goes wrong in the world, which motivates all xenophobia. The Doukhobor is a radical, a conchy, a nudist, he speaks Russian, he eats no meat, he is an odd duck from whatever viewpoint the average Canadian looks at him, a challenge to the common man's own colourless avoidance of eccentricity—and perhaps, unconsciously, a subject of envy because he fulfils the hidden desires of so many of the normal citizens.

At last we boarded the train, and left Nelson when it was already almost dark. The conductor persuaded us not to stop off at Yahk. It was only a one-horse station with a single mean hotel which would probably be full in any case. Another forty miles, less than two hours, and we'd reach Cranbrook, which was so full of hotels that we could get a room at any hour of the night.

The country through which we passed—the west shore of Kootenay Lake's southern arm, the declining orchards and mining country around Creston, and then the steady pull up into the Selkirks as we approached Cranbrook—all this was merely a black night which dashed its sheets of rain against the windows and was labelled now and again with the names of stations—names like Sirdar, Goatfell and Blake.

A young Englishman occupied the two seats on the opposite side of the gangway. He carried a little attaché case and now and again would slink with it into the toilet. After the third or fourth visit he returned in a state of benevolent intoxication and insisted on buying us something from the newsman. To make him happy we compromised on a nickel bar of chocolate. Then he persisted in shaking hands all round, at the same time delivering a rambling harangue, of which the burden was something like this : "I don't care whether you're an English Englishman—I don't care whether you're a Scotch Englishman—I don't care whether you're a Welsh Englishman—I don't care whether you're a Jewish Englishman, all Englishmen are jolly well Englishmen—thass right, isn't it—all Englishmen are jolly well Englishmen and they should jolly well stick together in this lousy country." Then he went to sleep untidily and noisily, and got out of the train two hours afterwards—to all appearances completely sober.

It was just before midnight when we reached Cranbrook, with rain pelting down the dark streets. We knew little about the city, except that it was the railway junction for the big Sullivan mine and also something of a hunting centre, but we found that the conductor's prophecy of the numbers of hotels had been quite correct, and we had no difficulty in finding an excellent room, with a private bathroom, for four dollars. Even at this late hour Cranbrook impressed us for two things. Firstly, an obstinate streak of local eccentricity had caused the city fathers to decree the perpetuity of daylight saving time, and we lived that night and the next morning in a state of continual temporal confusion between town clocks and railway clocks. Secondly, although Cranbrook is a relatively small town, it has several cafés which stay open all night and which seem, from what we could see when we went out for a midnight supper, to have a supply of teen-age nighthawks to keep them going indefinitely.

The proprietress of the hotel and the waitress in the café both promised us a superb view in the morning—if only the clouds would clear away—since, they told us, Cranbrook lies right in the centre of a number of impressive mountain peaks, of which one, Mount Fisher, is a handsome 9,000 feet in height. But Mount Fisher kept his cloudy cloak, and after breakfast we wandered aimlessly about the town—for the local experiments with time had got us out an hour earlier than was necessary. Without its mountains Cranbrook was a melancholy place, with a few hunters hanging around the hotel porches, a few old men ringing the spittoons in the cheaper lounges. Down by the railway there were decrepit streets dating back to the Kootenay Rush, but the main street was more substantial, and the town obviously owed its present livelihood partly to being, except for Revelstoke, the only big hunting centre in the Selkirks, and partly to its position as a railway junction and Saturday-night town for the Sullivan mines.

19.

Our train, when it at last arrived, was the most astonishing railroad antiquity we had ever seen in North America, particularly when one considered that it came from over the United States border—a single day coach attached to a train of box cars and refrigerator vans and dating, if one could judge from the dingy upholstery and the elaborate oddity of design, from the very first days of railways in the north-west Pacific area. The most overpowering of its decorations was a series of large ornate gas lamps suspended from the ceiling by great twisted cast-iron arms, like a file of metal octopi hanging above our heads.

The discomfort and ugliness of the coach was compensated by the prevalence of a free and easy atmosphere, reminiscent of an old-fashioned English country bus. Easily the most voluble of our fellow-passengers were a couple of old American middle-westerners, who maintained a peculiarly repetitive form of conversation throughout the day. A typical dialogue went something like this :

First American. Yes, sir, it sure seems a mad world when you stand back and take a look.

Second American. It sure does seem a mad world.

1st A. Look at this business in Korea. We spent Lord knows how much building that country up, and now we smash it all to bits.

2nd A. Yes, sir, I'll say we do, smash it all to bits.

1st A. Now look at Japan. We spent billions of dollars and hundreds of thousands of men smashing it all down, and then when we got it smashed, we start building it up again.

2nd A. We sure are building it up again. Don't that make you mad! Building up the Japs again!

1st A. Well, maybe it does, and then look at it another way. The Good Book tells us to do good to our enemies. And the way I look at it, what the Good Book says should be good enough for me.

2nd A. Yes, sir, if the Good Book says it, then you can't go wrong. What the Good Book says should be good enough for all of us.

1st A. It sure should be. But it still seems a mad world when we've got to smash 'em down before we build 'em up, and then start all over again smashin' 'em down. . . .

And so they would go on, never reaching any real conclusion, but always ending in a declining spiral of exhausted interest.

There was also an Indian family, very different from those we had been used to on the coast—a tall, lean woman, with a dark and rather handsome face, a boy of twelve in a Hopalong Cassidy hat, and a younger girl. The children seemed to be fascinated to the point of obsession by the conveniences which even this antiquated coach provided. The girl ran every quarter of an hour to lock herself into the women's toilet; the boy indulged in a positive debauch from the iced-water container, scattering the paper cups right and left over the floor of the coach. The mother watched the vagaries of her children with dignity, and talked banalities about Spokane with an elderly New England lady who knitted the journey away with implacable vigour.

9

Out of Nelson we ran down into the valley of the Kootenay, crossed it at Wardner, a decaying town with many half-ruined buildings and jetties collapsing into the river, and then began the steady climb of eighty miles through the foothills to the crest of the Rockies. It was a strange country through which we now passed—of decrepit farms, with old mossed orchards and buildings which were often falling to pieces and abandoned, of dead mines, of untidy second-growth forests—a country over which the flood of occupation had flowed and ebbed, leaving a landscape which on that rainy day, with the magnificence of the mountain tops completely hidden from sight, seemed far more forlorn and dead than the ghost country of the Cariboo. We passed the sites where busy towns had stood and had completely vanished, engulfed by the returning bush. There was Elko, a little flag stop on the railway, where nothing remained of a big mining community. The conductor told us that one could walk through the brushwood and stumble over the fire-hydrants of the main street, but hardly two boards hung together of the wooden city that had been ravaged successively by fire and rain and frost. Even Fernie, the largest town between Cranbrook and the Great Divide, had an air of pitiful seediness, with great stark brick buildings—built during its prosperity as a coal town—falling into decay and lines of crumbling and weed-grown coke ovens subsiding beside the railway line. Here the two old Americans intoned a lament to the theme of: "Yes, sir, I sure remember the days when Fernie was a real wild town."

After Elko we ran for more than thirty miles along the Elk River, a typical wide, shallow stream of the Rocky Mountain foothills, broken by sand banks and gravel bars, surging at times into wild rapids, occasionally pushing out backwaters which are dry except in the wettest season, and bordered for most of its course by marshy forests of alder and willow whose fallen trunks and up-torn roots often confer a singularly dismal raggedness upon its banks. When we left the Elk it was to run into a narrow, dark valley which led straight up into the Crowsnest Pass. It was a coal-mining area, and the towns of Natal and Michel formed a long narrow community in the bottom of the valley, stretching for about four miles along the railway, a single elongated town which, with its pitheads, its coke ovens, its sidings full of great iron coal-wagons and its streets of small dingy houses, reminded one of the Welsh coal valleys, Rhondda or Ebbw Vale. A group of miners

who came on the train spoke harsh Czech among themselves, and
the names over the small stores were almost all Slavonic or Hun-
garian. The more voluble of the two old Americans began to tell
a long and heavily embroidered story of how the whole mountain
had once collapsed on top of Michel, and how the sole survivor
had been a little baby girl who had been found perched on a pile
of rubble and playing happily by herself; even her name or
how she had so miraculously survived was never discovered.
This he variously interpreted as an example of the madness of the
world and as a sign of the inscrutable judgment and mercy of
God.

Beyond Michel we climbed steadily up through the wooded hillsides of the Crowsnest Pass. It was a comparatively gentle and
unimpressive passage through the Rockies, for the mountains that
we might have seen were all the time obscured by the low clouds
and the pass itself presented none of the terrifying magnificence of
its fellows to the north, the Kicking Horse and the Yellowhead.
We reached Crowsnest, the last station in British Columbia, a few
hundred yards away from the crest of the watershed. Here we
hurried out of the train across a bleak stretch of barren ground to
the station café—a bare, crepuscular shed with grimy wooden
tables, much more in the international tradition of high mountain
huts than in the chrome-steel manner of the usual Canadian snack-
bar, and while we blew agitatedly into our coffee railway workers
were stolidly eating dreadful-looking plates of stewed steak and
mash, rather like the meals which are served in inferior White-
chapel High Road eating-houses.

The slope into Alberta was much more gentle and regular than
that by which we had climbed from British Columbia. First there
was a rocky region of slate-grey mountain lakes, with occasional
quarries and small mines, then the landscape changed to little
craggy ranges of hills where mining villages alternated with cattle
ranges and small mixed farms. Right from the beginning, on this
drier side of the mountain, the forests were more meagre than on
the coastal face, and they quickly became more and more scattered
until we ran into a rolling prairie, rather like the Wiltshire downs,
where the only trees were the willows and aspens in the gullies and
in the valleys which the few rivers had cut into the deep prairie
soil. Here the rain of the west gave way to snow, the sky was shut
in with leaden clouds, and the thin fall of flakes increased in
volume as we travelled eastward. The ground, however, was still

too warm for the snow to lie, except in occasional pockets on some colder slope.

As the land began to flatten out into the long, imperceptible slope of the real prairie, ranching gave way to the great wheat-fields, with the tractors ploughing steadily over their surface and long strips of black soil alternating with the yellow of recently cut stubble in a barred pattern that extended far into the distance. At each little village station the grain elevators reared up high above the few stores and gas stations and houses, taking the place which the church towers had held in a less materialistic world. Now and then a bunch of saddled horses would be tied up to the poles of the empty station corrals, and sometimes, on the long flat highway that ran beside the tracks, a cowboy in mackinaw and jeans would jog along after the speeding Plymouths and Cadillacs—nothing here of the romantic dash that still survives in the Cariboo. At one station a tall, hawk-nosed Indian in a big black hat came on board and joined the family who had travelled up from Spokane.

The light began to fail as the snow thickened, and, tiring of the prairie monotony, we hoped to be able to read. But the iron octopi in the ceiling remained in darkness, and when the conductor at last lit one of them he explained that owing to some neglect at Spokane the gas tank had not been renewed, and he would have to make do as best he could with the small residue for the remaining two hours to Lethbridge.

Finally we reached MacLeod, the first settlement of any size in the Albertan plain; here we intended to alight and catch a train the next morning to Calgary, whence we could return by the main Canadian Pacific line into British Columbia. The station stood well outside the town, and we had to walk for nearly a mile to the nearest hotel, with the snow increasing into large, mushy flakes, falling over a flat twilit landscape.

MacLeod was typical of a hundred medium-sized raw prairie towns we had seen on our way across Canada two years before, with no charm of situation or architecture and little purpose except the supplying of the needs of the grain farmers and cattlemen who, now the depression years are past and almost forgotten—the average prairie man finds it hard to imagine that they will ever return—have only the desire to make their money quickly and re-tire early to some temperate climate. There is nothing here of the decrepitude of the old mining towns over the mountains—all has the appearance and the dullness of solid prosperity, of the land that keeps bearing year in and out and whose crops seem, since 1939, to have gained an apparently inexhaustible market.

The people of the prairies are quite a distinct type from the mountain valley and coast folk of British Columbia—even less disposed to eccentricity of dress and manner, and worn to a kind of uniform leatheriness and hardness of features by the rigours of broiling summers and winters well below zero. The vast riches of Alberta, with the great yields of its new oilfields complementing the solid wealth of the farmers, has given its inhabitants a peculiar smugness, and we found the atmosphere of MacLeod for this reason distinctly unsympathetic. The food, however, was surprisingly good, and I still remember with some pleasure the great meal of roast chicken, with an excellent banana cream pie to follow, which we were given for 80 cents each. The hotel was inhabited for the most part by resident workmen, who in this fabulously rich province seem to afford even relatively expensive accommodation; like most prairie people, they had little idea of other people's need for quiet, and kept shouting along the corridors and hammering at each other's doors well into the early hours of the morning.

20.

When we set out to the station, the snow was already lying inches deep on the chilled ground, and as a large flock of magpies flew among the bare trees on the edge of the town their harsh calls had a peculiar resonance in the muffled snow silence. The train north to Calgary was another single coach, with a fluctuating population mostly travelling very short distances to intermediate stations. The most spectacular were a pair of tall, bearded men, with peculiar suits of black alpaca and round black velour hats. At first sight they looked like an unfamiliar type of rabbi, but in fact they were members of the Amish, a sect of religious communists, descended from the Anabaptists of the sixteenth century, who have established in Canada and the United States a number of large pacifist and communitarian colonies, maintained according to a very strict rule of life which includes the uniform clothing our fellow-passengers wore.

The two Amish sat on opposite sides of the coach and talked to each other loudly across the aisle in an almost incomprehensible Low German dialect. All at once one of them received a visitation of the spirit, and began to intone a long declamation in which the name of Jesus Christ figured frequently. It seemed a joyful process, for he smiled happily and his friend looked at him with approval and occasionally mumbled an Amen. A little afterwards the conductor came walking down the coach, leaned over our seats, and whispered, "You seen the editors?" "What editors?" Inge asked. "Them editors," cocking an eyebrow in their direction. "Ah, you mean editors!" in a great wave of understanding from Inge. "Sure I mean editors," he mumbled, quite impatient with our density. How he could have mixed up the word "editor" with "Amish" is still a puzzle to me.

The country through which we ran was still devoted almost entirely to wheat-growing. Everywhere, now, it was thickly covered with snow, and as we went northward into more hilly land there were many farms on which the stooks still stood in the fields, as if the change in the weather had taken the farmers by surprise before they could get their crops thrashed or under cover. The land was very thoroughly cultivated, with little waste—a vast contrast with the areas of bush which isolated the comparatively small cultivated districts west of the Rockies. Every few miles there was a small settlement, always on the typical prairie pattern, with the elevators and corrals beside the tracks and the buildings of the single-sided main street facing out on the railroad. Often, in the flatter parts of the prairie, the towns were the only places where one saw any trees. But none of these places had any kind of individuality, and as I look back into my notebook for that day and read the names of the settlements once again—sometimes really memorable names like Okotoks and Midnapore—I can recollect no feature that distinguishes any of them from its fellows along the line. One would ride through an apparently boundless landscape of snowy stubble-fields, and then a town would come into view, with the same plan, the same kind of stores, the same petrol signs, the same styles of houses and the same species of trees as all the towns one had passed that morning, so that in the end all that remained in the mind was a kind of composite picture, with all the common features, and superimposed upon it the vast dreariness of the beginning of the prairie winter.

Calgary itself, of which, for some odd reason, the Albertans are often inordinately proud, is a dull, flat, characterless, shapeless, sprawling western city—a city in which the traits of all the little prairie hamlets are magnified to an urban scale and garnished with the facilities which would be economically impossible in a village.

We saw dozens of large box-like hotels, but all of them were reproductions in large of the hotel opposite any prairie railroad halt —with the opulent-looking ranchers and farmers sitting around in leather armchairs, their hats on and big cigars at Groucho Marx angles in their mouths, with spittoons on the floors and pieces of sandpaper nailed up in the corridors with notices begging smokers to spare the walls, with a bottle-opener fixed beside the door and a Gideon Bible on the dressing-table in every room. The streets were covered with thick slush which nobody tried to clear away; later it melted and combined with the underlying prairie dust into a slippery and treacherous mire.

There was nothing particularly interesting to be seen in Calgary —it blooms only once a year, for the great Stampede when the cowhands from all over Canada and the United States and even from Mexico come in to show their skill, and at other times it has little to attract the visitor. We tramped the streets from end to end, we looked in all the shop windows, we dropped into cafés at every hour for lunch, for tea, for dinner, for odd cups of coffee and slices of pie in between.

For almost every commodity the prices were higher than on the coast, even though transport charges are less. Shoes were the only exception, doubtless owing to the abundance of leather in this ranching area. The restaurants were as expensive as the shops; some, indeed, pseudo-Mexican places with wrought-iron grills and softly lit pink plaster alcoves, presented enticing menus which were startlingly beyond our pockets (three dollars for a single steak), and the restaurants we could afford, with one exception, served bad food with a minimum of politeness. We had the impression that Calgary was suffering from such a plague of money that very few tradesmen felt it necessary to be civil, since they were certain of custom in any case. It was the only Canadian town in which we ever encountered that take-it-or-leave-it arrogance from which we suffered so intensely during the war at the hands of the London shopkeepers.

During our shop-gazing we came upon the one thing in Calgary that really had the pleasant touch of the unexpected. Passing a show window of Eatons (one of the two big western Canadian chain department stores—its rival is the Hudson's Bay Company), we were startled out of our contemplation of shirts and chemises by three paintings in a dazzlingly familiar manner and technique. Reproductions, surely! Or passable imitations! No, they were a

trio of original paintings by Salvador Dali, going on tour as part
of an advertisement campaign for a perfume called Desert Flower.
The desert flower was the Yucca, and Dali had made his pictures
around the scarcely veiled theme of this plant as a symbol of
sexuality. They were smooth, facile paintings, full of devices dating back to the early Chirico. We waited around to hear some of
the reactions of spectators; several couples looked in, but all of
them ignored the paintings and were much more impressed by the
detached plaster arm and leg which the window dresser had suspended above them. It was a just comment. The show, despite
Dali's efforts to equal *Vogue's* imitations of himself, was clearly an
advertising failure, particularly in an overgrown hick town like
Calgary, and Desert Flower's proprietors, who seem to have become thoroughly convinced that the classic shock techniques of
surrealism offer a bonanza for the publicity man, carried out a
much more effective stunt when they persuaded the proprietors of
a Vancouver daily newspaper to mix several thousand dollars
worth of perfume with their printing ink and astonish the British
Columbians with a morning issue reeking of the desirable tangy
fragrance.

For the rest, we sat through half of a painfully bad mountain-
eering film, and did our best, by discreet questioning, to discover
whatever we could of the Social Credit government in Alberta,
which the followers of Major Douglas throughout the world regard with the same crass veneration as communists accord to
Moscow. What we found was that, while the Social Creditors had
proved themselves an astute group of politicians, well able to ride
the crest of a wave of prosperity, they have done nothing in
Alberta which a Liberal or Conservative caucus might not have
done had it been in power. Indeed, one lifelong Tory remarked to
us, "I've nothing against the Social Creditors. They went into
power with a good deal of radical talk, but they let it remain talk.
As for their practice, why, a businessman couldn't ask for a better
government. Even the bankers like them."

One cannot entirely blame the Social Credit Party in Alberta for
having done nothing concrete towards implementing the famous
Douglas programme of the National Dividend, since when they
made one attempt the Dominion authorities and the Supreme
Court vetoed their proposals as unconstitutional. But where their
supporters are wrong is in drawing so much attention to success
in such fields as the reduction of taxes and of the provincial debt,

and in trying to prove that the present prosperity in Alberta is due
to Social Credit principles.

The truth is far different. No party, in fact, has ever been more
fortunate in the historical circumstances which have attended its
rise to power. In 1936 the Social Creditors were voted in by the
Albertan farmers, tired of the economic rigours of the Depression,
attracted by the evangelical demagogy of the party's leaders, and
ready to give any policy a trial rather than remain in their present
condition of anxiety and poverty. Within two years of the election
the Depression was well on its way out, owing to international
recovery and the demand for farm products created by the on-
coming war—a demand which has not lessened appreciably to the
present day. Add to this the discovery of the great oilfields in the
north, and it becomes clear why Alberta today is the most prosperous of Canadian provinces. To claim that this prosperity is due
to the Social Credit government is little short of dishonest, for the
same good fortune would have assisted any government that happened to be in power at that time. The fact that the Social Creditors
were further able to gain popularity by reducing taxes and by cutting down the debt is due to the same causes. By a lucky provision
of Albertan law, almost all mineral rights were the property of the
province, so that the rich oil royalties went into the treasury at
Edmonton instead of into private pockets, and with this steady
flood of cash it was a simple matter to gain political credit by cutting taxes. The answer to the oft-repeated plea that no other
Canadian province has cut taxes can be found simply in the fact
that no other province has experienced an oil boom.

21.

Our second night in Alberta was even less restful than the first,
for a drunken party continued in the adjoining room until the
early hours of the morning. The next day we picked up the Dominion express along the main C.P.R. line through the Rockies. The
first few miles of our journey were rather like a recapitulation, in
reverse and without the coal mines, of what we had seen when we
entered Alberta through the Crowsnest Pass. We followed the
course of the Bow River right into the mountains, passing from
the rolling range country around Calgary into the scrubby foothills and at last into typical mountain valley landscapes. As we
went farther west the lying snow became thicker, but the sky

began to clear, and soon we could see the high peaks of the great range glittering in all their new whiteness. Here and there we would pass a small highland lake, but for the most part it was the country of rushing mountain rivers, and as we ascended higher the woods became dense, making a sharp black and white pattern with the snow that lay at their feet and hung on their boughs. Beyond Canmore we ran into the Banff National Park. We expected to see a great deal of wild game running freely in this protected area, but for some reason—perhaps the thickness of the woods and the relative distance of the mountain slopes—we saw none at all. It was somewhat disappointing after our experience in the Jasper Park to the north two years before, when we had seen whole herds of elk and mountain sheep, as well as bear and deer.

We debated, as we travelled farther into the mountains, whether we should stop for a day at Banff, the most celebrated of the mountain resorts in the Canadian Rockies. But when we reached the station the town was out of sight, a foot of new snow lay on the roads, and we realised that it would be foolish to expect any mountain excursions until the real winter began, while in this time between seasons the resort would certainly be at its most stagnant state. So we stayed on in the train and decided that we would make our break at Revelstoke, in the Selkirks, which we had been told was scenically very beautiful and where, on the western side of the Divide, the snow was as yet unlikely to be any bar to climbing.

Beyond Banff the journey began to assume its most impressive character, as the great peaks rose up on each side of the line— Ball, Eisenhower, Richardson, Hector, Stephen, Temple—the highest and most massive of all, reaching up to more than 11,600 feet. On the Albertan side the slope was steady and regular, but as soon as we crossed the watershed, the pass became steep and precipitous, falling far down into the deep valley of the Kicking Horse River. The scenery was really magnificent, whether one looked up at the great bulky peaks or down into the chasm beneath, and the way in which the railroad made its way through this fantastic landscape was an engineering triumph which I think can rarely have been equalled since it was completed in the 1880's. At one point, to overcome the difficulties of the terrain, the engineers resorted to the device of spiral tunnels, each more than half a mile long, in which the line turned almost complete circles, first under Cathedral Mountain and then under Mount Ogden. By the time we emerged into the Columbia Valley at Golden, the first settlement of any size on the western face, we had descended 2,800 feet in less than fifty miles. It was a singularly wild landscape in every way, for the Rockies have none of the sense of generations of settlement which one encounters in the Swiss or Austrian Alps. There are no Alpine meadows, no herds of cattle, no industry, no villages, few paths or mountain huts, and any attempt at serious climbing involves an expedition with equipment and packhorses. As I have already said, the very massiveness of most of the peaks robs them of some of the charm of the Alps, and I have yet to see a Canadian mountain with the challenging and beautiful outlines of the Matterhorn. Nevertheless, I imagine that for those who have the enterprise to attempt them, the very size, inaccessibility and lack of human settlement in the Rockies may add to the adventure and the sense of achievement. Yet, as a mere viewer and walker, and a lover of the incredible floral profusion of the Alps, I must admit to finding the Rockies less friendly and sympathetic than I had anticipated.

At Golden, which is a pleasant-looking little valley town, we saw a group of chalets and balconied houses away on a wooded hillside to the right. It was a little community of Swiss, we were told, who had here resumed their occupation of mountain guides in the vastly different terrain of the Rockies. Out of Golden we travelled north-westerly for a while beside the Columbia, which first runs from its source towards the Yukon, then fetches a great curve through the Selkirks—the Big Bend of the 1865 gold rush —and afterwards turns south to run through the Arrow Lakes and down into the north-west corner of the United States. The highway follows the river in its great curve, but the railway climbs up again into the mountains, and from a little decaying town called Rogers, lying below a massive peak of the same name, we ran up the Beaver Valley into the highlands of the Glacier National Park, through the long Connaught Tunnel under the ridge of the Selkirks, and then down a broad, magnificent wooded valley, with the bulk of Mount Dawson rising to the south. The valley narrowed into the cragged, dark confines of the Albert Canyon, and eventually we came out once again, at Revelstoke, to the Columbia, here in the full swing of its southward flow towards the head of the Upper Arrow Lake, barely twenty miles away.

Night had already fallen when we reached Revelstoke, but the sky was clear and we could make out the dark masses of mountains standing all around the city. The situation seemed excellent, and we made up our minds to stay for a day or two and try to explore some of the surrounding country. Finding an hotel was not altogether an easy process, for the largest were near the railway marshalling yards, which echoed with the bells of shunting engines, and the one we eventually chose by elimination was a stuffy Edwardian place with dingy brown wallpaper and dusty plush furniture. In our room the central heating created the temperature of a Turkish bath, the regulator would not work, and when we complained the proprietor snorted, "Most people grumble because the rooms are too cold. How can you please everybody?" Perhaps we did seem a little eccentric, for the average North American shivers in a winter room at much less than 70 degrees.

If the hotels in Revelstoke were surprisingly poor for a town that prides itself on being a mountain resort, the restaurants were even worse. We stopped a man in the street and asked him to direct us to a good eating-house. He was an Italian, and when he had finished laughing at what he evidently considered a highly amusing joke, he said, "There are no good eating-places, but there is one less bad than the rest just around the corner." The less bad café was closed, and in the one we did try the soup was inedible (though both our stomachs are tough and experienced), the meat was stringy and scanty, and the sweet an unidentifiable stodge. It was an experience which was repeated, with slight variations in badness, through the remaining three meals we took in as many different Revelstoke restaurants. It was not merely average dull food—it was a case of cooking so poor that one could hardly imagine it to be the result of mere carelessness or incompetence. Western Canadian cooking is rarely very good, but nowhere else did we encounter such a concerted effort to exploit the customers by scamping on the ingredients as we did in Revelstoke.

The town—and this made the bad food all the more incomprehensible—seemed rather cosmopolitan. For, besides the Italian, we encountered a family of Japanese, delicate-featured and friendly-looking people who must have been among those deported to the inner valleys during the war. And our sad first meal was enlivened by the presence of a resonant-voiced Indian who talked like an early Hollywood version of his race. Discussing an absent member of his party, he shouted, "He late, he no get car.

He no get car, he no go to dance. He no go to dance, he bloody-hell me."

The next day, when we arose, the clear sky of the last evening had vanished, and the outlines of the mountains we had seen as dark shadows were now tantalisingly closed in with cloud. The day looked altogether unpromising, but we decided to walk out in the hope that a good wind might clear the sky. Revelstoke, in daylight, was an extremely loose and straggling community, spreading a small population over the area of a relatively large town; there was a surprisingly well-designed city hall (anything bigger than a village is incorporated as a city in British Columbia), and one good modern church, but the residential districts were rendered horrifying by a curious passion among the inhabitants for covering their roofs with aluminium sheeting. We walked out for nearly four miles along a main road which led into a country of promising foothills. The mountain tops, however, were still wholly invisible, and soon it began to rain with an increasing intensity, while the clouds descended even on to the smaller hills. We returned into the town; our desire to make the closer acquaintance of the mountains seemed fruitless, and we did not feel prepared to face an indefinite period among the discomforts of Revelstoke in the hope of the weather clearing. So we hung dismally around the town for the rest of the day, and took the last train down to Vancouver.

Once again it was a black, rainy night, and we saw nothing until we awoke the next morning back in the Fraser Valley, looking out on Mission City and its flat, autumn-browned strawberry fields. By nine o'clock we were in Vancouver; to our surprise the two Amish brethren stepped out of the train before us, and two sleek black seals floated idly in the harbour below the station.

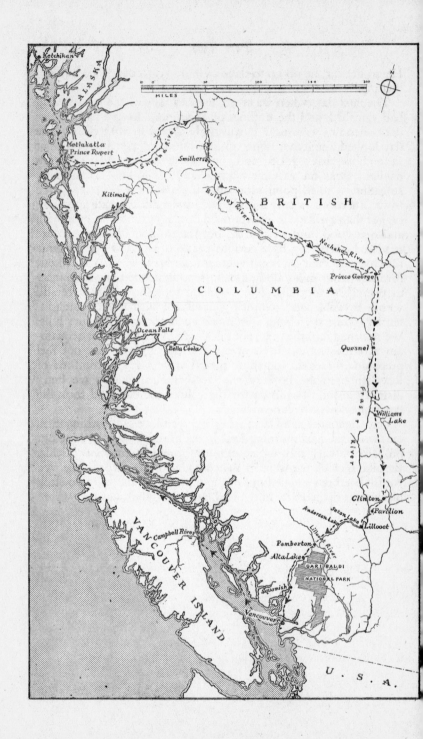

Part Three

FOR a thousand miles north from Vancouver the coastline of British Columbia and Alaska is shielded from the storms of the North Pacific by a screen of many islands. In among them runs the Inside Passage, a smooth but dangerous waterway through whose narrow and shoal-ridden channels the coastal shipping travels from Seattle and Vancouver to the northerly ports; the navigators of today follow the course which the Indians used in their great dugout sea-going canoes for centuries before Cook and Vancouver or the Spanish explorers came to this coast.

The ship on which we embarked on the 30th October for Alaska was the *Prince George*, a trim passenger boat, somewhat larger than a Channel steamer, and incomparably more comfortable. During the summer the Canadian National Railway run it as a cruise ship for American tourists, but in winter it is transferred to the regular passenger service between the coastal ports. To travel in a cruise ship during the off season is a rather pleasant experience; we had a most comfortable and spacious cabin with a private shower, there were plenty of half-empty lounges, the food was good, and we were relieved of that tedious social life which is stimulated artificially on such ships when the tourists reign. The passengers were ordinary travellers, returning home from weekends in Vancouver or going out on business trips up the coast, a few were Indians and half-breeds, there was one family of Chinese, and the rest were Canadians and Alaskans, for the most part quiet and unobtrusive people.

The boat was due to sail at midnight; we went on board during the evening and, having stayed on deck to watch the lighted mass of Vancouver recede behind us as we drew out under the Lion's Gate Bridge, we went down to our cabin. As we slept the boat sailed in a westerly direction through Georgia Strait, turned into Malaspina Strait behind Texada Island and, between three and four in the morning, drew into its first port of call, Powell River, a great isolated company town which centres around one of the largest paper mills in Canada.

The noises of berthing awakened me, and I got up to look out of the porthole. There was the inside of a warehouse, great piled rolls of newsprint, small petrol trolleys scurrying over the hollow-echoing deck of the wharf. As there was nothing else to see and the night seemed dark and bleak, I crawled back to bed and was asleep by the time the ship left the port.

When we rose next morning the *Prince George* had already made her way through the best part of the labyrinth of islands and channels which stretch between the mainland and Vancouver Island to the north of Powell River. Now she was sailing up Johnstone Strait, a serene fjord-like channel which runs for about seventy miles in an almost westerly direction, with the solid bulk of Vancouver Island to our left and a broken tangle of islands and extended tongues of the mainland lying off to the right at a distance rarely greater than three miles. There were low wooded hills on either side of the channel, but soon those on Vancouver Island gave way to a succession of mountains, rising almost from the shore to peaks nearly 6,000 feet high, with virtually untouched forests of gigantic Douglas firs climbing up the slopes and powdered with the glistening crust of the first mountain snow. In this area neither the Island nor the opposing mainland capes showed much sign of human settlement. One could see no roads, and it would have needed some ingenuity to build them or to find sites for settlement in many of the places where the slopes ran down precipitously into the sea.

Towards the end of the morning the mountains began to recede, and the coastline to the north was broken up by wider channels, running in and out of a series of smaller islands. One of the first we sighted was Cormorant Island—an appropriate name, since all the morning large numbers of these birds had swum heavily in the calm water around the boat or flown in low strings across the strait, with their black heads and bodies outstretched in an improbable stiffness.

Along a crescent-shaped indentation in the south coast of Cormorant Island the logging town of Alert Bay straggled thinly for a couple of miles, for the most part a one-sided street of wooden houses, overhung by the scrub which came down the hills behind, but thickening at the centre into a cluster of warehouses, jetties and aluminium-bright oil tanks, with the large brick building of an Indian residential school at the far end. The ship did not stop, but sailed slowly past, so near that in the clear morning we could

see almost every detail of the town, even the little park towards
the shore where a few memorial poles formed the last remnants of
what had once been one of the richest collections of Indian carvings on the coast.

Alert Bay stands on the site of an old Kwakiutl village, and it
marks roughly the southern limit of the pole-carving culture.
Below it began the territory of the Salish tribes, who never erected
poles and did not carve them until they found crude miniature
imitations were popular among the tourists, but to the north, as
far as Skagway in Alaska, pole building was an integral part of
every tribe's ritual life. Yet it was among the Kwakiutl that the
ritual pattern of Coast Indian life was developed to its highest
degree. Kwakiutl territory was the birthplace of the secret
societies, and particularly the Cannibal Society; the power of
these organisations became so strong here that the tribal year was
divided into a summer devoted to fishing, food gathering and war,
when the dynastic chiefs held sway, and a winter of feasts, dancing, drama and craftsmanship, when the secret societies usurped
power, and precedence was counted, not by birth, but by religious
initiation. It was in the miming art and oral poetry of ritual, in the
preparation of the ingenious liturgical masks of the secret cere-
monies, that the Kwakiutl tribe excelled. Their poles never
equalled in design and craftsmanship those of the Haida, yet there
was a force in their relatively crude carvings which undoubtedly
sprang from the intensive cultivation of drama in their elaborate
ritual—a ritual so formalised that one single false step in a dance
might result in misfortune for the people or even death for the
performer.

Alert Bay became a rich centre of craftsmanship because it was
visited by Europeans at a comparatively early date. Before their
arrival the Indians carved laboriously with stone tools, and poles
could therefore be erected only occasionally, by rich clans; but the
advent of metal tools not only brought about an immense increase
in the number of carvings, but also liberated the imagination of the
workers and produced a great enrichment in fantasy and design.
Thus the greatest period of coastal art extended from the first
arrival of the Europeans at the end of the eighteenth century down
to the decay of the coastal culture which started between 1860 and
1870, the era when white settlers began to scatter all over British
Columbia and the missionaries commenced their intensive attack
on the native social order.

10

Alert Bay was one of the earliest points at which that attack began, and indeed the present logging and fishing centre was first an Anglican mission. Under the influence of the clergy, the islanders abandoned their pagan ceremonial and social customs, and, though the dances and the secret ritual are said to survive in some of the less accessible mainland inlets, they are certainly practised no longer at Alert Bay. Moreover, the clans here allowed their poles to be taken away by visiting anthropologists and curio collectors; the few we saw decaying near the beach were a tiny remnant of the veritable grove that dominated the shore even fifty years ago. There is one consolation for this despoilment, however; the poles are at least preserved in their museums in every corner of the world, and do not present the dismal spectacle of neglect at the hands of their creators which we had seen in Kispiox.

We had hardly passed Cormorant Island when we came in sight of the larger bulk of Malcolm Island; it was more cleared of wood-land than its neighbours and wide areas were covered by purple stretches of fireweed and autumn-brown deciduous brushwood, among which occasional ragged and broken clumps of fir stood out as survivors of the forests that had formerly covered the low hills. There were large fields and pastures, white barns and farm-houses, and a generally tranquil air of settlement about the shore along which we sailed into sight of the little harbour of Sointula, once again fringed by jetties, gleaming oil tanks and clusters of white fishing boats.

The very name of Sointula suggests Malcolm Island's curious history; in Finnish it means Place of Harmony, and this was the site of the only socialist Utopian community of any magnitude that was ever founded in British Columbia. It belonged to a con-siderably later date than the classic Utopian era of the eastern United States, for it was conceived by a group of Finnish émigrés in 1900, and it was not until the end of 1901 that the first group of pioneers landed.

The subsequent history of Sointula reads like that of many a similar venture, with the peculiar circumstances of the Pacific North-West superimposed thereon. The community began on credit, and never ceased to be heavily in debt. There was no clear land for farming, and the felling of the heavy timber by inexpert workers was a slow and exhausting process; not until the very end of its life did the colony become self-supporting even in farm products. Attempts to sell lumber and fish were unencouraging, since the prices at that period were excessively low, while a contract to build bridges on the mainland merely ran the community into debt. There were never enough weatherproof houses, the cattle died from exposure in the winter, and a fire killed eleven of the settlers and caused irremediable damage. Added to these material difficulties were those of personality. The leader, Matti Kurikka, was a brilliant thinker but a poor organiser, with a gift for making enemies and an inability to appreciate the viewpoints of other members; he provoked endless schisms on points of socialist dogma and its practical interpretation. Furthermore, the original intention of applying a selective principle to the membership broke down when people began to stream in from all parts of North America and even directly from Finland. Many of them were theoreticians who had no intention of working, others came expecting a Utopia in full flower and found that they had to face the winter in tents and with little food. It was not surprising that many of them departed quickly; during the four years of the colony's existence no less than three thousand people lived in it for varying periods, yet the average population was little more than two hundred.

Indeed, in all the circumstances, the cause for wonder is that the community lasted even four years. At last, the perpetual economic threats, the lack of any real improvement in living conditions, the failure of harmony, all helped to tarnish the Utopian vision, and when, in 1905, the creditors at last moved in, there were only thirty-six members left to carry through the dissolution.

But the end of the Utopian community was not the end of Finnish colonisation at Sointula. Many of the former members, when they had somehow repaired their fortunes in the outer world, moved back and bought or pre-empted land on the site of their old failure, and today Malcolm Island is almost wholly inhabited by survivors of the colony or their descendants, who have now cleared much of the land and live in a balanced economy based on farming, fishing and logging. But they are no longer a community and live on no more radical lines than their neighbours. The Russian Revolution roused a flutter of interest in old ideals, for a while there was renewed talk of a community, a band of enthusiasts raised the red flag on the village hall. But it all faded away, and today the only approach by the Sointulans to their past ideals is to be found in their fishermen's co-operative, one of the earliest on the coast.

Unfortunately, like Alert Bay, Sointula was not one of the ports at which the *Prince George* called. About a month later we tried to reach it from Vancouver Island, only to receive a salutary lesson in the difficulties of travelling to these remote spots in winter. The small freighter from Vancouver which visits the island every fortnight would not take any more passengers when we tried to board it on its midnight stop at Campbell River. The fishing boats that often touch Sointula were all in port because of the gales; a boat-load of Indians had been drowned off Alert Bay that morning. Our last resort was the taxi-plane company, but they demanded £85 for the return flight of about sixty miles—so we never reached Sointula.

After Malcolm Island the ship left the narrow waters of Johnstone Strait and began to veer to the north-west and thread through the scattered islands of Queen Charlotte Sound. We left the mountains and the great stands of Douglas firs behind, and the softly rounded hills were now covered with spruce and hemlock.

Meanwhile an evanescent social life had begun to crystallise on board, not so much the forced *bonhomie* of cruise days as a kind of natural drifting together by the accident of acquaintance, of sharing the same table or cabin, or by some tentative remark about the scenery or the gulls which escorted the ship in large numbers. Many of the passengers were regular travellers up and down the coast, who greeted each other on this 500- or 600-mile voyage in almost the same casual manner as season-ticket holders travelling from Bexley Heath to the City.

We sat at the Captain's table, and our companions were a nurse from Prince Rupert, a technician who was travelling north to manage a new wood-processing plant, and a young married woman from the company town of Ocean Falls. The captain was a genial, irrepressible man, with an irreverent turn of mind, an impulse to prick any bubble of inflated sentiment that might float in on the eddies of conversation, a taste for water-colour painting and a knowledge of literature that sometimes surprised one by its ramifications; in addition, he had the two essential qualities for a master on a cruise ship—a long and expert knowledge of every angle and inlet and islet on the coast and of how to manage a fairly large ship in such constricted waters, and an abundant social tact, which enabled him to set chance acquaintances at their ease, to stimulate conversation, and to entertain his guests, if necessary, from an endless fund of jests and tales. He confessed that for him the winter was a holiday; then he could shed the cloak of amiable but reserved dignity which fitted the tourist's idea of a good sea captain, and for a few months he could live easily among people who had no desire to be impressed or overawed, but merely wanted to get from one place to another in as pleasant a way as possible.

One at least of the captain's tales remains in my memory with a dogged and rather illogical persistence. It deals with a letter which he was entrusted by a friend to deliver to a young lady in one of the coastal towns. It was a squally night, and as the captain approached the lady's house, a sudden gust tore the envelope from his hand and sent it sailing into the darkness. He searched up and down the street with a flashlight, he peeped stealthily into front gardens, but no trace of the letter was to be found. So he had to call and explain the curious accident that had befallen him. The lady received his explanations coldly, and a moment afterwards retired to her room; the crestfallen captain was contemplating a return to his friend with the report of a failed mission when she hurriedly returned, carrying in her hand the very same letter which the wind had stolen a few moments before. She had found it lying on her bed, where a freak of the wind had carried it through the open window—a window which, he would have us believe, was open only three inches.

Late in the afternoon we drew near to Ocean Falls. In the meantime we had crossed the rough open waters of Queen Charlotte Sound and then, sheltering behind the bulk of Calvert Island, had sailed up Fitzhugh Sound, passing mile after mile of thickly wooded mountains and headlands, of islands and entrances and narrow fjords probing deep into the heart of the mainland, until the very monotony of the scene began to pall. There is hardly a spot along this coast which, taken by itself, has not some grandiose beauty, but when the same abundant scenery is consistently repeated, mountain and forest and deep blue waters, one begins to long more impatiently every hour for some bare hillside or green valley spreading its meadows down towards the water's edge.

There was hardly even any settlement, for in all that day's sailing between Sointula and Ocean Falls we only caught sight of one isolated canning post. The intense aboriginal activity which once flourished in this labyrinth of channels and passages is ended, for white men's diseases have reduced the Indians to a third or a quarter of their former numbers, and nearby villages like Bella

Bella and Bella Coola, once great cultural and religious centres, have now declined to mere fishing settlements.

23.

Ocean Falls lies at the pinched-in end of Cousins Inlet, a singularly desolate spot, with the dark mountains coming close on every side. As we put in, the ridges were already blackening with the onset of night, while the white houses and the large modern apartment buildings stretching up the hillsides were given an unreally exotic appearance, so that for a moment of shifting half-light one could imagine that a Mediterranean town had been scooped up out of the sun and landed in this gloomy northern channel.

Drawing near the quay, we could hear the crackle of explosions echoing through the town; it sounded almost as if a minor revolution had broken out, and it was only when the ship was mooring that we remembered it was Hallowe'en, which in Canada takes the place of the Fifth of November and gives the children—and some of the older people as well—a chance to let off fireworks and to play tricks which often show a singularly ingenious malice. It acts as a kind of Saturnalia, a releasing of resentments too long concealed, and it was significant that the manifestation which greeted us as we entered the closed town of Ocean Falls was of an unusually violent kind. Down on the quay there was the large crowd which always gathers when a boat enters a port whose only connection with the outer world is by sea—people expecting friends, others waiting to board the ship for its next destination, and an abundance of gazers who had come merely to be reassured that there really was a way of escape whenever they might choose to take it. In among them a company of boys were throwing lighted squibs and crackers; not content with this, they were lobbing them on to the roofs of the sheds, and the usual quayside confusion was vastly increased by the noise of the explosions and the antics of people trying to avoid the fireworks.

Beyond, in the open space outside the dock gates, groups of adolescents piled pyramids of miscellaneous fireworks a foot high and set them alight; the ensuing explosions sounded like volleys of machine-gun fire. Later, when we went into the town, we found that no corner was immune—even in the restaurant and in the lavatories of the hotel the battle went on.

Ocean Falls is a paper-producing town, to which vast booms of logs are brought in from the coast and the islands, to be chewed up in the great mill and changed into newsprint and paper bags. The mill lay across the inlet, blazing with lights and humming loudly in its unending twenty-four-hour processes, but the dam which closed the channel and provided power formed a kind of visual link which symbolised the unity of Ocean Falls.

For the town is wholly dependent on the mill, and almost every one of the 3,000 people there is either directly employed by the company or a member of an employee's family. Everywhere, indeed, we were treading on company territory. The houses and dormitory buildings, the hotel, the restaurant and the department store, the very streets were controlled by the mill, and equally surely its hand was behind the town's social institutions, the hospital, the cinema, the recreation buildings, all company-controlled and operated by Community Relations Supervisors and Recreational Supervisors, as if even leisure could be planned as mechanically as a tree was turned into toilet rolls.

By now we had acquired the knack of scraping up an acquaintance at a coffee-bar by means of some fatuous conversational token, and in this way we managed to gain at least some idea of how people in this town reacted to such a closed and isolated existence. In particular there was one clerk who expressed it rather thoroughly.

"You get the feeling that those hills are crowding in on you, and you know there's no escape except by leaving altogether. Think of it—it's two hundred miles to Prince Rupert and three hundred to Vancouver, and not a place worth a damn in between. No, there'll never be a road in here, with all those mountains in back of us. Why, we're so cramped in that the town can't even grow any more—there's no ground left on which to build."

It was not difficult to feel the vast boredom of such a life, of seeing the same faces and every day walking the same streets—or rather the same wooden stairs up the hillside—and there was a sense of isolation in this town quite different from that in distant inland communities. Those have usually a periphery of open country; there is space, and therefore a feeling of freedom. Here people were turned in towards each other, like men in an outsize lighthouse, with only the periodical relief of the visiting ships.

We heard that, although the working conditions were good, there was an unusually high turnover of labour. The single men in particular tended to stay a few months only and then move on.

They might have no specific grievance, but they could not endure the isolation, ultimately, I suppose, the lack of a sense of freedom in a monopoly town.

Indeed, we ourselves felt relieved as we sailed out of the inlet and left the frustrated town behind us. It seemed too much like a realisation in miniature of the monstrous Utopian visions of the past, like Icaria, in which life is completely planned and unified, a reminder, indeed, that every day in some stultifying respect our own contemporary life becomes steadily more Utopian.

24.

By the time we had returned on board it was already late, and during the night the boat nosed on through further long and twisting channels towards Prince Rupert. After breakfast we stood on deck and watched the rocky, wooded shore of Kaien Island, on which the city stands, appearing to our right. There was a railway—the first in 500 miles since Vancouver—running by the shore; then a cluster of fishing boats behind a snug stone breakwater and a clump of white buildings on the waterfront—this was the Prince Rupert Fishermen's Co-operative, the biggest fishing plant on the coast. After that we swung round the island into the great natural harbour, with the city rising above the lines of wharves and docks.

Prince Rupert's harbour is said to be the third largest in the world, exceeded only by Halifax and Sydney, and from the spread of its waters one could imagine that this was true. A fisherman who was standing beside us, waiting to go ashore to his home in the city, told us that it had been discovered almost by accident. Up to the end of the last century all the navigators had held the theory that a ledge of rocks stretched right across the entrance, and nobody had the enterprise to make a trial until 1904, when an exploring party sent by the Grand Trunk Pacific Railway stumbled upon the entrance. The possibilities of such a harbour were evident and the railway immediately bought the land from the Tsimshian Indians, and so Prince Rupert began. Did we know how it got the name? They held a competition in 1910, and some woman from back east sent it in and got the prize. It was a name like any other, he thought; perhaps Rupert had been a bit of a rogue, but not much worse than some of the local politicians after whom some of the other towns were named.

"Talking of politicians," he went on, "now there's what a person might call a politician's folly." He pointed to a colossal grain elevator standing on the wharf at the beginning of the city, the biggest we had seen west of Winnipeg. "That God-damned thing will hold a million and a quarter bushels of wheat. But do you think that much wheat has ever come to Prince Rupert? Not in a lifetime. Nobody in their senses ever thought it would. Why should the folks on the prairie send it out here when they can get rid of it much more easily back east? Sometimes that damned tower stands empty for months on end, but they still spend thousands of dollars a year to keep it in repair. It's what they call pork-barrel politics down in the States—trying to make the voters think they've got Prince Rupert's interest at heart. They have to keep it up, just to save their faces. But do you think Rupert people are taken in after all these years?"

The *Prince George* was due to spend the rest of that day in the port, so we decided to use the time in making our first survey of Prince Rupert. From the wharf we walked up through a park where the Canadian National Railway had erected a whole cluster of Haida poles from the Queen Charlottes; later, in the city itself, we found another group of these enormous heraldic carvings. They were all in a reasonably good state of preservation, and, although their setting on the grass slopes among the trees was very different from the offal-strewn beaches on which they had originally been placed before the tribal community houses, it doubtless even enhanced their spectacular appearance. All of them had been carved out of massive cedar trunks, from the drenched forests of the Queen Charlottes, and many of them were four feet in diameter and about forty feet high. Such a large collection demonstrated admirably the qualities which made the Haida the greatest woodworkers of the coast—their exceptional power of handling masses of wood to make the best sculptural use of its natural qualities and the great versatility of design which they achieved within a convention that was strictly bound by tribal ritual, by considerations of prestige, and even by individual copyright in certain motifs and images.

Beyond the park we came on to a piece of waste ground which sloped up towards the first buildings of the town, and here we were greatly entertained by a jackdaw which was hopping to and fro on a rickety wooden shed, thrusting beakfuls of an apple he had found on the road into a wide crack in between two of the roof timbers. He regarded us with a great air of circumspection, and there was a delightfully smug avarice in the way in which he thrust every additional fragment of his highly perishable hoard into its hiding place.

As we walked down the shabby main street of Prince Rupert, with its unpainted façades and its shops, unlike those of its rival Prince George, always a little out of the fashion, we felt something of the down-at-heel atmosphere of a town that had been left behind the times. Nor was this impression lightened when we penetrated into the outskirts. Here the peculiar alternation of rock and swamp which characterises Kaien Island, and which has been covered up by the streets and buildings in the city itself, gains a dismal dominance over one's outlook. The trees nurtured on this sour ground are ragged and scanty, and between them there are stretches of rush-grown bog, broken here and there by stark boulders and outcrops of grey rock. The roads are built on piles and sometimes even carried on stilts above the surface of the ground, and the small modern houses which were erected hastily during the war years stand dismally in their gardens of brown peat through which the marsh water seeps away slowly and reluctantly.

Combine such aspects of the town and its surroundings with the leaden autumn skies and the steady drizzle which fell for most of the muggy day on which we first saw Prince Rupert, and it will not be difficult to imagine the sense of desolation which overwhelmed us as we explored it.

But our first impressions were not wholly accurate, since, as we quickly learnt when we talked to various people in the city—the local railway officials, the editor of the little daily paper in his office where the newsboys came in to pick up their supplies in the room where he chatted with his visitors, the secretary of a businessmen's organisation in his real-estate office above the main street—Prince Rupert, with its 10,000 inhabitants, is in fact one of the most prosperous communities in British Columbia. It is a considerable logging and fur-trading centre, but the greatest part of its present income, in the region of 10 million dollars a year, comes from the fishing industry, one of the largest in the world, of which it is the pivot.

Yet the impression of some lag in the city's development was not entirely unfounded, for the people who originally built Prince Rupert had thought in terms of a really large city, a second Vancouver, and had laid their plans accordingly, so that today, despite prosperity, it contains many reminders of how much greater it might have been if only history had played into the hands of its early dreamers—so many fine possibilities that have failed to develop. There is the harbour, capable of holding the largest seagoing ships and nearly 500 miles nearer to Japan than any other large North American port; except for the war years it has been used only by fishing boats and coastal steamers. There is a drydock of 20,000 tons capacity and a shipbuilding yard where, during the last war, the Canadian National Railway built vessels up to 10,000 tons; since then the shipbuilding industry has been hibernating for several years. There is the white elephant of a grain elevator, built to hold the wheat which never came over the railway from the prairies to be sold in the Orient.

Thus, all its expectations of becoming a great seaport being destroyed by circumstances, Prince Rupert has remained merely western Canada's foremost fishing port, making the most of its qualified good fortune, yet never quite forgetting the dreams of grandeur among which it was born. Once the north really opens up, one is told on every side, Prince Rupert will at last be a great city. Soon the rich coalmines and farm lands of the Peace River will be linked by road with the rest of British Columbia, and that is bound to add further to Prince Rupert's development. And, sooner or later, the country along the Skeena Valley, with its long, twenty-one-hour summer days, will be farmed properly, and then there will be plenty of grain and seeds to export—and plenty of dairy produce and fresh vegetables, say the local patriots as they drip tinned milk into their mid-morning coffee.

Of more concrete significance than these dreams of the future has been the arrival of large-scale industry. When we reached Prince Rupert work was almost completed on a 35-million-dollar cellulose plant. This industry will undoubtedly give a new direction to the economic life of this north-western area, yet in many ways it illustrates the complicated balance of benefits and disadvantages which accompany such developments.

For instance, it will provide employment for nearly 2,000 workers, and thus add probably 5,000 people to the urban population of the district, while it will undoubtedly stimulate the secondary industries in Prince Rupert. If one regards the urbanisation of the wilderness as beneficial, this may be placed on the credit side. On the other hand, its perpetual demand for more and more wood will involve the denuding of large areas of the coastline; even this, if it is not excessive in any one point, may be of value, by reducing the heavy rainfall and clearing land for farming. A third consequence of such a development is the temptation of the local Indians to become absorbed into the new industrial life. Some of the Tsimshian have already worked as labourers in the building of the plant, and many will be persuaded by the prospect of relatively high wages to enter into permanent employment. Here is no question, as in South Africa, of the aboriginal population being forced to work as helots at a low economic level, for in British Columbia the Indians who leave their reservations receive the same wages as their white fellow-workers, and they are free to come and go as they wish. It is rather a question of whether one prefers to see them pursuing an old tribal life which has little economic foundation or social relevance in the modern world, or becoming involved in an industrial society for which their traditional values and attitudes have fitted them very poorly. It is, as we were soon to discover, a problem which admits no facile or clear-cut solution, once the first triumph of the alien over the aboriginal culture has taken place and shattered its social hierarchy and its natural economic basis.

Similar doubts were raised in our minds, as they have been in the minds of many British Columbians, by another plan of which the people in Prince Rupert were speaking with great anticipation. That is the scheme, estimated to cost eventually about 500 million dollars, to establish a huge aluminium factory at Kitimat, which lies at the end of a long inland channel about seventy miles from Prince Rupert. Undoubtedly, if the scheme is carried out—as now seems certain—it will completely change the tempo of life in this north-west corner of British Columbia. On the other hand, there are several ways in which it may interfere with the region's natural equilibrium; its power dams will prevent the access of the salmon to many of their breeding waters, will flood large areas of rich potential farming land, and will make a whole district as large as Wales subject, once again, to control from afar by corporations which will inevitably be much more interested in receiving the maximum possible amount of products at the minimum cost than in regulating their work so that it will fit in with a balanced development of the country.

Such were the anticipations which we found filling the minds of the businessmen to whom we talked in Prince Rupert, and it certainly seemed as though, for most of them, the prospect of immediate profit was much more attractive than any vision of development which would conserve the resources of their land for posterity and produce, in time, a balanced and integrated society. Indeed, such considerations, when one put them forward, quite evidently aroused a certain suspicion. It was the kind of talk in which the local radicals indulged, and the businessmen who hoped at last to ride to prosperity on the wave of the new developments looked at it as an unjustified and rather impertinent interference with their prospects of grasping the great chances for which they had waited so long in vain. How much they were like the jackdaw gleefully augmenting his perishable load!

Most of our day was taken up with such conversations, and by the time we sat down to tea in a dismal Chinese coffee-shop—for Prince Rupert is singularly poorly graced with eating establishments—we had become more than a little exasperated with the short-sighted desire for immediate profit which still seemed, from all we had heard that day, to characterise the small-time Canadian businessman in a developing frontier area. But our mood rather changed when we went on to see the local Indian Agent, from whom we intended to get some enlightenment on the survival of coastal traditions and ritual.

His office was in the basement of the Post Office building, and we waited for a while in an anteroom where some clerks were working and interviewing a stream of Indians who came in with requests and problems. Then we were ushered in to the Agent. We had been rather apprehensive of meeting an administrator of the old, unimaginative type, concerned only with following the letter of the law and very little interested in the Indians as human beings. But it is one advantage of such specialised departments that they frequently give opportunities to men who are concerned less with the minutiæ of bureaucratic rule than with the more fundamentally human aspects of their work, and we were relieved to find a man passionately interested in the Indians, who had worked among them for a quarter of a century with every desire to understand as well as to administer them, who had been a friend of Franz Boas, the most important scientist to study the Coast Indian culture, and who himself had made a close study of anthropology in connection with his daily work. Indeed, he was so devoted to the Indians that he welcomed anybody else who showed an interest in them, and gave us a lecture conducted so energetically and packed with so many facts from his personal experience that we only realised at the end that we had kept him nearly two hours after his office time.

He told us that the Indian tribal customs had in fact survived to a much greater extent than most people imagined. It was quite true that potlatches took place; he himself had sat in on dozens of them since he came to the coast; and the Indians had shown a great deal of ingenuity in circumventing the laws that forbade them. The legal definition of a potlatch was that of a celebration at which feasting, dancing, speechmaking and giving occurred at the same time and place. The Indians got round this very simply by just inviting their guests to step out of doors to receive their gifts, or by postponing one of the functions until the next day.

He went on to describe some of the potlatches he himself had seen. At one of them a tray full of gold coins had been given away, at another a hundred Singer sewing-machines. Those had been ordinary potlatches in which the gifts were strictly returnable with interest. But such was not invariably the case. One chief, for instance, felt the need to prove that he was above material considerations, so he armed his young men with butchers' knives and on the potlatch day he ordered them to rip to pieces a thousand bags of flour and throw the contents into the sea. By this means he impoverished himself materially, but he gained greatly in the all-important prestige.

Other features of the ritual life also survived, such as the secret societies, though it was not very often that white men would know anything about them. Indeed, the whole of Indian culture presented such a complicated unity that it was difficult to imagine any part of it flourishing in isolation, and the dance festivals still continued during the winter months at many of the isolated villages of the coast. He himself had been present at one festival in which no less than 140 masked dancers had taken part.

Yet, despite these survivals, the institutions of the Indians were changing rapidly. Take that most important of them all, the clan or phratry system. The tribes from Alaska down to Bella Bella are divided into phratries which descend through the maternal lines and which extend over tribal barriers, embracing clans within each nation. Within these phratries marriage is considered incest. Thus a Raven from Sitka in Alaska cannot marry a Raven from Prince Rupert, although they have no evident relationship and may not even understand each other's language.

How this system arose and why it preserves its rigidity is an unsolved mystery, but it is still a powerful influence in Indian life. Nevertheless, such western influences as the school and the cinema have fostered the emergence of romantic love, a concept hitherto almost completely unknown in their society, and the young people are no longer content with the old marriage customs.

"Here is a good example for you. A Tsimshian boy of the Eagle phratry fell in love with an Eagle girl. The parents refused to sanction a wedding, so the couple went to live in common law marriage. The girl's brother felt that she had brought shame on the family, and one night he went out and shot up the house in which they were living. The couple fled into the bush and stayed there for three weeks, until we persuaded them to come out and transferred them to a more peaceful district." This, the Indian Agent added, had happened only two years previously.

Many of the older people still clung obstinately to their inherited conceptions of property, which neither missionaries nor education have been able wholly to eradicate. He called to mind one instance in which a wedding was about to take place in a nominally Christian village. The bride had actually reached the church door when her maternal uncle (the guardian under the tribal matriarchal law) took hold of her veil and prevented her from entering until the bridegroom's family had paid over to her relatives a present of 2,000 dollars in accordance with the ancient custom.

The I.A. went on to describe the general conditions of the Indians today, and the way in which these had improved during the time he had known them. Early in the present century the Coast Indians were at their lowest point, economically impoverished, physically degenerated and spiritually demoralised, so that many authorities thought that they would die out from mere lack of ability to cope with a modern world so different from that conceived in their own highly spiritual and ritualistic culture. The great epidemics of the nineteenth century had not only reduced their numbers, but had also lowered the physical standards of the survivors and their ability to provide for themselves, and so malnutrition had followed, laying them open to yet other diseases. Moreover, they had been treated as inferiors by the white population, and had endured the indignities of a subject people, not so much exploited as ignored and allowed to rot away in the scanty reservations.

Today the situation was very different. The Indians were no

longer despised by their white neighbours, and they had made themselves economically secure by the adoption of modern fishing methods. At the same time, despite their comparative prosperity, the problem of sickness remained, and this was due largely to ill-balanced feeding, since the more money an Indian earned, the more likely he was to live entirely on tinned foods.

Politically, the Indians were still treated as second-class citizens. They could vote in the provincial but not in the federal elections, and they had fewer social benefits than other Canadians. For instance, their old-age pension was one half of that given to full Canadian citizens, while the provision for hospital treatment of tubercular Indians was completely inadequate.

The I.A. finally asked us whether on our return from Alaska we would like to get in touch with him again, and then he would take us to Metlakatla, a mission village in one of the neighbouring inlets, where we should be able to see a group of Indians in an advanced stage of adaptation to Canadian life. We accepted gladly, and went away a good deal more pleased with that discussion than we had been with our earlier interviews.

25.

During the night the *Prince George* left Prince Rupert and sailed up towards Alaskan waters, past Dundas Island, across the rough seas of Dixon Entrance, which marks the division between Canadian and American territory, and then through Revillagigedo Channel into the dense archipelago which stretches all the way up the southern end of Alaska as far as Skagway. Scenically it was a continuation of the country through which we had sailed all the way up the coast from Vancouver—the heavily forested islands, the mountains more or less covered with clouds, the narrow, relatively sheltered channels—and there was nothing, before Ketchikan, the first Alaskan city, to distinguish the land we were passing from that we had left.

At Prince Rupert a number of Alaskan Indians had boarded the ship to travel up to Ketchikan. Physically they were not unlike their southern neighbours, broadly built, with wide, Mongolian faces, but they had an open and expansive air which was very different from the rather sullen demeanour of the Indians we had seen in Prince Rupert. Our waiter, a very precise German, regarded their advent with dissatisfaction, and asserted stoutly that they never washed, smelt always of smoked salmon and slept in

Company Houses at Ocean Falls

Ketchikan

Waiting for the Boat at Ketchikan

their clothes. I am quite sure his statements were mostly unfounded, particularly when I remember their expensive, well-pressed suits, but I record them as an expression of the prejudices which still survive.

As the boat sailed through the last channels towards Ketchikan, we sat on the promenade deck near a group of these Indians. The most irrepressibly talkative was a sturdy old gentleman with a brown, wrinkled face and white hair *en brosse*. He talked in a loud, thick voice, and laughed continually at what he said—not always without reason, since he had quite a vivid turn of phrase. He spoke at length about the Alaskan towns, and about the waters between, of which he claimed to have "gotten to know every darn stone", in his occupation as a fisherman. Indeed, it was from him that we gained our first conception of Ketchikan.

"Anchorage, there's a real city," he declared, "nice and square. But Ketchikan—an old piece of driftwood left lying on the beach. I know every darn hole in Ketchikan, every snake's alley. There you can have good times, hard times, a little crime, loving up, plenty drink, in the morning someone pick you gently up." He spoke with a rhythmic utterance that gave his images all their full value. The talk of the amusements of Ketchikan led him to philosophise on the universal brotherhood of man, which he based on the opinion that "the craze for drink lead 'em all into one mud puddle".

Age was one of his bugbears. "When a man get old, he need windows to his eyes." And again, "When a man's young, he want to do all wild things, get drunk, travel at sixty, but when he's gotten old, what he most enjoy is plenty good friends."

However, the conversation seemed to run mostly on relationships. The old man suddenly stopped before a fat, comfortable, fur-coated woman who looked almost as old as himself, and shouted, "I remember you! You're my grand-daughter!" The statement was accepted with equanimity, and there followed a long discussion of various absent personages, all of whom turned out to be cousins or nephews. The old man became so enthusiastic about this plethora of kinship that he stamped up and down the deck, shouting boastfully that he had relatives all the way from Skagway down to Oregon. We listened with astonishment to the ramifications of these Indian families, wondering how a people that had declined in numbers and no longer bred freely could run to such a wealth of cousins and aunts and nephews. Only

11

afterwards did we realise that many of the so-called cousins must in fact have been fellow-members of the same clan rather than blood relatives of any real closeness.

Almost as fascinating as the problems of relationship were the names which we heard bandied about that morning. For these broad-faced, jolly Indians and their distant relatives rejoiced in a selection of names that sounded almost like a Jacobite directory, a roll-call of the Forty-Five. There were Stuarts and Camerons, Macdonalds and Hamiltons, and many another ancient Scottish name. Indian surnames on the Pacific coast are almost as interesting as the place-names, and the nationalities and predilections of the various missionaries, and even the lack of missionaries, can often be traced by such clues. In Anglican mission stations you will usually meet the names of the solid English shires; among the people of the northern Interior, where European Catholic priests were all-powerful, there are Indians with names like Rossetti and Lazare, and on Vancouver Island, where epithets were often bestowed before the missionaries began their work, I have met Indian families with surnames like Charley and Joe. Along the coast, however, the Scottish names are more common, and there is even a legend among the fishermen of a village of Indian Macdonalds who wear the clan tartan and play on the bagpipes the tunes of their Highland namesakes. I have never met anybody who actually heard the pipes, but it is the kind of thing which may very well happen on this strange coast, particularly as most of the Indians have a remarkable musical aptitude.

As we neared Ketchikan the wind which had been blowing all morning increased to something very near a gale, and the rain began to fall in tearing sheets, while the clouds blew in ragged wisps through the very treetops by the water's edge.

If one had seen it from the air, Ketchikan would doubtless have answered fairly faithfully the old Indian's description, for it was a long, narrow town, crowded together on a level strip between the turbulent water and the steep, wooded hills. A whole fleet of fishing boats lay along the waterfront, a couple of coastal freighters stood against the wharves, a tiny sky-blue seaplane bobbed on the heavy sea, and there were the usual coastal congregations of warehouses, of white cubical cannery buildings, of glittering oil tanks, and, behind all that, a town which seemed rather neater than the raw, shabby settlements with which, from neglect rather than poverty, the Canadians tend to plant their coastlines.

The boat was berthed skilfully, among great shouting from the longshoremen, in a spot where little space had been left, the American customs and immigration men came on board, and, after the most formal of investigations, we went down through the sheds into the plank-laid streets of the town. It was a neat, compact little settlement, with a tendency, in so far as its hilly and constricted situation would allow, towards that grid-iron pattern which is the downfall of American city builders. But there was too much cause for deviation, there were too many breakings of the vista, to allow the depressing effect which this formal planning produces in the larger cities.

Our first task was to find out how it might be possible to go farther up the coast. We had already, in view of the lateness of the season, abandoned a plan to go down the Yukon River, since we should almost certainly have struck Whitehorse after the steamship season had ended. But at least it might be worth travelling as far as Skagway, in the angle between the two sections of Alaska.

We had heard down the coast that there was a steamship strike in Alaska, but we hoped that it might be ended by the time we arrived. However, the clerk in the travel office told us that it was still in progress, and there was no immediate chance of its ending. We asked if he could suggest any other course.

"There's one Canadian boat that goes to Skagway. But you can't board it here. American laws forbid Canadian boats to carry passengers between two Alaskan ports. You'd have to go back to Canada and start again." Owing to the infrequency of the Canadian boats, this would involve waiting more than a week down the coast.

"Is there no other way of getting north?" I persisted.

The clerk shook his head. "You *might* get a fishing boat to take you, if the weather calms down a little. But that will probably go only as far as the next port, and then you'll have to wait for another one to carry you on. It might take three or four weeks, depending on the weather, to get to Skagway, and then you'd have to get back. The only other way is by plane. But even they aren't flying today. It may be a couple of days before they do if this keeps up." He cast a totally pessimistic eye out to sea.

"What will the plane to Skagway cost?" we asked. The sum was staggering, more than 500 dollars for the double return trip, and that was a good deal more than our budget would allow. The alternative, of waiting in this expensive and notoriously rainy city until some fisherman took it into his head to move north, and then perhaps repeating the process two or three times over at different ports, seemed unattractive, and we decided to abandon the idea, to return to Prince Rupert, take the train through to Prince George, and then try our luck on the Pacific Great Eastern's back-woods line through the coast mountains. The *Prince George* was due to leave in less than three hours, and we had no difficulty in arranging our return. Indeed, we seemed almost to be expected, and there was a general suggestion in the purser's air of "We could have told you all this if only you'd cared to ask."

Meanwhile we made the best of our time by walking through the stormy streets of Ketchikan. Wet weather, indeed, seemed such an institution here that most of the pavements were covered by permanent awnings, and it was only at the crossings that one had to plunge out into the full, lashing force of the squall-blown rain.

Perhaps the feature that pleased us most about Ketchikan, after two years of the odd, Calvinistic liquor laws of British Columbia, was the number of bars and private liquor shops which flourished in all the streets, but particularly down by the water. We dropped into the Goldrush Bar; it was full of bearded men drinking hot grog, slapping silver dollars on the counter, and looking as though they had been hired from some theatrical agency to impersonate Alaskan old-timers for the benefit of tourists—actually most of them were longshoremen. We drank Californian wine, and the pug-faced barman treated us with an unexpected generosity, re-filling our glasses as soon as they were empty for no extra charge, with the hospitable excuse that the bottle was almost empty and we might just as well finish it off.

Afterwards, when we walked through the town and entered some of the shops, we found the people expansive and pleased to talk with strangers; a bank clerk told us in detail the history of his own emigration from Scotland, and a shop assistant from Montana lamented the inconveniences of Alaskan existence and the cost of living. Milk, she said with disgust, arrived only once a week, and then it cost 30 cents (more than two shillings) a short American quart. The price of everything except cigarettes was much higher than in Canada, and we were warned that the farther up the coast one travelled, the worse it became, so that in such northern towns as Anchorage or Fairbanks one might pay, particularly for fresh food and restaurant meals, at least twice as much as in Ketchikan.

Very few of the people, we found, were either Alaskans or permanent residents of the territory. There was an enormous turnover of population: during the summer many seasonal workers came up from Washington State and even from Vancouver to work in the fishing and lumbering industries, and most of the residents were Americans who came for four or five years and then went home with what they had made. The Alaskans had many grievances; the principal was that political interests in the United States had persistently kept them in a semi-colonial position, as a territory subordinate to the Federal Government, and had refused them the relative autonomy of statehood. With more regional self-government, they all fervently believed, they would become even more prosperous than they were at present, and they would acquire a more permanent population. But perhaps their most burning grouse was not so much the material difficulties under which they laboured as the feeling that they were regarded as second-class citizens, less fit to manage their own affairs than people in states like Tennessee and Mississippi, which are in every respect much more barbarous and backward than Alaska.

To remind one of the real, aboriginal Alaskans there were large Tlingit heraldic poles at various street corners, massive in form and not unlike the Haida carvings; many of them had been retrieved from decay and restored under W.P.A. projects during the palmy days of the New Deal, which even brought about a temporary revival of native craftsmanship. But, like so many arts which are fostered artificially by patronage, woodcarving disappeared again as soon as the support was withdrawn during the war, and nowadays there is very little work of this kind being done among the Tlingit, a tribe whose individuality has largely been ground out between the millstones of Presbyterian missionary activities and American progress. That some craftsmanship indeed lingers we saw clearly from the very delicately made baskets which were exhibited in a shop devoted to Indian work, but we looked in vain for any example of the beautiful Chilcat blankets of mountain goats' wool which, up to comparatively recent times, were woven by the Tlingit and bought eagerly by the other northern tribes for the ceremonial clothing of their chiefs.

26.

Back on the *Prince George*, the waiter consoled us with the remark that we had not missed a great deal, since the Alaskan coastline was not very exciting once the fishing season had passed its peak. The towns, he said, were all much the same, though it was a pity we had missed the Russian cathedral at Sitka. We endured a painfully rough trip back across Dixon Entrance, where the waves had now reached North Atlantic proportions, and late at night we arrived back in Prince Rupert, over which a dense fog had descended. Here, by some error, there was no customs official on duty; in Ketchikan we had only bought one carton of American cigarettes, since we imagined that we should only have to pay duty on them, and now that we saw a clear gangway before us, and a taxi standing on the other side of the open gate, with not a single government uniform in sight, we felt bitterly cheated at having missed such a chance of foolproof smuggling.

We took a room in the largest hotel in Prince Rupert, since we had been warned solemnly by everybody on the boat that it was the only possible place to stay; nobody had exactly praised it, but they had all recommended it in a rather negative way by saying that all the other hotels were much worse. Here, at this superior hotel, they gave us a miserable, tiny room, with ancient, grimy wallpaper, whose drabness was only accentuated by a picture of an improbably vivid green parrot. The bed was one of the most antique and creaking pieces of furniture I have ever encountered, and as we spent the night rolling against each other in its great central concavity, we tried to visualise how bad, if this were the best hotel in Prince Rupert, the worst must have been. If our stay in the city had extended over more than one night, I am sure we should have sampled the horrors of some of the less urbane hostelries; as it was, we discovered that there were only three passenger trains a week on the east-bound Canadian National line to Prince George, and if we did not catch that which ran on the following night, we should have to stay three more days in Prince Rupert. So we decided to rise early the next morning and do our best to cram into one day the visits we had already planned.

One of the places we were anxious to visit was the plant of the Fishermen's Co-operative, which is one of the largest and most successful producers' organisations in western Canada. The secretary of the Chamber of Commerce had undertaken to arrange this visit on our return, and when we rang him up early in the morning he promised to see that this was done immediately. However, by the time we arrived, his conscience as an official in an organisation of businessmen had evidently been at work, and we found that instead he had arranged for us to visit a privately owned packing plant. Since he was hospitable to the point of chartering a taxi to take us the two miles out of Prince Rupert, it seemed churlish to protest at the genial Machiavellianism with which he had tried to frustrate our aims, and we merely made up our minds that we would find other means to see what we desired before the day was out.

The packing plant lay in an unusually beautiful little cove around the corner of Kaien Island, out of sight of the main harbour. It was a smaller establishment than the co-operative and it was evident from the few fishing boats lying in front of it that little work was going on. Indeed, we found that their season had finished about a week before. A Scottish foreman took us through the almost deserted rooms and sheds, setting in motion for our benefit the silent packing machines, demonstrating with dumb show such processes as mild curing and smoking. His eagerness to help us with information and demonstration was boundless, and his factory seemed a model of efficiency and cleanliness. But it was still not what we wanted to see—a successful producers' co-operative in action. Our guide, indeed, was an open and bitter enemy of the co-operatives. The plant he supervised had been formed by the amalgamation of a number of small capitalist concerns which had been forced by co-operative competition to rationalise their own methods, and we could tell from his remarks that a new skirmish in the war between the rival organisations was even now in progress. The capitalist packers, whose low payments to the fishermen were the original cause of the urge towards co-operation, were now trying to turn the tables by offering prices which in the short run seemed uneconomical, in the hope of undermining the strength of the co-operatives which, our guide suggested, had not the capital to buy fish at a loss and hold on to it in a falling market. His attitude had the reverse effect to what he must have desired, for it merely enhanced our idea of the importance of the co-operative and made us all the more resolved to see what it had done.

Meanwhile, however, we had rung up the Indian Agent, who told us that he would have his boat ready in the late morning for the trip to Metlakatla. We arrived in time, drove down from his office to a quay crowded with fishing boats and launches, and climbed on board a high-bowed, snub-fronted little motor cruiser.

Her skipper—and entire crew—was already on board, a quiet-spoken Tsimshian Indian from the northerly village of Fort Simpson.

The boat made its way across the choppy harbour and nosed through a tangle of islands and shoals, past scrubby headlands where long-vanished Indian villages had stood, until we came to the natural harbour where Metlakatla lies, a great wooden church, a string of white houses along a low cliff-top, a red-painted jetty stretching out from the shore. There were few boats at their moorings and the I.A. concluded that many of the men must still be out on fishing and lumbering expeditions. But most of the women would be back from their summer work in the canneries and fish camps, so that we could be sure of someone to welcome us. If we had come a month ago, he told us, we should probably have found only a single watchman in the village.

Here I should at least sketch the rather fantastic history of what is still often called the Holy City of Metlakatla. In 1859 the Anglican missionary William Duncan arrived on the coast at Fort Simpson, then a Hudson's Bay post surrounded by a great village of communal houses, inhabited by 3,000 Tsimshian, who had moved their villages from the original sites on the surrounding channels in order to live conveniently near the trading centre.

Duncan was a thorough man, with a tormenting sense of purpose. He first shut himself up with a Tsimshian Indian and, except for his few necessary conversations with the trading officials, he spoke only the native language for nine months, until he had learnt it completely and was ready to start his mission. Like many missionaries, he acted with a strange combination of fearfulness and impetuosity. He believed that the people he had come to convert were very monsters of evil, he was convinced that the ritual of the Cannibal Society involved the actual slaughter and eating of human beings (an error, as he later admitted), and he thought his own life in such perpetual danger that he would return every night to sleep within the stockades of the trading post. Yet the very depth of sin which he saw in his potential flock made him all the more determined to master them and win them to his faith.

He soon made many converts, for the Indians, versed already in the tortuosities of spiritual symbolism, were very ready to show interest in the European doctrines and divinities. Unfortunately, from Duncan's point of view, the new Christians had a wicked tendency to seize upon the similarities between Anglicanism and

their native beliefs, to regard the communion feast as a new kind
of potlatch, to see baptism as an initiation into another secret
society, and to make Christ another guardian spirit among their
animistic pantheon. A Catholic priest would have accepted the
situation and turned it to his advantage. Duncan, whose evangeli-
calism was strongly laced with Calvinistic inflexibility, could not
tolerate any adulteration of his gospel; he refused to be content
with a merely nominal acceptance of Christianity, and he saw that
in order to achieve his aim of total conversion it would be necessary to detach his followers from every vestige of pagan life.

So he decided to found an entirely new town where he could
centralise his flock and isolate them from the associations and
temptations of their original villages. He persuaded almost half
the Fort Simpson tribes to follow him, and Metlakatla, the result
of his efforts, became to all intents and purposes a model Victorian
village. There were carefully arranged streets of houses for individual families, and the place was dominated by a vast sham-
Gothic church which became known as Duncan's Cathedral.
Indian dress and customs, secret societies and potlatches, dances
and songs, communal houses and heraldic poles, all were swept
away, for Duncan's aim was to make each Indian as nearly as
possible an exact copy of a pious English working-man of the mid-
nineteenth century. Even the tribal clan organisation was ended
and the institution of chieftainship was abolished; Christ was to
be the only chief and the church militant the only clan.

The Indians were trained as carpenters and blacksmiths, and the
new town hummed with the industry of sawmills, canneries and
soap factories, rope walks and weaving establishments. Over it
Duncan ruled as an inflexible theocratic dictator who surrounded
himself with armed constables, who, if he thought it necessary,
would flog offenders with his own paternal hand, and who coaxed
and bullied the Indians into a nineteenth-century cult of hard work
which has influenced their descendants even today.

The village at which we landed was only the shadow of
Duncan's Holy City. Scrub was advancing over the land where
streets had formerly stood. A patch of rough grass and weeds
marked the site of two great residential schools. The workshops
and mills had vanished. The change began in 1887, when Duncan
quarrelled with the church; among other disagreements, he had
refused to allow the Holy Communion at Metlakatla on the rather
diplomatic grounds that it might encourage the Indians to revert to

the rites of the secret cannibal society. Eventually he set off with many of his converts to found a New Metlakatla in Alaska. But Duncan's departure by no means meant the end of old Metlakatla. Still, at the turn of the century, it was the centre of an Anglican diocese, with no less than four schools. But gradually its inhabitants died in epidemics (like the influenza of 1918), or moved away, and now less than two hundred people remain.

As we began to climb the narrow slippery path to the cliff-top, a tall old Indian, with walnut-brown, wrinkled features, came up to us. He was an eighty-year-old carpenter who could remember Duncan and the great schism that preceded the migration to Alaska. He spoke slowly, but, unlike the old men in most Indian villages, in excellent English, and he accompanied us to a decaying wooden house, the first along the path, from which echoed the sounds of sawing and hammering. Inside we found two men, dressed in fishermen's jerseys, who were ripping out the cedar lining of the rooms. When they stopped work and greeted us, we could not help being puzzled by the unusual conformation of their features, for they were the first coastal Indians we had yet seen with aquiline noses and long, definite chins. They had a very frank bearing, but it was less like the expansive affability of the Alaskan Indians than the open but slightly reserved bearing of a friendly English countryman.

They told us that the house on which they were working had originally been a residence for women teachers who had come to help the missionaries during the 1890's, and the old man remarked that he himself had helped to build it before Prince Rupert was even thought of. Over the floor a whole library of discarded books lay scattered; I rummaged among them and recognised some of the titles of those mawkish moralistic tales which were published by the S.P.C.K. at the turn of the century.

The two younger men were taking the wood for a house which one of them was building, and he invited us rather proudly to take a look at his progress as we went on through the village. The old man at the same time asked if we would call on his wife, who had just come out of hospital and would be glad to receive visitors.

Before we went into the village itself we called at the school, a little square building on the cliff edge, from which we could hear the slightly tinny sound of children's voices singing some very conventional English tune. Our guide wandered around the outside of the building with a tape, taking measurements for some alteration. Then we went inside, the children shouted in chorus, "Good morning, sir", the white teacher came hurrying over to welcome us, and we were embarrassed to hear the I.A. make a speech about two people who had been commissioned by the British Government to write a book on Canada and whose first impulse on reaching Prince Rupert was to visit Metlakatla, of which the fame had spread even to England. The reference to the British Government was due to a rumour, based on some verbal misunderstanding, that floated around Prince Rupert during our three days of contact with the city. We had not realised until this moment that it had reached the I.A., and now it seemed rather late to disabuse him, particularly as the older Indian children seemed already to have seized upon it as an added sign of their own prestige.

All the children struck us as remarkably clean and well dressed, even by the high Canadian standards, and they seemed an unusually alert group. But what impressed us most was their variety of physical types. Some were typically dark Indian children, with the straight black hair and rather opaque brown eyes, the high cheek-bones and wide flat faces of the coast; but these were in the minority. At the other extreme was one boy with fair hair and ice-blue, Scandinavian eyes, and between was a whole range of intermediate colourings and facial shapes. We found this evidence of mixed blood running throughout the village. Later, when we asked the I.A. how it was to be explained, he became unexpectedly taciturn, and though he remarked that this had been a problem right from the beginning, we could get him to express no opinion about its origin. Had Duncan's iron hand failed to quell the sexual weaknesses of the Tsimshian women, or did the trouble date from before conversion? We angled in vain for an answer, but whatever the original cause may have been, the people had evidently benefited by it, for a more intelligent and attractive group of Indians we saw nowhere else on our travels.

The teacher, indeed, was full of praise for her pupils. They were enthusiastic to learn, and much more diligent and quick of apprehension than most of the white classes she had taught in the past. As we had yet seen few of the adults, we were curious about their attitude towards education. The teacher said that she had experienced no difficulty whatever from the parents, who, like all Indians, were devoted to their children and wished them to have the best and most modern education that was available. The difficulty, indeed, was to keep up with their demands.

The only building remaining from all the activity of the past was the great barn-like church, the successor to Duncan's Cathedral, which had been burnt down at the turn of the century. The present building was neither so massive nor so ornate as its extravagantly bepinnacled predecessor, yet it was as large as many a parish church in an English market town, and the elaborate font and pulpit, the rows of carved pews, still reminded one of the days when a Bishop ruled in Metlakatla. But it is ten years now since the church was used, for the villagers are no longer very strong on religious practices and content themselves with a little shed which is easy to heat, and the foundations of the great building were already beginning to decay, its floor to sag, its great timbers to strain apart in the first deceptively slight motions of collapse. In a very few years this last monument to the missionary era will have disappeared.

At the end of the chancel was a garish stained-glass window, which had been erected in 1903 to the memory of a certain Lydia Ryan, who had died at the age of one hundred. The decay of the building was endangering it, and the I.A. told us that the ecclesiastical authorities were anxious to preserve it as a relic of Metlakatla's past. But here they had encountered an obstinate survival of primitive conceptions even in this apparently fully converted village. The Indians regarded it, like a memorial pole, as the property of the family, aad the family refused to consider its removal without a feast. But they saw no reason to spend any money themselves; it was the Bishop's idea, and he should see to it. The Bishop in his turn thought it none of his business to stand treat to the villagers of Metlakatla, and so the matter remained in deadlock.

Almost all the houses were large two-storied structures, even more spacious than those in Kispiox and Moricetown and, for the most part, in a much better state of repair. We went into the home of the old carpenter; an adolescent girl—she looked more Latin than Indian—answered the door, and took us into a parlour where a fragile old woman with a creased leathery face and wispy white hair received us with much dignity and an astonishingly prim English accent. Her house was as clean as any Dutch housewife could wish. It was sparsely furnished, in the ornate late-Victorian style which the missionaries must have introduced, with a few elaborate pieces of mahogany and plush furniture; the shelves and tables were cluttered with the kind of ornaments one sees in

country cottages, great shells murmuring of the sea, photographs
of the mission class in 1890 framed in faded purple velvet, a pair
of chipped china dogs. The old woman spoke in a quiet, detached
voice of the kindness which had been shown to her in the hospital;
the girl, her grand-daughter, told us that she found the village too
dull and would like to live in a town. It was a conversation that
might, but for the dark skin of our hostess, have taken place in
almost any remote village in England.

The younger people had lost their fathers' craze for big Victorian dwellings, and the house of the young carpenter was a little
wooden bungalow as modern as any on the outskirts of Victoria,
with an up-to-date electric stove and an elaborate chrome and
white enamel sink. A shift in the conceptions of prestige was
occurring, and it had become praiseworthy among these Indians
to own a modern rather than a large house.

The only way in which the Indian character obtruded itself was
in the untidiness of the gardens. Outside the houses there were
usually piles of tins and other rubbish, while it was rarely that the
fertile soil, in which Duncan had taught his flock to grow their
own vegetables, was ever cultivated. The convenient and ubiqui-
tous can had obviated, in the eyes of the Metlakatlans as well, the
need for any such work. They were far from being idle people,
but they preferred to put their toil into something which made a
show, a new house or even a communal building like the large
village hall which they had built for themselves by voluntary
labour.

We visited several more houses; often the people had not returned from the fishing, and where we were received it was by the
women, invariably courteous and hospitable. One of them I remember particularly, doubtless because, while so many of the
others reminded one of English housewives, she was undeniably
Indian in appearance and character alike. She lived in one of the
large old houses at the far end of the village; an aged woman in a
rusty black satin dress, with white hair straggling down on either
side of her wrinkled Tsimshian face. She shambled before us into
a room which, in comparison with those we had already seen, was
chaotically untidy, with open drawers and their contents lying
scattered all over the place under a generous layer of undisturbed
dust. She apologised with demonstrative regret, and began to
weep as she told us that since her husband died two years ago she
had not felt like keeping her house in order. Her weeping rose

into a crescendo of sobs as she recounted how her husband had been a deacon, a saintly man who had translated the Gospels into Tsimshian and had spoken Latin; she insisted again and again that she herself was a good Christian, and had lived with the missionaries in childhood, never once having been punished. It was a heartrending display of sorrow into which this tirade dissolved, rendered all the more poignant by the pathetic appearance of the old woman, with her dark, contorted face and her despairing gestures. Inge and I went away full of pity and ourselves almost ready to burst into tears, but the I.A. took it all with great equanimity, and expressed satisfaction that one of his Indians should have so ably demonstrated to us the dramatic talents of her race, since he was quite sure that her excessive manifestation of sorrow need be attributed to no other cause than the presence of a new and unexpected audience.

We walked back towards the beach, and our companion told us more about the administration of the village. The institution of chieftainship had never been revived, and the villagers elected their own council, which managed their local affairs and levied taxes for communal needs. There was a water supply, piped from the hills above, and an electricity system. But the most interesting fact he recounted was that the Metlakatlans have been chosen for an experiment in citizenship. Very shortly they would be enfranchised, admitted as full Canadian citizens with complete rights, and allowed to administer their own affairs without governmental tutelage.

For ourselves, we had been much impressed by the relatively thorough adjustment to modern society which these Indian fishermen had attained. Personally, I am not fond of missionaries, and I do not like the dictatorial methods or the frustrated personalities of men like Duncan. Yet it seems a melancholy fact that the Indians who cling to their old customs and still attempt to build a communal life around them are trying a compromise between two incompatible ways of life, while the Metlakatlans have reached the position when they can break out of their isolation, with all its social tensions. If only a similar opportunity were brought to the rest of the Indians, it might yet be possible for their cultural heritage, their dramatic, artistic and musical aptitudes to take their part in and leaven the dry mass of contemporary Canadian culture.

27.

We returned to Prince Rupert during the afternoon; if we wished to see the Fishermen's Co-operative, we should have to do it very quickly, and we bethought ourselves of the secretary of the Civic Centre, to whom the Captain of the *Prince George* had given us an introduction. He proved very friendly, immediately rang up an acquaintance at the Co-operative, and then, in the hospitable manner which everybody displayed in this city, insisted on taking us in his own car the three miles over a rough gravel road to the plant. His kindness was ill repaid by a flat tyre as we reached our destination, but he still hoped we would return and look over his Centre during the evening, before we caught our train.

One of the administrative officials of the Co-operative was awaiting us, and he hurried us into the plant, explaining that as the afternoon was well advanced the work would soon be over. It was unfortunate, he added, that we had not come at a time of full operation. A certain amount of work is done all the year round, but now the volume was relatively small in comparison with the height of the season, when as much as 350 tons of fish might be unloaded and processed in various ways in one day. However, there was plenty to see, and he suggested that we should visit the various departments, and on the way we could learn something of the history of the Co-operative and its place in the life of the area.

The process of deep freezing has revolutionised the fishing industry in western Canada by enabling its products to be kept for many months and sold as they are required, and we started off by visiting the cold-storage plant. We stepped into a lift, like a great rough wooden box, and as it rose we entered the abrupt chill of an atmosphere hovering around the zero mark. At each floor the lift stopped and we went out into chilly corridors whose floors glittered with rime. The icy handles of massive doors were opened and we gazed into chambers stacked to the ceiling with fish—stiff, brittle-looking creatures which it was hard to imagine had ever crowded in the sea or fallen to the lure of a trolling line. The most impressive were the white, glistening halibut, some of them higher than the workman who exhibited them, but there were many other kinds—salmon, of course, in large quantities, and ling cod, black cod, tuna, red snappers, an odd sturgeon, and so on down to herring bait packed in frozen blocks ready to be taken to the fishing boats. Altogether, we gathered, the Co-operative put away about 14 million lb. of fish into cold storage every year.

We were impressed and somewhat revolted by this great fish mortuary, and glad to leave its icy atmosphere and return to the lower and warmer regions of the plant. In one room we found a number of white-clad girls standing at benches and deftly filleting sole. The speed with which they worked was astonishing to our uninitiated eyes, and we were told that 60 lb. an hour was a fair average output for an experienced hand. Farther on we encountered men packing mild-cured salmon in great 400-lb. casks. Then we went into the liver oil plant. At first sight the enormous green-painted cylinders, the large tanks and various gadgets connected with them looked as complexly incomprehensible as any other modern machinery seen for the first time. However, the process of extraction seemed a relatively simple one of breaking down the protein and extracting the oil by a centrifugal separation process. For a time the liver oil meant a large addition to the income of many Prince Rupert fishermen. Some would make as much as 1,500 dollars a season from this source alone, but in the last two years the situation has been changed by the competition of cheap Japanese oils and the cash return has fallen to a tenth of what it had been two years ago, a loss which has been largely offset by increased sales and prices of fish.

Afterwards we went to the ice-manufacturing plant and watched the great rectangular blocks being lifted from their moulds by a crane and sent slithering down a complicated series of runways to the store where 3,000 tons are kept on hand for the use of the fishing boats and for packing fish which is sent directly to the retailers. Then there was the smokehouse and finally the laboratory, where the chemists not only carry out the necessary routine tests, but also initiate research into the problems of the fishing industry.

This complicated plant, we learnt, was only the processing end of the activities carried on by the Fishermen's Co-operative, and, indeed, only came into existence after the association had been working for more than ten years. It all began in the early 1930's, when, owing to the world depression, the prices which the fishermen received through ordinary marketing channels had fallen so low that they faced starvation and insolvency. During the 1930's red salmon and halibut were both fetching between 12 and 15 cents a pound. By 1931 the price for salmon was 4 cents and that for halibut dropped as low as 2 cents.

Trail

Part of the Doukhobor Colony at Brilliant, before the fires. Note the regular groups of houses near the Koobenay River

A Doukhobor Gathering

Rather than run heavily into debt and mortgage their vessels, the salmon trollers decided to form a marketing co-operative. In 1938 their first floating depots appeared in the Prince Rupert grounds, to collect the catch and at the same time to supply the crews with food and equipment at non-profit prices. The venture proved so successful that in 1943, when fishermen in other parts of British Columbia were receiving $8\frac{1}{2}$ and 10 cents a pound for their cohoe salmon, those who operated through the co-operative received between $13\frac{1}{2}$ and 14 cents. In 1944, because of the lack of cold-storage facilities and the need to provide means for expanding the industry, the co-operative began to build the processing plant through which we had just been shown, and the whole of its varied departments have been opened since that time.

The membership, at present about 2,500, is restricted to active fishermen and employees in the plant; each member owns shares in the society, but no dividend is paid, and he has only one vote, no matter how many shares he may possess. One fact which impressed me particularly was that the co-operators have set out to combat racial prejudices, and have made a special effort to bring the local Indians into their society.

There is no doubt that this organisation has enabled many fishermen to remain independent and to earn a great deal more as a result of their own work than was the case before it existed. The fishing fleet has increased in size and prosperity, and this in its turn has helped to prevent Prince Rupert from suffering a slump after its temporary wartime expansion had ended. But, apart from these local advantages, there was something very encouraging in seeing here, as in the fruit industry in the southern valleys, the rise and growth of a form of voluntary association for mutual advantage which, in this age when some form of collective organisation seems inevitable, offers a much preferable alternative to the rival monsters of the state and the capitalist combine which today threaten our freedom. Throughout British Columbia the fishermen and farmers are tending more and more to handle their own affairs by means of such co-operative bodies, and to my mind this represents a far surer and more stable guarantee of liberty and prosperity than any amount of political coercion.

In Prince Rupert we turned to the Civic Centre, where the secretary immediately proceeded to take us round the building and explain its functions. The Centre is in fact another example of the extension of the spirit of co-operation in western Canada, for it is

12

run directly by the people of Prince Rupert, for recreational and cultural purposes.

The building seemed to have endless rooms in which all manner of activities were going on: there were three gymnasia alone; there was a large auditorium with a stage and film projectors, and a restaurant which we found by experiment to be the best in the town; there was a surprisingly good library and an elaborate dark-room for amateur photographers. In one room a group of small children watched nature films, in another a leatherwork class was proceeding, and as we went back into the main hall a crowd of musicians was assembling for a rehearsal of the city's symphony orchestra.

That more than a fifth of the city's population are members of the Centre—and the proportion is increasing steadily—is a good sign of the work it has done towards humanising social life in this remote city; in particular, it has done a great service in easing the problem of aimless adolescents which afflicts so many North American towns.

As a final gesture, the secretary insisted on taking us down to the station and seeing that we got safely on board our train. We had decided to break our journey at Smithers, where the railway touches the main road along which we had travelled nearly a month before. Unfortunately, we should have to travel by night over the whole 230 miles, for there are no easterly daytime trains along this part of the line, so we took a sleeper compartment and enjoyed at least a more comfortable night than we had endured in the best hotel in Prince Rupert. By the time the porter awakened us next morning, we had passed through not merely a night, but also a whole transition in seasons, for, while Prince Rupert had been mild and damp, the landscape over which we now looked was white with snow; the winter of the Interior had begun, and we knew that the farther inland we proceeded the more extreme it would become.

28

We reached Smithers at about half-past seven in the morning. It seemed as though the whole Indian population of the town was attempting a migration, so many of them stood waiting on the platform, either to travel farther east or out of mere curiosity, the old men wearing shabby trilbys, the young men skiing caps or

Hopalong Cassidy hats, the women invariably using the bright scarf tied, gipsy fashion, around the head.

The main street of the little town was now a river of snow churned into several inches of liquid slush, while the old wooden sidewalks were slippery and treacherous. We had decided to visit the settlers in the mountains once again, since we were interested in the progress of their venture, so we checked our suitcases at the station and bought a duffle-bag into which we put the few necessary toilet items for a couple of days in the wilderness; what space was left we filled with stores, so that we should not be a burden on the resources of our hosts.

Then, once again, we took the road to the north, where, since there is no bus service on the 500 miles of highway between Prince Rupert and Prince George, we should have to rely on the generosity of motorists for our transport. Fortunately the main road was in a much better condition than the streets at Smithers, the snow was dry, and we could walk with little discomfort. The air was crisp and invigorating after the heavy coastal dampness, and there was an unexpected beauty in the snowy landscape of thin low woods, with the mountains, whiter than ever, circling us in every direction. Nevertheless we were anxious not to walk too far, since heavy clouds were once again gathering, and we anticipated that if we were too long on the road, we might very well run into bad snow on our climb up the mountainside. But there was remarkably little traffic, and it was almost an hour before a powerful American car drew up and a thickset, whisky-faced man barked an invitation that sounded almost like a command.

He seemed at first a solid, forbidding individual, but he soon softened into almost garrulous conversation. He was curious about our apparent eccentricity in trying to hitch-hike about the north country at the beginning of winter. And then, when we explained ourselves, he became even more actively interested. "So you're a writer!" he began in his gruff voice. "Well, you might be able to give me a bit of advice."

I said that I would gladly do my best. "I'm a sea captain," he went on—it was so evident in his manner that I wondered why I had not realised it the moment I saw him. "Now I'm in the coastal business—I retired once, but I couldn't stand the feeling of rotting my days away in small-town tittle-tattle, so I went back to sea. It's a quiet life, just keeping interested until I die. But back in the days before the war I ran into plenty of excitement, and I was thinking that some day I might make a book out of it. I can't stand writing, though, and that's my problem."

I suggested that he might talk into a dictaphone and then get somebody else to shape his account into a book.

"Yea, a dictaphone, I hadn't thought of that. I'll ask about one next time I'm down in Vancouver."

With a little prodding he was soon off on the tale of his adventures. "Well, I guess it ain't copyright," he laughed. "I ran liquor into the States for sixteen years. I used to take whisky out of Hong Kong to California. I had a big depot ship that lay out of territorial waters, and then we'd run the stuff in to the beach by fast speedboats. For a start we had the revenue people beat every time—they never could catch up with us in the old three-mile limit. But then they had a limit based on the speed of your boats, and that was when the fun really started.

"No, sir, I never once used violence, and I never resisted when they really had me cornered. I should have been plumb crazy when there were other ways of getting out of trouble. They had me up in court three times, but I always fixed it so they couldn't pin anything on me. Of course that cost money, so we always made a good run and only let them catch us when there was no alternative."

"How did you get rid of the whisky?"

"No difficulty about that, with every other household in California clamouring for the stuff. No, I had that all carefully arranged. There was a very efficient organisation which took the drink up on the beach, paid on the nail, and that was the end of my side of the affair."

I surmised that the organisation which handled the liquor so promptly and had such a beneficial influence with the American courts was probably a branch of the Capone syndicate. But there was a finality to the captain's words which seemed to preclude any too close questioning.

"I was the last of the runners on the Californian coast," he volunteered in a moment. "I carried on even after prohibition was ended. Then the liquor was so cheap down in Mexico that it was worth bringing it up from Lower California by speedboat just to beat the duty. I enjoyed that part of the game—Mexico is a fine country, and the Mexicans are good people, if you treat them fairly. But towards the end things began to get too hot for the business to be worth while. The Federal authorities even slapped an indictment on me, and do you know what happened to it? The

Attorney-General's office got in contact with me and said they'd wipe it out for twenty-five thousand dollars. I wouldn't bite, and they came on down, thousand by thousand, until I wiped it out for seven thousand spot cash." It sounded an odd story, but as the improbable is a characteristic of all North American administration, it may very well have been true.

"The funniest thing that happened to me on the coast was when I bought an old windjammer to carry a load of Scotch out of Macao. There was a hitch, the whisky wasn't there, and someone came with a proposition to take a cargo of illegal Chinese immigrants. Well, I was a businessman, and once I was in the smuggling trade it didn't seem to matter what I took on board, so I agreed. Everything went fine until we got near the American coast, where we were supposed to make a rendezvous off Pasadena with the fellows who were taking the Chinks to land. Nobody appeared, and we had to hang offshore for a couple of days. That spoilt everything: a fisherman saw us, and the story got around about a suspicious-looking craft. The newspapers splashed it up and down the coast with the headlines, 'Vice Ship Anchors off Los Angeles'. You see, the Chinks had been wearing their long robes, and the fishermen who sighted us took it into their heads that we had a cargo of women. Of course, that was the end. The coast guards began to prowl about to keep us out of territorial waters, and the Press men came out in motor boats, with their movie cameras ready to start clicking. I had the satisfaction of keeping them off, though; I stood the Chinks along the side with pots of filthy water and told them to throw it over the heads of any dirty little reporters who got too near. The next day I pulled up anchor and took my passengers back home. It was the last time I ever touched anything but liquor."

The familiar curved bridge arrived all too soon, and we had to stop him in a narrative which fascinated us and which he was enjoying thoroughly. Then he made the most amazing remark of all: "I read a good deal myself. I've just been reading Boswell. Now that Johnson, he seems to have been a regular fellow!"

Off the highway the lane was at least six inches deep in snow, and where the first camp had stood—now there was only a cache of boxes under a tarpaulin—the aspen copses were stripped and spindly. Gazing down into the valley, we saw a Breughel winter landscape stretched out beneath us, a bleak Breughel without human figures to bring the canvas to life.

As we began to climb the mountainside our premonitions were fulfilled; the snow began to fall thickly, in large, cold, melting flakes. Higher up it cleared, and we walked the last half-mile in a pale sunlight that pierced with difficulty through the thinning clouds.

John B. was just coming in along the opposite path when we reached the tent, his Alaskan packboard on his back, and at his shout of welcome the whole family came rushing out to greet the first visitors from outside since we had left a month before. We were taken in and regaled with stew, which afterwards we discovered, to Inge's secret horror, had been made out of one of the horses, killed for a rupture that destroyed its value as a working animal. We wondered whether this meant that the settlers were in really serious straits, but John assured us that this was not the case—it was merely a logical avoidance of waste, for, though their fortunes had taken a very promising turn since we left, it seemed almost like tempting providence to throw good food away. Never having had any prejudice against horse meat, which can be cooked to taste as well as any other, I agreed with him, but Inge could not be persuaded to accept the logic of this argument.

We asked about their good fortune, and John explained that it meant nothing short of the economic assurance of the community. Since they had arrived the demand for timber had increased phenomenally, prices had risen fast, and now the very man from whom they had bought the land was offering as much for the privilege of cutting down a limited area of good timber as John had originally paid him for the whole farm. Furthermore, he had offered to employ John as a faller* as soon as the work began. But this was not all. The Provincial Forestry Department had decided to cut a trail through the property for the use of woodsmen going to the forests in the mountains, which would provide a ready-made road to the site of the permanent settlement.

It was impossible to imagine a better material turn of events. Henceforward there would be no economic problem, and there only remained the question of recruiting new members for the community. John himself felt convinced that, now he could present a sound and going concern, people who had before been a little scared of living in the wilderness would flock to join them.

---

* A faller, in British Columbia logging terminology, is the worker who actually fells a tree.

During the next two days we led a relatively idle life around the camp. The great tent, with snow piled against its walls and two stoves burning full pelt, was more cosy than many a house, and I was able to assemble and type the notes of our travels. I also spent a good deal of time sawing and splitting wood, a task which was singularly gratifying in the high, cold air, and I was interested by the woodpeckers and camp robbers (grey and white birds akin to magpies) which gathered around the joints of meat that had been hung from the branches of a tree beside the tent, to keep them cool and safe from the dogs, cats and foxes. These relatively large birds would swing on the pieces of meat like bluetits on a lump of suet, but I noticed that, while the woodpeckers contented themselves with tapping the marrow out of the bones in the same way as they would attack a piece of rotten wood, the camp robbers tore away the shreds of meat in the true manner of carrion-eating birds.

After dark we would sit in the tent around the big stove—hearing Mrs. B.'s reminiscences of her youth on a pioneer homestead farm, arguing with Pop, who put forward an orthodox behaviourist viewpoint, on whether animals had reasoning power, and discussing with John his student days at Chicago and the gradual shifts of opinion which had brought him almost inevitably to his pastoral anarchism. He suggested that we should join their settlement; we replied that we had been scared by too many failures among communities to be good recruits for any such venture.

During these days in the mountains we were regaled with several items of North American pioneer fare which we had not encountered before. There were such things as corn bread and bran muffins, but the *pièce de résistance* of the open-air larder was a quarter of moose, and one evening we ate steaks cut from this great haunch. Alas, it turned out a labour of politeness, for the animal must have been a very aged bull and the meat was some of the most leathery I had ever tried to chew, while in flavour it was much inferior to the venison and particularly to the bear meat we had eaten during our life on Vancouver Island.

On our second night the snow fell heavily once again in the mountains, and next morning there was more than a foot around the tent, submerging the wood piles, but providing an unlimited reservoir from which the children would fill huge cans to melt on the kitchen stove. It looked as though at this high altitude the winter had begun its time of isolating severity.

After breakfast John invited us to take a walk through the

woods to the site of their future settlement. The distance was little more than a mile and a half, but the clearing of the trail had not been very thorough and under the thick snow lay many roots, brambles and formidable taloned briars, known as Devil's Clubs, which tripped us continually and made our progress necessarily cautious and slow.

The forest had a remarkable stillness, muffled under its thick shroud of fluffy snow; for a great part of the way we trod quietly in the hope of seeing game, and then the only sounds were the sliding rustles of snow falling from the branches. But, for all our caution, we saw no animals, and the only tracks in the snow were those of such small cattle as weasels, squirrels and wood mice. The larger animals had evidently been scared away by the noise of the foresters at work.

At a turn in the path we came to a tent, with boarded-up sides and a black stove chimney sticking out of its canvas roof. This was the camp in which the forest service men lived while they worked on the road; we were invited inside, and found a comfortably large room, with a board floor, camp beds, a roaring cooking-stove and a large wireless receiving and transmitting set. The genial camp cook was pottering around with saucepans and dishes; he offered the usual backwoods hospitality, providing mugs of hot and welcome coffee for us all, cracking incomprehensible jokes with John, and explaining the radio telephone system by which the forest men kept in touch with their headquarters 130 miles away. The two other men had gone down to the main road to pick up the week's supplies, he explained, so there would be little work done that day. Indeed, we gathered that the foresters' life was altogether a rather pleasant one, for even a camp with two men had its own cook, and the tempo of work seemed very much slacker than that of loggers who were working for commercial outfits. The financial return was admittedly lower, but the real outdoor man will always prefer a leisurely life in the woods to the mechanised haste which the Stakhanovism of the crack fallers has brought to the logging industry.

We went on, now by a narrow, barely defined path, scrambled over a rocky creek of clear mountain water, and came out into open meadowland at the bottom of the smooth slope where the pale brown seed stalks of cow parsnip and other weeds stood out above the snow. We climbed to the top, where the houses of the settlers would eventually stand. There was an astoundingly beautiful view on that winter day, with the tall black and white slopes of the mountains merging into the white valleys, and we could hardly imagine a situation in this wilderness better endowed with the advantages of plentiful water, clear land and an inexhaustible fuel supply. Indeed, we were moved to speculate whether the Indian village in this valley might not have stood in this very situation and whether the clearing was in fact as natural as it appeared. But in the thick snow it was impossible to seek for signs, and we retraced our steps, Inge and I bidding our farewells at the camp and John accompanying us down the mountainside to pick up his share of the foresters' stores.

29

As we descended, the snow lay less thickly than in the higher valley, but there was still a fair covering on the highway; very little traffic had passed that day. Most of the drivers were evidently waiting until the snow had packed and frozen into its usual and dependable winter surface—the best surface, as local people will tell you, that these rough northern roads ever have. Eventually, when we had begun to calculate in how many hours we should reach Smithers on foot, a taxi which had already gone northward some time before pulled up beside us and the driver offered us a lift. He had three passengers, Indian youths from Moricetown. They were very withdrawn and taciturn, and it was difficult to carry on more than a monosyllabic conversation with them, but the taxi-driver made up for them in volubility. He seemed to take us for potential settlers—it was probably difficult to imagine any other reason for strangers to be wandering about this part of the country on foot in winter—and he went into a long account of how some unfortunate newcomer had been persuaded to buy a stretch of land for two thousand dollars, only to find that if he had waited a few weeks he could have bought it for two hundred in a tax sale, for the original owner, a logger who had taken away the valuable timber, had already made up his mind to relinquish it in this way, rather than pay his taxes.

The Indian boys insisted obstinately on treating us as their guests for the ride, and paid the driver from a great wad of dollar bills. I do not know whether they were motivated by generosity or by a sense of prestige, but I think it was a combination of the two, for such considerations are, to an outsider, very curiously mingled in the Indian mind. What, however, really fascinated us about their behaviour was that they spent their time in Smithers at such occupations as lounging in the pool room, which was patronised almost entirely by Indians, leaning over the bar in the Chinese café, and standing at the street corners eating popcorn.

For such entertainment they had gone to the expense of a taxi journey which, counting the trips both ways, must have run to about sixty miles. It was an action whose illogicality in our eyes underlined the total difference between European and Indian attitudes towards money, enjoyment and a host of other things. To them, clearly, it was even here a question of prestige, the prestige to be gained from being able to spend, ostentatiously and on complete trivialities, relatively large sums of money which they had probably earned by some unusually hard spurt of exhausting work.

In Smithers there was little to be done. We already knew the place as thoroughly as we wished, and so we engaged a room in a little hotel which had a veritable hedge of cacti in the plate-glass window of its small lounge, and behind them a row of easy chairs in which elderly men sat all afternoon looking out on to the slushy and almost deserted street, talking in monosyllables, and occasionally breaking off for a game of the inevitable cribbage. As our room was better than we had anticipated in such a typical backwoods hotel, we decided to devote ourselves to an unusual evening of reading, only going out to dine at one of the small cafés in the main street, where the waitress annoyed us by behaving arrogantly to an old Indian. "Why don't you go to Sung's?" she snapped—Sung's being the Chinese restaurant which was principally patronised by the Indians. It was the only incident of this kind that we encountered in British Columbia, and the very fact that it made an impression is perhaps a good sign of the absence of the cruder types of racial discrimination. Conflicts exist, but they are no longer expressed in open insults.

Our next day's journey was barely 240 miles, but it took us five minutes less than ten hours to reach Prince George by train. Such railway travelling seems almost unbelievably slow by European standards, but in western Canada, where it is necessary for the few trains to stop at every halt, expresses in the European sense are almost unknown, and one comes to accept as inevitable the everlasting crawling and stopping at an average speed of somewhere between twenty and thirty miles an hour. This also happens in many parts of the United States, and in the eyes of the new arrival it rather tarnishes the North American reputation for hustle. But it is an unavoidable disadvantage in a thinly populated country.

The train passed through the same country we had traversed a month before by road, but it was only occasionally that the highway and the railroad came together, and rarely was the view from both identical, for often, to avoid steeper grades, the train would creep along the bottom of a valley while the road climbed over a range of hills or on to the heights of a plateau. Thus we kept much more closely to the course of the Bulkley than on our first journey, and beyond Fort Fraser we descended into the valley of the Nechako and followed that river to Prince George, avoiding the dreary plain over which we had originally travelled for seventy miles to Vanderhoof. Altogether, indeed, the railway journey is scenically much more pleasing than that by road.

Of all the people with whom we travelled in the day coach, one dour old nuisance stands out in my memory, a veritable ancient mariner who spent the journey buttonholing any of his neighbours who demonstrated the least weakness of will and pouring into their ears a rambling story of the ailments which seemed to have descended on him with all the weight of Job's torments. He caught up with us during that long lunchtime halt which is customary on Canadian trains; the day coach had almost emptied and its occupants had crowded the dismal shed which served as a coffee shop at this isolated point. Here the old man cornered us and, with the barest prologue, began a recital of how travelling affected his heart, building up a formidable pyramid of symptoms to the final breast-beating revelation: "You know what's wrong with me, folks? I'm a victim of Vagina Pectoris!" Fortunately, he interpreted our too ill-concealed levity as a sign of callous glee at his condition, and left us severely alone, except for an occasional look of canine mortification, for the rest of the journey.

Though hotels of every type, from the spittoon and aspidistra grade to the expensive sporting hostelries, were numerous enough in Prince George, they were mostly full, and it was with difficulty that we found a room—a dismal room at that, but at least an improvement on Prince Rupert. Since there would be another interval of two days before the first train on the Pacific Great Eastern Railway departed from Quesnel, we decided to spend the whole of the next day in Prince George, in order to find out a little of the development of the north country of which it had become the pivotal centre.

We supped in a café which seemed to be a backwoods equivalent of Dupont's in the Boulevard St Michel, for it was patronised almost entirely by the elder high-school students, surprisingly well-dressed girls, with a high proportion of handsome Swedish blondes among them, and youths, old for their years, among whom it seemed fashionable to shave their budding whiskers into those tenuous fringes which have been affected by Parisian students since the liberation. We were at a loss to explain how such a fashion had penetrated from the Left Bank to Prince George, and nobody to whom we talked could enlighten us further than to say that it had suddenly caught the fancy of a circle of youths who liked to enliven northern life by their eccentricities. Last year it had been bowler hats, next year it would be something new, and foreign beards would be totally forgotten.

Towards ten o'clock, when the crowd of students was already thinning out, a solitary and singularly ugly girl wandered into the café, dropped a nickel in the juke-box, and went over to drink a milk-shake at the bar. The record she had chosen was a tune then fraying out of popularity—"I'm the loneliest girl in town." As the throaty voice of the crooner sobbed out of the Wurlitzer, the girl at the bar looked the very woebegone prototype of the song. The record ended, and a moment later a youth walked up to her and, with the brassy jauntiness which passes for gallantry in these parts, started a conversation; they departed together a few minutes afterwards.

30.

By next morning the temperature had fallen quickly to three degrees below zero. This would not have been particularly uncomfortable in the dry air of the plateau, if a razor-edged wind had not begun to blow down from the north, raising miniature dust storms in the snowless streets and locking our unprotected cheeks into aching grimaces. But we put on every spare pullover with which we had stuffed our suitcases against such turns of the weather and set out to make our researches into the past and present of the little city.

The first man we met was the editor of the bi-weekly local paper, who regarded our arrival as a lucky news item in a dull week. He was a typical English newspaperman who had once been a Balkan correspondent, had gravitated into Prince George four years ago by one of those series of chances which bring unlikely people into

remote Canadian towns, had bought himself a share of the newspaper, and had trebled its circulation in two years, a fact he attributed to no talent of his own, but to the rapid growth of his
potential public. When he arrived, Prince George had still been a
settlement of untidy shacks with mud roads; now, as we had seen,
it had already the beginnings of a modern city.

From this point we went into a long and agreeable discussion
which covered a vast number of points only distantly connected
with Prince George and its history. There was, for instance, the
editor's theory that the ancestral Aztecs had originally made their
way southward from this plateau, a contention which he argued
with a great deal of ability and which certainly seemed to have as
much substance as any other theory I have heard on that obscure
subject. There were his revelations on the enormous liquor con-
sumption of the area—it reached more than a million dollars a year
for a total of about 15,000 people, including women and children;
and his accounts of the Seventh Day Adventist colony over towards the Rockies, whose members showed such commercial
ability, while awaiting the Second Coming, that they had pushed
half the local old-timers out of the sawmill business by their
vigorous competitive methods. Out in the backwoods, he further
declared, there were little communities where ecstatic religious
cults—as strange as any that Erskine Caldwell had written of—
still flourished, accompanying their piety with odd variants of
sexual promiscuity.

But apart from these amiable hors-d'œuvres, we gathered from
him a great deal about the contemporary growth of the city and
its surrounding area and, with what we later learnt from a wholesale merchant who could tell us more of the past, we were able to
piece together a fair sketch of our subject.

Back in the early 1800's Prince George, which was then called
Fort George, was one in the northern chain of posts founded by
the fur companies, and for a whole century it remained a trading
point with two or three white inhabitants and a small Carrier
Indian village. Then, when the Grand Trunk Pacific Railway was
planned to pass through Fort George on its way from Edmonton
to Prince Rupert, a group of promoters studied the map and
realised that, if the north were ever developed, the site of Fort
George would be its logical centre. Two speculative companies
immediately pre-empted rights on large areas of virgin forest and
began a world-wide publicity campaign for the non-existent city,

which they already called "a second Chicago". It was 1910, a time
of restless movement, when people were seeking new frontiers to
re-enact their fathers' searches for happiness and fortune, and the
suckers rose in such numbers that one company alone sold twelve
thousand lots (through the mail), most of them in impenetrable
forest country where no roads or even Indian trails existed. Many
of the unfortunate purchasers accepted the loss of their savings
and went away after having had one look at the wilderness, but
enough remained to form three rival towns along the Fraser, with
brothels, banks, Chinese gambling hells, two mutually contemptuous newspapers, and a hotel which claimed the longest bar in
the world. Land prices soared steadily, and the final mass shearing
of the sheep came when the railway was completed in 1914; then
the Provincial Government entered on the crest of the wave of
speculation and sold a block of public land for prices which
reached as high as 13,000 dollars a lot. Altogether the politicians
cleared 800,000 dollars out of that one sale alone, for land which
later became virtually worthless; afterwards they tried to placate
uneasy public opinion by remarking: "It was a speculative time
and the Government took advantage."

One of the leading promoters in this artificially stimulated boom
was a Toronto lawyer named Charles Miller, who combined an
astute business capacity with a few vaguely radical social ideas.
Among other things, Miller was devoted to the emancipation of
women, and to the spread of birth-control propaganda as a means
to this end. He decided that he must carry out some outrageous
satirical joke to draw public attention to the folly of indiscrimi-
nate breeding, so he made a will in which he left nearly a million
dollars to be given to the mother in Toronto who, within ten
years after his death, should produce the largest number of
children. The "Baby Will" was published in 1926, but its author
had not made his satirical intention sufficiently clear, and his testa-
ment was taken by Press and public alike as an exhortation to
produce larger families than ever; during the following decade the
hopes of the Toronto poor led to a fantastic increase in the working-class birthrate of that eastern city, more than 2,000 miles away
from the place where Miller's money was made from fleecing
other members of the poor.

To return from this digression, the great boom of Prince George
failed to develop into anything more than a matter of real-estate
speculation. The potential wealth of the country was certainly

there—in timber, minerals, good farming land and water power—
and in this at least the promoters had not lied, but there was little
demand for it in a world where the existing and more easily available sources of supply were still far from exhaustion, and no
financier was prepared to lay out capital on such a remote frontier
area. Two of the three towns along the Fraser withered away;
Prince George remained, a typical frontier town whose mayor and
corporation began their work in a superannuated bawdy house, a
fact which gave rise to a stubborn British Columbian legend that
Prince George kept a municipal brothel. But even such eccentricities died away as the city settled down to the somnolent stagnation of the years between the wars.

Its present growth dates entirely from the last ten years. Since
1941 its population has grown more than five times; it is often
difficult to get exact and up-to-date figures of what such an increase means in local productiveness, but it will give some idea of
the rate of progress when I say that the timber production of this
district increased in four years, from 1944 to 1948, almost three
times. Today there are nearly four hundred sawmills working in
the surrounding country.

This rapid growth has already made Prince George the largest
city in Canada's northern latitudes (53 degrees), and one of the
three or four largest cities in the interior of British Columbia.
Furthermore, it is a development which shows no signs of
decline, but rather seems destined to continue with a growing
momentum. For the difference between the boom of the 1910's
and the present process is to be found in the fact that today the
economic world is more conscious of shortages than of sur-
pluses; sources of minerals, timber and farm products, which had
once seemed inexhaustible, are now barely sufficient for present
needs, and certainly not enough for the future. A relatively
undeveloped area like central and northern British Columbia
constitutes a great reservoir of these much needed materials. As
an example, the almost untouched coal measures alone amount to
at least six billion tons, and the reserves of many other valuable
substances are proportionately large.

Only the transport is lacking, and even this is gradually being
provided in a series of lines of communication which radiate from
Prince George like the threads of a spider's web. To the east and
west the Canadian National Railway already runs. To the south
the Pacific Great Eastern Railway is expected to link Prince George

and Vancouver within two or three years and a little later the Cariboo highway will be completely resurfaced. To the north-east the new highway to the Peace River is almost ready for use; besides opening a great stretch of new country and connecting the Peace River area for the first time with the rest of British Columbia, this will give a shorter alternative route from Seattle to the Alaska Highway, saving 500 miles for the freight lorries and incidentally bringing a new contribution to Prince George's growing importance. The only link now remaining to be realised is a road going northward from Prince George to Alaska; up till now it has not even been planned, yet it is inevitable in the relatively near future.

Unfortunately there is at present no reason to hope that the process of opening up northern British Columbia will develop into anything better than the wild scramble to tear as much from the earth as it will profitably give, which has characterised so many similar economic movements in the past, for, though there are plenty of Canadians who are conscious of the need for conserving natural resources by a balanced regional development, they are at present neither powerful nor very vocal. The slogan we heard most often in Prince George—"There are endless opportunities for making money"—is likely to drown out for many years to come the voices which put forward any more reasonable counsel.

In the evening when we walked back to the hotel, the street was filled with the smell of woodsmoke, and we found a man calmly burning a red glowing pile of timbers about thirty feet long by ten feet wide on a vacant lot between the wooden houses. His action seemed to arouse no concern, either among the people or the authorities, although the danger to the rest of the town, in the event of the wind suddenly freshening, seemed quite alarming. We went to our hotel expecting every moment to hear the fire siren announcing the beginning of a town fire on the grand scale.

31.

We left for Quesnel next day by bus, which is still the only public transport southward from Prince George. By now the route had become familiar, but the extremely cold weather—for the temperature had fallen even lower during the night—had given another new aspect to the landscape, an unusually soft greyness from the thin scattering of rime on the forests which stretched out towards the Rockies. Some of the smaller creeks were already completely congealed into their winter stillness, and the Fraser itself, when we looked down from the hills, was a white jumble of jostling ice cakes. "It's an early winter, even for these parts," the driver said. "It'll be a bad one, for sure."

In the bleakness of winter Quesnel was a much less congenial town than it had appeared on our last visit. No town, indeed, could have seemed very agreeable in that searching wind, and in any case we were tiring of the eighty-year-old decrepitude which passes for age in these early frontier towns. However, we had the whole afternoon and evening to spend and we set out once again on an assiduous interviewing of local personalities.

We found an interesting difference between the attitudes of people in Quesnel and those in Prince George. Quesnel had no prospect of being a centre of the north country, and even its present situation as a minor railway terminus would be superseded when the Pacific Great Eastern was finally connected to Prince George. So its inhabitants tended to decry the latter town's spectacular progress. "Quesnel grows naturally with the country around it," one old man told us. "When I was a kid here I went to a school with only seven pupils. Now there are nearly two thousand people here and it keeps expanding steadily. And that's a good deal better than being like Prince, which is always growing up fast and then falling away."

This same old man, now a garage proprietor, had once run a business carrying goods by covered wagons from the south up to Barkerville. It had ceased to be profitable only in 1922, when the railways finally reached the town. He described the change in the economy of the country since his boyhood. Then mining, mostly placer work, had been the principal industry, followed by trapping. Farming had been a chancy business, since the poor communications made the farmers reliant on a local market, and this in its turn was subject to the constant vicissitudes of the mining industry. Now it was different: logging had become the main industry, farming, established on a permanent exporting basis, was second, and mining was third—hard rock quartz mining rather than the placer mining of the past. Trapping had declined, owing to the decrease in fur-bearing animals, to negligible proportions. This, from what we gathered elsewhere, was a fairly just analysis of the situation in all this area of the old Cariboo.

13

A further point which distinguished Quesnel people from their neighbours eighty miles north was their consciousness of an interesting historical past as well as a promising future. One of the places we visited was a little growers' co-operative, run by about three hundred local mixed farmers. They had nothing like the spectacular plant we had seen among the fishermen in Prince Rupert, since they confined themselves to a common system of wholesale distribution and a service for providing cheap equipment, seeds and fertilisers for their members. But one feature which we had certainly not expected to find either in a producers' co-operative or in a little frontier town like Quesnel was a historical research committee.

A short, heavy-moustached farmer, covered with meal from loading sacks on to his truck, was pointed out as the leading man in this venture. "It's something to do in the quiet winter months," he explained deprecatingly. "But we really are concerned with the amount of material which is lying about unrecorded in this part of the country. Most of it is stored up in the memories of the old-timers, and they are dying out fast, so we want to get their stories down on paper before it's too late. And then we are thinking of preparing a reliable history of the Cariboo which will tell just how people lived and acted during the early days. Nowadays some facts have been made sensational, and the rest of the picture is left out, but we want to give people the whole story."

We were intrigued by the idea of farmers in a remote country town setting out on an experiment in objective history-writing; it showed, if nothing more, a preoccupation with something deeper than the craze for unbounded opportunities of making money which had afflicted so many of the people farther north, and it did not seem impossible that some really interesting result might be achieved by such co-operative research.

But the farmers were not the only people in Quesnel who were fascinated by the past. As we returned into the town we saw a little shopfront bearing the legend *Cariboo and North West Digest*. A few exercise books and guides to the Cariboo were on sale, and there was a pile of magazines bearing the title which appeared on the shopfront. We went inside and a young man in Harris tweeds, with a weathered face and a broken nose, came up and began to talk to us in a quiet voice which at times we found it difficult to overhear. He was the editor of the magazine, and when we told him about our reasons for travelling, he immediately brought out a pile of back numbers, explaining that they might give us an idea of the country's background. The magazine was a curious mixture of historical articles (some of them very conscientiously prepared), of old-timers' tales which seemed to verge on the apocryphal, of news about the area between Clinton and the Yukon, and of editorial comment which grappled intelligently with the problems of growth and conservation. It was a surprising publication to find in such a little town, and we asked the editor how he had ever set out on such a venture.

He explained that he had lived in the Cariboo since his childhood. Before the war he had been one of that almost extinct breed, the hand loggers (i.e. men who fell trees by the old cross-cut saw instead of the power saw), and later he had become a truck-driver, travelling over the north country wherever there were any roads on which to run. In the meantime he had put in odd spells as a guide, and his experiences had shown him not only the wealth of unpublished historical material, and a number of local problems which needed ventilation, but also the interest these questions aroused among the people he met. So he decided to publish a quarterly magazine about the Cariboo. The first issue he printed himself on a small hand-press and peddled it in the streets of Quesnel. In five years he built it up so that it now paid its own way, with a slender margin which enabled him to spend six months a year travelling about the back country and gathering information. He was never at a loss for articles, since people were becoming more conscious that their memories might help to create the history of important social movements.

It was interesting to see how powerfully the legend of the Cariboo past seemed to be implanted in the minds of the people in Quesnel, for it must certainly need some strong emotional impulse to inspire loggers and farmers to start founding magazines and embarking on historical research. I think the reason can perhaps be found in the highly dramatic nature of life in all frontier movements. It is not without reason that such historical phenomena as the gold rushes have found their place in folk literature, for their essential elements of tragedy, disillusionment and plain human folly and weakness inevitably appeal to ordinary men as a representation in reality and on a grand scale of their own everyday fantasy lives.

We had dinner—a passably good one—in the Nugget Hotel, a kind of exaggerated dormitory for transient workers, with a

restaurant patronised by cowboys and Chilcotin Indians from
the cattle country to the west, who wore black ten-gallon hats
decorated with bead bands that had been worked in the vivid
geometrical patterns which belonged to the tribe before the
advent of the degenerated floral patterns we had encountered
on our earlier journey. Inge thought that both—hatbands and
cowboys—were very handsome.

Then, in the darkness, we stumbled through the ill-lit streets
down to the Pacific Great Eastern station, a little apple-green shed
with a single wooden platform which forms the terminus of this
grandiloquently named railway serving a stretch of country longer
than from London to Land's End. The train stood waiting, a large
and powerful orange diesel locomotive for pulling up the steep
gradients, a day coach with wooden benches, a sleeping coach and
a kind of general-purpose coach, comprising a lounge, a small
dining compartment and the kitchen. But even this little train
allowed vast room for the passengers who travelled that night;
there were three in the sleeper and four in the day coach. The
porter, who seemed pleased at having so little work, explained
that in the summer it was another matter, since many people
travelled on this line solely to see the magnificent mountain
scenery.

For the early part of the evening we sat and smoked in the day
coach. Occasionally the train stopped at some tiny station and we
would see the snow falling through the beams of the single platform light. One or two people would sometimes get on or off, but
the actual number of passengers did not increase until the next day.
Now and then a man would come through to rake and stoke the
great black cylindrical stoves which stood in the vestibules of the
carriages. These were rather pleasant arrangements, for the air
never became really over-heated, and one could always get warm
very quickly by standing in the corridor beside a scorching hot
stove.

32.

When we awoke next morning the train was past Clinton, descending from the 3,000-foot-high point of Kelly Lake, and running around the edge of Pavilion Mountain, into the Fraser Valley.
It was typical southern Cariboo desert scenery once again, grey
mountainsides, sage brush, stunted trees in the sheltered corners,
with the Fraser milky green in the valley bottom and already

narrowing between its arid banks as it flowed towards the Canyon. This was the part of the river which we had previously missed when the road swung north at Lytton. Once again a night had brought a change of climate, for here there was no longer any snow, and even a few remaining leaves still splashed an occasional golden touch on the grey landscape.

Lillooet was our first morning stop; the railway lay on a wide ledge above the town, and, since we were anxious to use our half-hour's stop to breakfast at the single café opposite the railway lines, we had no chance to examine this relatively old town which was once the beginning of the Cariboo road. All we saw was a small fruit-growers' co-operative warehouse by the railway, and, over on the far side of the valley, a mass of gravel heaps which were a relic of the placer-mining era. On a shelf between the river and the lower mountains were orchards and gardens, for Lillooet, its gold days ended, survives as the centre of a small but very productive agricultural district whose irrigated fields are an example of what might be done in the rest of this desert region to emulate the horticultural achievements of that other natural desert of British Columbia, the Okanagan Valley.

Beyond Lillooet the railway left the Fraser and began to climb again into the coast mountains, through which we were to travel for the rest of that day. Here, for the next sixty miles, we followed the route of an old trail which had been used by the fur traders who did not trust themselves to the dangers of the Fraser Canyon on their way down to the coast, and which became the first route for the gold-miners travelling to the Cariboo. It then involved a long and arduous journey, including a passage up the rapid-strewn Lillooet River and the crossing of four lakes. When the Cariboo road was built this route fell into immediate disuse, the busy villages to which it had given birth mostly fell into total decay, and the trail itself in many places vanished completely under the returning bush.

A few miles out of Lillooet the narrow valley opened up to Seton Lake, a turquoise-blue water lying in a trough between mountain ridges which at places rose between 7,000 and 8,000 feet above its surface. Like the other lakes in this mountainous region, it is a resort for Vancouver people to escape from the city summer; there are small holiday camps of tiny garish cabins on its shores, shabby little bungalows, and brilliantly painted rowing-boats bobbing on the water, all helping to build up an atmosphere of leisure and holiday, which seems to linger even in the winter months among the permanent residents-pensioners or the kind of small rentiers who gravitate to these raggedly amiable encampments on the edge of the sea or the wilderness, where there is at least the illusion that one can just step over the frontier into the world of primitive nature and escape completely from the cares of civilised life, the life of duns and bureaucrats, bank-managers and employers. For adults, I suppose, these consolations must often grow rather thin; for children, those supreme illusionists, I imagine there is little more satisfying than the easy outdoor life of such places.

There was a settlement of Lillooet Indians along the lake shore (it seemed incredibly poor and filthy after Metlakatla), but the only place of any size was Shalalth, near which there was a big uncompleted power plant. Its huge pipelines hung like overgrown anacondas down the mountain, and emptied into the concrete building on the lakeside. The latter was an unusually pleasantly designed structure and, although the conduits had caused a temporary marring and scarring of the mountainside, it was on the whole one of the most innocuous examples of industrial intrusion into the wilds that we had yet encountered.

At Shalalth our first contingent of passengers came on board. They were miners from the workings at Bridge River, now the most prosperous gold mines in British Columbia, but they had nothing of the appearance or manner of the old-style prospector, for modern gold mines are thoroughly mechanised industrial plants whose workers are wage-earners very much like those in any other industry. There is a road for about fifty miles from Shalalth up the Bridge River, at the end of which a whole cluster of busy little towns lie isolated in a mountain valley, the outposts of European settlement in this part of the country, with only a trackless expanse of mountainous country westward to the coast, more than a hundred miles away.

Beyond Shalalth only a short stretch of rising valley separated Seton Lake from Anderson Lake, yet there was an amazing difference of temper between the two sheets of water. Around Anderson Lake the high mountains crowded more jealously, and its surface was dark, almost black, and stirred by a heavy, sullen swell, on which the pale yellow leaves of the willows were gathered into a thick golden line which swayed to and fro a yard from the shore, never scattering on the waves, yet never washed up on the scanty beach below the narrow rock ledge on which the railway ran. It seemed altogether a stern and unfriendly place, but this aspect may well have been due to the rapid change in the weather, for an angry wind was rising and the sky clouded over as the mountains drew in more closely around us.

The line ran upwards through a belt of thick forest land to Birken Lake, and then fell away through a rather bleak upland country until it reached a stretch of valley land which was inhabited mostly by Lillooet Indians. One of their villages was a fairly large settlement of several dozen poor cabins, with a school, outside which the children were playing as the train stopped at the little halt. What immediately impressed us about them was their strict sexual segregation. The boys and girls were gathered in opposite corners of the playground, and there was also a totally different spirit in their activity, for while the former played football with a grim and conscientious intentness, as if it were a ritual to be performed adequately and exactly, the latter were engaged, with much shouting and laughter, in burying each other under piles of fallen leaves. They were very spontaneous in their frisking, like young animals, whereas the boys had already that sullen solidity which so often repels one on first encounter with the Indian male.

The only European settlement worth the name between Shalalth and the sea was a little jimcrack village called Pemberton, a veteran of the early gold trail, which now survives by a mixture of farming, logging and trading with the Indians and the local settlers. It lies in a broad and almost completely waterlogged valley which seems at one time to have been fairly heavily settled. One could see the lines of rotting fences leading down into fields which had long lapsed into marshes, and all along the track there were melancholy deserted homesteads. Even those farms which were still occupied were almost unbelievably decrepit; green, mossed-over buildings, gates patched up with haywire and string, ancient wasted fruit trees on which the tiny deformed apples hung unpicked. The cattle were thin and dejected, the pigs were armoured with mud from rolling in the boggy farmyards, the chickens were scrawny and ravenously busy in their search for food, and the whole farming knowledge of the people seemed to be on the most primitive level, for even the hay was thrown into rough and almost shapeless piles which only extreme flattery could dignify with the name of stacks.

Some of these farms were occupied by Indians, who are always unenthusiastic and inefficient farmers, but the homesteads of the white settlers were little better. Most of the people, indeed, seemed extremely poor by the standards of the country, and there were many cabins, inhabited usually by old people who evidently eked out their pensions by growing their own food, which could not even be classed as homesteads.

The decay of this countryside was probably due to economic factors, and particularly to the lack of any readily available market. That it was not due to poverty of the soil is shown by the fact that the provincial authorities have recently embarked on a project for reclaiming about forty square miles of the marshland about Pemberton, and when the railway is finally connected with Vancouver this derelict valley may well become a prosperous farming district.

Meanwhile, here was one sign of its present condition. On the fence beside the railroad one of the smallholders had optimistically—or desperately—fixed a pencilled notice: "Turnips, cabbages, carrots for sale." Doubtless he had heard of the customs of farmers on the Fraser Valley highway, and having no road before his door, had hoped that now and then a train might stop to allow the passengers to buy his goods. In this he may have been encouraged by the waggish legends which say that the initials of this line have a second esoteric meaning, Please Go Easy, and which tell of occasions when the train has stopped to pick up the dolls which children dropped from the carriage windows. Nevertheless, I cannot imagine that he has sold many of his turnips and cabbages in this way.

Out of Pemberton the line rose rapidly into the mountains, 1,400 feet in the nineteen miles to Alta Lake, with the white-topped peaks of the Black Tusk and Garibaldi ranges coming into sight on either side. Alta Lake lay on the crest of the Coast Range, 2,100 feet high, its waters flowing away both east and west, towards the Fraser and Howe Sound. It was a small, pleasant lake, whose forested shores were dotted with sawmills. Here indeed began the heavy forest of the coastal slopes, which accompanied us all the way down to the sea, except for the patches of scarred mountainside where it had been logged off to feed the numerous lumber camps and the pulp factories on the seashore.

It was a wild landscape of high peaks with blue glaciers glittering in their clefts, of deep valleys and ravines, with swift torrents and churning cascades. Brandywine Falls, whose name had charmed us, were an annoying disappointment, since we travelled above them and saw only the water pouring over their lip instead of the legendary beauty of their 200-foot descent. But we had plenty of compensation elsewhere in this magnificent and almost completely uninhabited country, and particularly when the track wound its course for several miles along the crest of a deep ravine in which the creamy waters of the Cheakamus River boiled and thundered towards the coast. To the east the mountains formed the Garibaldi Provincial Park, a preserve in which, once more, we optimistically hoped to see some big game. But again the animals were evidently much more frightened of the trains than the self-possessed bears and elk at Jasper, and the only gratification which we had was to see several large eagles gliding in vast sweeping circles above the crags and the forests.

At last we came down into the broadening Squamish Valley, a green, damp place, soaked by the coastal rains, which had flooded much of its meadow land. There were extensive orchards, some of them completely neglected, the trees bearded with long grey hanks of moss and the apples lying in rotting circles underneath. But there were also a number of very well-kept farms, with lush fields and herds of sleek cattle, and it seemed certain that this area, with good sea communications, had not suffered the same economic difficulties as the farming country back in the mountains.

Squamish itself was no more than a village—even smaller than Quesnel—dominated by its large railway sidings full of lumber wagons. The port lay a mile farther on, and we ran down to the edge of Howe Sound, a great fjord which probes nearly forty miles into the land from Georgia Strait, its broad waters edged by sheer mountain slopes. Finally we reached the end of the line, climbed out at the tiny port station, and boarded a small steamboat which was lying at one of the jetties.

The three hours' run down to Vancouver took us through the same kind of coastal scenery as I have already described amply enough at the beginning of this chapter, with the only difference that the Sound was rather more thickly populated. Our only stops were two company towns. The first was a white settlement like Ocean Falls, centred around another pulp mill, with its quays full of lighters and of barges carrying loaded railway wagons. The second was dominated by a large metalliferous mine, whose aluminium-sheeted mill buildings sloped like a great glittering fungus up the mountainside. Here the boat filled with miners going back to Vancouver for the weekend, and the saloon became noisy with the slapping of cards and the shouts of the gamblers.

A gaudy sunset fell over the water as the Sound broadened towards the sea, and then a fast-blown wrack of clouds covered the stars and the rain began to fall suddenly and fiercely in the manner with which we had become very familiar during our two years on the Pacific coast. But it ended quickly, and by the time the lights of Vancouver came into sight the sky was clear and starry once again.

While I have been writing these pages about our journey through the mountains from Lillooet to the coast, I have been acutely conscious of the lack of incident and of human activity. The travel writer, unlike the novelist, can only exercise his inventive powers in a very limited manner; his narrative is determined by the experiences which the chance of the journey thrusts in his way. On this particular trip we were given scenery in abundance, and of as magnificent a kind as one could hope to discover, but all too little in the way of human contacts to bring it alive. And the Ruskinian age, when the writer could dwell indefinitely on the beauties of nature without mortally boring his reader, is ended.

This time our stay in Vancouver, the city where all our journeys seemed to end, was mercifully brief. We were now to begin the final stage of our travels, in which we intended to return to the Doukhobor settlements in the Kootenays, to traverse some of the mountain roads and valleys we had missed on our previous trip and, as we came back towards the coast, to visit some Mennonite settlements in the Fraser Valley of which we had recently been told. It would mean going over some ground we had already covered, but that is inevitable in a country whose mountainous nature severely limits alternative routes.

We had in mind to travel first down the whole length of the Okanagan Valley, which previously we had merely touched at its southern end. Once again we had to catch a night train, this time on the Canadian National Railway, and since the next day was Saturday, and for some peculiar Sabbatarian reason trains are not allowed to run down the Okanagan Valley on a Sunday morning, it was a matter of leaving the same night or of killing a couple of aimless days. So we seized a taxi at the wharf, and were shuttled through the alleys which run like long mews behind the main streets of Vancouver, and reached the station with an hour to spare. We dined hastily in a coffee-bar where two fairies were engaged in some deep and bitter consultation. Then, since we knew that the next part of our journey would involve us in a fair amount of hitch-hiking into areas where the railway did not run and where buses were infrequent, we transferred a few necessities into a rucksack we had bought in Quesnel, stored our suitcases in the baggage office, and boarded the night train for Kamloops.

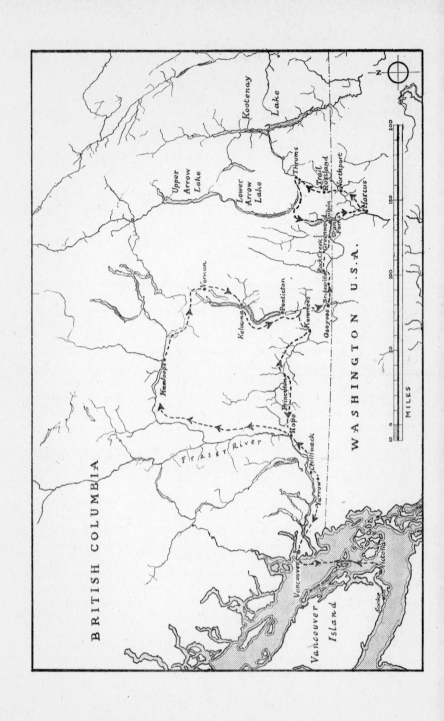

Part Four

KAMLOOPS remains for me the one elusive town in British Columbia, the one place to which I look back with a tantalised expectancy. It is not that we ever failed to reach it; on the contrary, during two years in Canada we passed through it three times, but on each occasion in the middle of the night, so that all we ever saw of the town was a railway yard illuminated by floodlights, a few houses and the lights of a restaurant across a kind of square decorated with spindly trees. Beyond that, all I can say of Kamloops belongs to hearsay and history—that it lies on the Thompson in a valley where the winds blow in such contrary manners that even the daring pilots who fly in the mountains often find it difficult to land, that it was one of the largest fur-trading depots a century ago, that it has had its turn as a smaller mining centre and now lives partly from its position as the largest railway junction in the interior of British Columbia. What Kamloops looks like, how its people live in their windy valley, are still as unknown to me as they were before I ever heard of the place.

It was the pitch dark of early morning as we alighted at Kamloops Junction on that Saturday morning. Once again the snow was falling with gentle persistence and lying in a cold slush on the platform. We stumped about in it for half an hour while a new train for the Okanagan was assembled, and then climbed on and tried to resume our broken sleep. Eventually, by the time all the shunting had been done and the train had finally started out along the southern branch of the Thompson River, dawn was breaking over another landscape of barren hills and cattle ranges.

Only seventy miles farther on, in the northern Okanagan, did we begin to see any intensive agricultural activity. There, around Armstrong, were the first orchards and dairy farms, and at each station the warehouses of various co-operative societies. Some of these organisations were surprisingly specialised, and at Armstrong we saw one which was restricted to pea-growers and another to cheese-makers. Indeed, as we were to have ample evidence during the morning, we were in an area where the

197

producer's co-operation had reached a very high degree of organisation, for through the whole length of this great valley (150 miles by road from Armstrong down to Osoyoos on the American border) co-operative marketing depots seem almost entirely to have replaced the capitalist wholesaler.

A few miles farther south we ran into lake country, and passed a chain of small sheets of water (small, that is, for Canada, since they would have looked large enough in Cumberland) among which the railway coiled its way, picking always the side which provided the most suitable ledges. Although this is a comparatively thickly farmed and populated district, there were many stretches of rocky forest along the shores of these waters, which carried a large winter population of ducks and other wildfowl.

Towards midday we ran through the thick belt of apple orchards which surrounds Kelowna. Now, in their winter bareness, they were as dull as only regular orchards of dwarf trees can look in the season when they carry no leaves or flowers or fruit. In the town itself we had to walk for nearly a mile down a long road which was bordered by many large co-operative warehouses where the packing and sorting of fruit from the whole valley is concentrated. Today they were lifeless, not a single workman moving among them, but for that whole mile the smell of sweet ripe apples was thick and penetrating on the air. Down the long, monotonous main street a dismal little Armistice Day procession of veterans moved to the tune of a pipe band, but most of the townspeople, wandering home to lunch after their holiday morning, paid them little attention. We went to the post office, expecting a letter from our Doukhobor friend in the Kootenays, but the building was closed for the day and we had to take a chance on whether our visit would be convenient. We crossed by the car ferry to the opposite side of Okanagan Lake, and here we took to the road.

At first we were rather fortunate in catching lifts. An old man with a tall Stetson and long drooping moustaches (the amiable elder of many a western film) carried us a couple of miles in an ancient Ford, recollecting as he went the bad winters of the past thirty years and the times when the ferry had been frozen hard in the lake. And then there was a hair-raising drunkard with a couple of bottles on the floor of his car, who was completely incapable of keeping a straight course on the road, which was covered with a thin icy sheet of snow; we were thoroughly relieved when he dropped us in a few minutes at the first of the lakeside settlements.

Now began a long stretch of walking, for, though there was a busy spurt of traffic every twenty minutes, corresponding with the times of the ferry, it consisted almost entirely of cars crammed full with people out to enjoy themselves for the day. Even the Indians were in a holiday mood, for a little horse-trap packed with a hilariously tipsy family overtook us, with a grave mounted cowboy, perched in an enormous Mexican saddle, bringing up the rear.

We walked through a belt of small craggy hills, covered thinly with trees and thrusting bare stone shoulders through the mantling snow. Here and there were pools, thick with bulrushes, between which the surface of the water was streaked with the first needles of thin ice; by the roadside the tall seedspikes of giant mullein stood up above the snow, with a peculiar resemblance to aloes standing out of the sand. At one spot we heard many bells tinkling, and a flock of several hundred sheep came over a hillside and down through a vast sloping orchard where the little trees stood out blackly against the snowy ground. We stood to watch the leading files, and then more and more came over until the little valley echoed with their bleating and the slope was alive with their moving bodies. Yet although we saw the last stragglers come down, no herdsman appeared, nor even a dog. The sheep had evidently been moved by some habitual impulse to seek the safety of the valley and the farmyard before the night fell and the wolves and cougars began to hunt.

Not far beyond this orchard a young scoutmaster picked us up and took us the rest of the way to the end of the lake. When we told him that we were thinking of hitch-hiking the whole way into the Kootenays, he looked grave. "You'll have to cross some bad mountain roads," he said. "There's only one way east out of this end of the Okanagan, and that's through Osoyoos over the mountains. It's a dirt road most of the way, and very narrow, and it'll be pretty dangerous with the snow. I doubt whether there'll be much traffic going over it at all. But if you do intend to travel that way I'd advise you to take the bus. It can hold the road much better than a car. And if the buses aren't running, give it up and go by the railway from Penticton."

We were a little dashed by this warning, since before we reached our destination at Thrums we should have to cross not one, but three ranges of mountains. However, we decided to push

on and to see for ourselves and, after leaving our pessimistic
scoutmaster in Penticton, we resolved to reach Osoyoos that night,
so that we should be able to set out first thing next morning across
the mountains.

The road towards the border was more crowded than ever with
packed cars of holiday-makers, coming so thickly that we had
little chance of attracting the attention of the few motorists who
might have room to take us, and after a while we began to despair
of getting very far that night. But eventually a trio of men stopped
and signalled us into their car. In dress and appearance they might
have fitted well into small gangster parts in a Hollywood film,
but actually they were three orchard workers, two Italians and a
Swede, who were out for their evening ride, and they very kindly
went several miles out of their way to put us on our road. As we
drove with them along the west shore of Skaha Lake—we recognised the white house of our German hosts of a month before
glittering high above the opposite bank—the Swede talked about
the autumnal beauty of the lakeside, which had lasted until a week
ago, and about the colour and perfume of the valley in the spring,
as each tree, with its special tint of pink and white, took its turn
in the flowering sequence. Only in the winter, he said, was the
valley dull and dead, for then the seasonal workers would depart
and the growers who had made anything like a reasonable profit
would lock up their houses and go to spend the winter in some
less extreme climate.

At the end of Skaha Lake the Okanagan River falls in a series
of cascades, and then it broadens out into marshy pools, which
have been turned into a game preserve. Here the wild swans
sailed white and sedate over the dark mirror of the calm waters as
we walked beside them. Then a last lift from a fruit-packer took
us down into the single sloping street of Osoyoos just after nightfall.

The hotel was a slightly gaudy, pink-washed place, with a beer
parlour on the ground floor which was packed with a crowd of
Armistice Day revellers. From the outside it did not seem at all a
promising place, but it proved one of the best hotels we ever encountered in Canada. We were given a very large room, with a
balcony overlooking a tree-shaded corner—there were still leaves
on the branches for the street lamp to shine through—and the
whole place was pleasantly furnished and had been decorated by
someone with an exceptionally good sense of colour.

In the restaurant a trio at the next table was engaged in a

noisy scene. A little fair man was cantankerously drunk, while his flashy sham-blonde wife was proposing to go off for the evening with another man, who made a rather sheepish and self-effacing third in the debate. After a long and incoherent argument, the woman and the second man departed, and the drunkard, left to himself, began a fantastic conversation, explaining his sad plight to a non-existent listener at whom he gazed fixedly across the table, and then replying in a totally different voice, with the answers which this interlocutor might be expected to make. At times the other person seemed to be his wife, at other times there was a third person to whom he appealed for support, and so the dialogue —or triologue—mounted into a grand confusion, until he suddenly fell asleep with his head hanging forward and his hair trailing down into the plate of stew before him.

We passed the evening in a little barn-like cinema, watching a satirical film on the American army. Between the main film and the shorts a notice was flashed on the screen; it was an appeal to the people of the town to gather for a building bee to complete the house of a man to whom the community owed a debt of gratitude for having rescued a drowning woman. I was reminded of the passage in *Typee* where Melville describes the natives working in common on one of their neighbours' houses. I do not know how the bee originated among the pioneer settlers in North America; it may have been born of necessity, but it may equally well have been borrowed from the Indians who, where they had houses at all, almost certainly helped each other to build them and equally probably accompanied their work with the feast which usually forms an added attraction at a working bee. But whatever the custom's origin, it seemed to me a much more sensible way of acknowledging a service to the community than by bestowing a Humane Society medal.

An old Indian walked out of the cinema before us when we left —at least, he looked old, for his aquiline face was lined and set, a gift for an academic sculptor. This face was crowned by a tall battered Stetson, and the bandy tightly-trousered legs ended in a pair of elaborately worked leather half-boots with high Cuban heels. But what really drew one's attention was a beautiful pair of shining silver spurs with many-spiked rowels, which glittered and chinked against the pavement as the Indian strutted down the street before us, the cynosure of all curious eyes in Osoyoos that evening.

14

He was a true plains horseman, probably a Kootenay who had strayed west into the Okanagan to get ranching work. The Kootenays, who still inhabit the district which bears their name, were originally a prairie tribe who had been driven over the Rockies by the Blackfeet and who, as long as the bison lasted, went through the passes every season to hunt the herds in the Albertan plains. They were the only tribe in British Columbia whose customs were not in some degree modified by the powerful influence of the Coastal culture; in so far as the new mountain environment would allow, they retained their old way of living and also the democratic social organisation of the prairie tribes. Their horsemanship was their salvation, for when their country was colonised fairly late in the nineteenth century, they took very easily to ranching and adapted themselves so quickly that they suffered neither the moral degeneration nor the physical diminution from which the other British Columbian tribes have only recently begun to recover.

Beyond the hotel, where the black waters of Osoyoos Lake heaved and sucked and threw back the broken reflections of lights in houses a mile away, we found a café where the buses stopped, and went in to ask the time of the service over the mountains to Rock Creek. There was only one, and, as our past experiences should have led us to expect, it went at three in the morning. Then and there we decided to put an end to night travelling, which had already robbed us of so much of the countryside, and to try our luck on the mountain road tomorrow. As we went out we looked over the lake to the east, and saw a light cutting a steep angle across the distant darkness. It was a car coming down from the pass, and it meant that the road was still open.

34.

Early next day, in brilliant sunshine, we skirted the lake and crossed the bridge over the Okanagan River, where a timber lorry picked us up and carried us over the valley flats to the base of the range. There we started our walk uphill; the road ran steep and straight along the side of the mountain. Contrary to the fears which the scoutmaster had planted in our minds, it was a wide new road, but we did not know how far it would continue in this manner, and already it was covered with snow which in places had packed down into a glassy, slippery surface.

Soon we could see the whole valley laid out beneath us. Snow had fallen again during the night, but now only a few thin bars of cloud obscured the glistening ridges of Snowy Mountain and Windy Peak on the far side of the valley. Southward we could just distinguish Oroville, the first town over the border; Osoyoos, with its tiny main street and its few side roads crammed in among the orchards, lay exposed like a map beneath our feet. We could see every car that came out of it; there were not many at this early hour, and some of them stopped at farms or sawmills outside the town. Even those which came up the mountainside defied our hopes, since their drivers had evidently no desire to halt upon this glassy slope, and when one eventually stopped it was a lorry which could only offer a perch on the flat open deck. Needless to say, it was a bitterly cold trip. By the time the driver let us off at the head of the pass, after half an hour's ride, we were almost relieved at the necessity to walk for another half-hour through the thick snow, until a couple of hunters stopped and took us the rest of the way over the mountain into Rock Creek. We were glad to reach this spot, since on the downward slope the road had in fact degenerated into the narrow, dangerous track the scoutmaster had predicted; the day before a lorry had somersaulted down into a ravine, killing the driver.

Rock Creek was no more than a hamlet with a hotel and a store. Now it is the depot for the loggers who work in the mountains around the higher reaches of the Kettle River, but during the last century seven million dollars in gold had been taken from the stream beds in the vicinity. That was chickenfeed in comparison with the Cariboo, but it was apparently enough to create a tantalising legend of a hidden mother lode which, so the hunters told us, almost every man bred in the neighbourhood had sought at least once in his life.

Mother lodes are to gold maniacs what mirages are to desert travellers. Even now, when the rich diggings of the past have long been worked out, and when no new strike of any significance has been made in British Columbia for a decade, one will still meet men—and not merely old men—who go out doggedly into the mountains in search of gold. And, though they may keep body and soul together by labouring frantically for the little piles of dust which just "make wages", this is not what they are really seeking. They are led by the theory of a great lode away up in the mountains from which the gold in the streams and the gravel beds was originally washed down in the distant past. I do not know enough geology to express an opinion whether such a mother lode exists, but I am certain that no trace of it has ever been found. Yet every prospector, when he sets out to work on a new spot and sees the "colours" glinting in the bottom of his pan, allows himself the brief thrill of believing that here at last he may have found the key to Eldorado.

Just outside Rock Creek we encountered one of those pieces of luck which make up for all the discomforts of hitch-hiking. A little orange truck drew up beside us and the driver shouted, "Where you folks headin' for?" When we said Thrums, he replied, "I'm going right through to Nelson. I'll drop you on my way." So the remaining 180 miles of our journey were assured.

He was a road contractor, a solid Ontarian with no eccentricities or peculiarities to fix him very deeply in the memory, but his knowledge of the country made him a pleasant travelling companion. For instance, he helped us to piece together the story of Greenwood, a little town at which we stopped about forty miles along the road.

We had already travelled through it by railway, but from the train we had not seen enough to make it appear more than an ordinary decayed mining town. The approach by road up the other side of the valley and into the centre of the settlement was a good deal more spectacular—though under no circumstances could one call it other than an unlovely place. It lay cupped among bare and fume-scarred hills, with a huge black slag-heap filling up a segment of the valley, and the rusting remains of the deserted smelter plant behind it. Perched on the hillsides were big empty Edwardian houses, with rococo belvederes and Gothic turrets and fretted porches—a disused set from an Orson Welles film. And in the streets there were many deserted shops and a couple of large brick buildings which looked as though a demolition gang had got tired in the middle of pulling them down.

Yet the town seemed fairly well populated, and most of the people, we were surprised to see, were Japanese, clearly distinguishable from the Chinese by their paler and more delicately cut features. They ran many of the shops and restaurants, and though they looked rather out of place in this dour valley, they had clearly made themselves very much at home there.

We learnt that they were the remnant of a group of 1,200 Japanese who were brought here from the coast after Pearl

Harbour. This forced emigration was, to say the least, a rather un-savoury incident. It is, indeed, quite possible that some of the émigrés were spies and fifth-columnists, but most of them were industrious market gardeners, fishermen and shopkeepers, and many were even Canadians by birth. No attempt was made to dis-criminate between good and bad—or hostile and unhostile—Japanese, but the worst feature of the whole affair was that the businesses and farms and fishing boats of these uprooted people were forcibly sold to their white and Chinese competitors for a mere fraction of their true value, and the deportees, when they reached Greenwood, had to start again almost from nothing.

The town itself was one of the old mining towns which had come down very far in the world. A prosperous copper centre in the early days of the century, it had begun to decline when the mine was closed down as unprofitable in 1918, and for many years it had lived on the edge of extinction, a few storekeepers and a handful of old people surviving precariously in the half-deserted streets. The Japanese came into this derelict town and gave it new life. With little capital they began logging in the hills, then they founded a sawmill and a box factory, and started to open up the dead businesses of the town. The natives of the place were at first hostile, but when they realised that the Japanese were ordinary trustworthy working people just like themselves, the tension dis-appeared and a co-operation was established between the two races which has continued to the present day.

Out of Greenwood we ran easily over the low range of moun-tains into Grand Forks. From here the Canadian road goes on over Cascade Mountain, but the roadbuilder was not anxious to travel that way; he said that it was no better than a crumbling lane, much more dangerous than any part of the road from Osoyoos to Rock Creek. Instead, he proposed to drive down over the Ameri-can frontier and make an eighty-mile loop through Washington State, which would run us around the bottom end of the range and bring us back to Canadian territory in the neighbourhood of Rossland. So we crossed into the United States at Laurier, a small frontier station with two pairs of officials sitting in their re-spective wooden sheds on either side of the border. The Canadians looked officiously through our wallets in the hope of finding smuggled currency; the Americans asked merely where we were going, exchanged a few wisecracks, and let us through. "You can consider yourselves lucky you don't have a Russian name," the roadbuilder commented as we drove on down the American end of the Kettle Valley. "I came over with a colleague, a man whose family have been in the Canadian prairies for more than sixty years. But he had the bad luck to be called Morosov, and didn't they put him through the mill! Ever since then he's preferred the bad mountain roads to that kind of treatment."

The countryside in this northern part of Washington was little different from that over the border—the same mountains covered with dark forests of spruce, the same deep, narrow valleys, the same patches of land denuded and scarred by the logger, the same apple orchards and little shabby wooden settlements. American prosperity had certainly not reached this corner.

Just beyond its confluence with the Kettle River, we crossed the Columbia and turned north to follow it back towards the border. We ferried across at a place called Northport—once again ramshackle houses, muddy main streets, and more dreariness and dirt than we had seen anywhere else. Apart from the scenery, which at times was excellent, the only good thing about this part of Washington was the well-surfaced roads; Canadian territory made itself immediately felt by a great squeaking and straining of the springs as the truck lurched into the first of several miles of deep potholes. Nearer to Rossland, indeed, a certain amount of reconstruction work was going on, and for a while we had to leave the highway and traverse a complicated network of old logging roads, barely wide enough for a single car to find its way through the returning scrub of the side woods. Even the roadbuilder found his professional loyalty wearing thin, and began to curse the fluctuating pattern of political interests which, he claimed, always tended to interfere with any rational programme of road construction in the province.

Rossland is another example of the mining town that has been saved from becoming a ghost by the advent of some unexpected outside influence. At the turn of the century it was one of the greatest and wildest boom towns in this part of North America. The prospector Ross Thomson found the rich copper and gold lodes in the middle of a primeval wilderness, and even in 1894 the site of the mines was still almost impenetrable bush. Two years later a whole frontier city had arisen, with forty hotels and saloons and three theatres—a larger and even gayer and more reckless city than Barkerville had ever been. In Sourdough Alley the bands in the saloons and dance halls played twenty-four hours a day, dog

fights were staged in the streets, and there were brutal boxing
matches in the theatres. In one year four million dollars in gold
alone was taken out of the mines, but gradually over two decades
the veins became exhausted. Rossland would have died, and its
buildings fallen into complete ruin, if the clear atmosphere had not
tempted the workers in the smelter plant to get away from the
fume and smoke of Trail, and so in the past twenty years it under-
went a rehabilitation as a dormitory town. Today it is a place of
not unpleasant bungalows, with a core of hideous masonry buildings which have survived from the boom days and a few derelict
mine sheds in the outskirts.

"But there's still plenty of gold there," our companion asserted
excitedly. "It's just built on gold. There was a guy who bought a
little house there not long ago, and he decided to dig himself a
basement. He had a hunch about the soil that was coming out,
and he started to pan it. He cleared four thousand dollars and half
paid for his house." This was the kind of story we had already
heard in some of these old gold towns, and it probably had only
some slight foundation in fact, for if it had been completely true
the whole population of Rossland would have burrowed like
moles into their gardens in the hope of making small fortunes in
their spare time. It was much more likely that he had come across
a few small nuggets and that the story of the four thousand
dollars had grown snowball fashion from this small beginning.

By the time we ran down towards Trail it was already growing
dark, with tier after tier of lights falling away from the monster
plant towards the streets below. We skirted the town, drove
through Castlegar and past Brilliant with the roadbuilder talking
hard about his adventures among the knife-toting white trash of
Georgia. Eventually, more by instinct than by any ability to read
the roadside signs on such a pitch-dark night, we pulled up dead
opposite Pete M.'s house, and parted from our genial companion, who stood by the wayside and bade us farewell as if we
were ancient comrades instead of chance acquaintances of the
road.

35.

Pete was expecting us after all, and a great Doukhobor meal
was immediately placed on the table. G.B.S. had just died, we
were told, and there had been a Puerto Rican attempt on the life

of Truman. We had been so much out of the currency of daily news since our travels began that the events struck us with a surprising force, like the intrusion of a world of death and violence upon the little globe of observation and criticism we had placed about us, like deep-sea scientists, in travelling.

During the next days, Pete told us, we should be meeting plenty of people, and he thought we should be able to get a fair idea of what was going on in the minds of the average Doukhobors. It was a pity that we had not come a couple of days ago, since there had then been a large meeting of the orthodox members of the sect to discuss the re-founding of the Christian Community of Universal Brotherhood.

I was very interested to hear that the Doukhobors still talked in terms of community, and asked him whether he thought anything would come of the discussion.

"Perhaps not for the present. But I believe that some day the communal life will be resumed, and then it will strengthen and unite the Doukhobors, and turn them once again into a moral force in the world."

The evening ended with Pete talking about his years in prison, and when he said that he had benefited from them by having for the first time in his life the leisure to read widely and to set his thoughts in order, I was reminded of the words of another, more celebrated prisoner. "I know ten times more than I knew three years ago, and everything ten times better; I realise positively what I have gained, and truly I do not know what I have lost." It was Proudhon, a man whose ideas were in many ways not far removed from those of the Doukhobors, and it showed, as the experience of Pete and the other Doukhobors had demonstrated, that imprisonment may demoralise the weak, but the independent man is often made stronger by it.

All the next day visitors were coming and going in Pete's home. Though no reference was made to the fact, I think most of them had come out of curiosity. The first, as we were at breakfast, was a cheerful old woman who was dressed in the peasant clothes of the older generation. She spoke only a few words of English, but with the help of the others who chipped in here and there to translate a sentence, we got along very well with her. She told us that she lived by herself, and grew vegetables and fruit in her garden to sell in the towns. When Inge asked her if she did not find it very hard, the old woman gave her a very shrewd look of conspiracy. "I hate housework," she laughed, "but it is good to work with the earth."

Her attitude was actually not an unusual one among the older Doukhobor women, who were brought up to regard work as a natural and inevitable part of life, who rarely developed any kind of intellectual interest, and who to this day carry on working in the fields and gardens so long as they are physically able. It was the women of this heroic generation who, when the Doukhobors first arrived in the prairies and had no money to buy horses, hitched themselves to the plough in teams of twelve and tilled the soil while their men went away to earn money on railway construction work.

This old woman had been a girl of eighteen when the Doukhobors emigrated to Canada, and for her, after all these years in a foreign land, Russia was still home, the country she loved and remembered most vividly by the flower-strewn meadows in the Caucasian mountains. Neither the iniquities which the Tsars had inflicted on her people nor the trials of the Doukhobors who remained in Communist Russia had dimmed her desire for her homeland or the hope that her sect might return to their native valleys before she died.

We found, indeed, that many of the orthodox Doukhobors had this attitude towards Russia. They were far from being Communists, at least in the Marxist sense, but they still regarded Russia as the land in which their sect would eventually fulfil its messianic role—the salvation of the world. One of them remarked, with that lapse into an irrational belief in prophecies and portents which one comes to expect even in the most rational-minded Doukhobors, that Peter Chestiakov, the son of Verigin, had foretold that after the death of Stalin they would all return to complete their destiny in Russia.

After breakfast two more visitors arrived. The first was a man with a gentle, clear-skinned peasant face and long grey drooping moustaches; his companion looked more like a Paris-Russian art dealer than a sectarian enthusiast. Pete went into a long discussion with them in Russian, during which the newcomers kept looking towards us with great curiosity. In a little while he came over and explained that they were Sons of Freedom from the village of Gilpin, and that if we would like to visit them the next day, they would call the villagers together to meet us. We accepted, and the peasant invited us to stay in his house. After they had gone Pete explained that he had asked the two Sons of Freedom to make sure that there was no undressing at the meeting, since the enthusiasts of both sexes were liable to divest whenever they became a little excited. We rather regretted this, since we had wished to meet the radical Doukhobors freely, and as near to their natural state of behaviour as we could. "What did they say when you asked them?" I put in. "Oh, they said they'd do their best to persuade the other people. But they couldn't guarantee anything. It all depends how excited the meeting gets."

Pete's land, we had already seen on our past visit, was covered with a small village of cabins of various kinds and sizes, and this time we discovered their purposes. Some were storehouses, one was a workshop, and one was a bath-house, where Pete suggested we might care to take a Russian steam-bath, a custom of which the Doukhobors are very fond. Having already found by experiment among the Vancouver Island Doukhobors how exhausting these exercises can be for those who have not been reared to them by a lifetime of practice, we gently declined.

Others of the cabins were inhabited, some of them by members of Pete's family and one by a saintly-looking recluse, a Czech mystic who had been attracted to the Doukhobors. He lived without money, and Pete gave him whatever he needed in return for any services he chose to render, such as cutting wood or occasionally helping in the garden. He was as shy as a deer, and though he always smiled with the greatest benignity wherever we saw him, he never gave us the least opportunity to talk with him.

That morning Pete and his sons were busy laying pipes from a spring in the hillside, in order to provide a direct water supply to the house, and Doukhobors from the neighbouring houses came strolling out in ones and twos to help and to give advice. They were very amiable, but it was not always easy to talk to them, since some of the older men had only the most broken English, but we learnt enough to assure us that, here at least, the traditions of the sect had a very strong influence upon their lives. They retained all their old distrust of authority, and their pacifism was still a central point in their faith. Indeed, it was perhaps the most persistent of their beliefs, for even among those who had relaxed some of the other Doukhobor tenets there was a very obstinate objection to taking any part in military activities. I have yet to hear of a Doukhobor who compromised on this fundamental issue, and the ambiguities of accepting partial service which one finds among many other war-resisting sects, such as the adventists, are quite unknown among these dogged Russian sectarians.

The puritanical rejections of smoking, drinking and flesh-eating are no longer consistently followed by all members, though many Doukhobors still consider such a renunciation as essential for the proper practice of their faith; our hosts were particularly strict on all these points of abstention, and, while we enjoyed their vegetarian food and were not in the least concerned about the absence of liquor, both of us suffered under the extreme moral pressure which was exerted on the question of smoking. With their belief in individual freedom, they would never have thought of actually prohibiting one to smoke in their house, but the atmosphere of disapproval was so strong that we would sneak out like schoolboys into the more secluded parts of the garden whenever we felt the desire for a cigarette becoming too strong to resist.

In the evening one of the younger men came in with a gramophone and a bundle of records. He thought we might be interested in some of the Doukhobor psalms. We would hear many of their traditional songs when we went to the Sons of Freedom the next day, but these were recent examples which he and some friends had recorded in California.

Hymns and psalms play a vital part in Doukhobor life; they are the poetry and music of the sect, the repository of its religious beliefs, and the means of transmitting its historical traditions. Both tunes and words are transmitted orally from generation to generation, and some of the hymns certainly date from the very beginnings of the sect, while the principal events of its past, the moral and physical struggles, the persecutions and migrations, are all celebrated in these memorised chronicles. But it is not merely a question of honouring the past; the hymns and psalms represent a living and actually growing folk tradition, since, down to this very day, the adventures of the Doukhobors are perpetuated in song. The psalms we heard that day described a demonstration against war which the Sons of Freedom had conducted in Vancouver during 1940, and told of the way in which they had been attacked and beaten by the police and then taken away to serve their years in prison. To anyone who understood Russian it must have seemed much more immediate because the singers were men who had actually taken part in the event and who had made the song for their fellows and for posterity. We, unfortunately, could not follow the words, but were fascinated by the strange, half-Asiatic music, with its unfamiliar harmonies and a kind of tragic wildness which seemed to symbolise all the rebellious obstinacy of this sect of God-intoxicated rebels.

36.

We set off for Gilpin the next morning; having formed a theory that no road is as bad as the pessimists assert, we proposed to hitch-hike over the road over Cascade Mountain which the road-builder had refused to take two days before. Our hosts, however, were appalled at the idea. They impressed on us that it was the most dangerous road in the whole of southern British Columbia, and that even in the summer nobody travelled that way if he could avoid it. It was not merely the road itself: no settlement of any kind existed for the forty miles between Rossland and the Kettle Valley, and if a blizzard came on and there were no traffic—both of which possibilities were very likely—we might well be caught in the middle of the mountains with no shelter at hand. At last we were convinced and agreed to take the railway from Castlegar.

The young Doukhobor who had played us the records of psalms the previous evening drove us down to Castlegar, and on the way took us through the old community village of Brilliant. Now very little was left of this centre of Doukhobor activity, and this was due largely to the internecine struggles which broke out during the 1930's between various factions of the sect. Of the communal buildings only the co-operative store was left, still carrying on its original function, but where the house of Peter Verigin had stood, and on the sites of the warehouses and factories, only the vestiges of concrete foundations remained. These buildings had all been burnt down, at one time or another, by Sons of Freedom who had chosen this rather dramatic and drastic way of trying to detach their fellows from the materialism which they felt was clogging the sect's activities and preventing a return to the original purity of its intentions. Up on the hillside above the settlement was the ugly concrete mass of Verigin's tomb, and this too had suffered at the hands of these puritans, who had carried their iconoclasm, with the aid of dynamite, to its logical end of destroying a symbol around which orthodoxy and stagnation might be built up.

Our companion was rather contemptuous of this extremism. He thought that though the ideas of the Sons of Freedom might be right, their success was only negated by the use of such violent means, which merely brought discredit on the Doukhobor movement as a whole. My impulse was to agree with him, but I decided that it would be much fairer to reserve my opinion until we had actually met the Sons of Freedom and discussed these matters directly with them.

So we boarded the train at Castlegar and travelled in reverse the same trip, beside the Arrow Lake, over the mountains and down by Christina Lake, as we had taken when we first came to the Kootenays. A new element was given to the fascinating colouring of the Arrow Lake by the snow which whitened the beaches and flecked the yellow rocks, while the drifts on the mountainside more than once revealed the tracks of deer which concealed themselves in this upland wilderness. Late in the afternoon the train ran down into the valley and we alighted at the halt of Gilpin, a tiny shelter beside which one stepped on to the gravel of the track.

On this side of the river there was no settlement, but we could see the little brown Doukhobor houses on the far side and walked down over a pasture dotted with rotting tree-stumps to the edge of the wide ravine which the water had scooped out at this spot. Across the hundred-yard gap a couple of disquietingly thin-looking wires stretched between wooden tripods on either shore, and we realised that we should have to make the trip by an aerial ferry which looked of the most primitive kind. There was nobody to meet us, and we waited for a moment, at a loss as to how the apparatus was operated. Then we saw a little group of people running down through the field on the opposite side, shouting and waving to us as they came. They gathered around the tripod, and then a kind of crib came swinging over the chasm, and in a moment the peasant we had met at Pete's house two days before stepped out and invited us to take our places in the aerial boat, as he called it. It was nothing more than a shallow, rickety wooden box, about six feet long, with half of one side missing. We crouched apprehensively in it, and then it was running back, tilting precariously as we leaned sideways to avoid the wire that whizzed beside our shoulders; fifty or sixty feet below the river ran shallowly but tumultuously over a bed of sharp and massive rocks, and we were relieved to step out on solid land and shake hands with the group of men and boys in overalls and old women in black shawls who had gathered out of mingled curiosity and hospitality.

During our day at this settlement we met many people, but I

certainly cannot remember all their Russian surnames. However, the Doukhobors are a simple and informal people, and I am sure they would be the last to object if I call them by their Christian names alone. The peasant-like man who was to be our host was called Alexei, and we set off with him down the mile-long road of the village towards his house.

All the dwellings in this village of radicals were low, single-storied houses, covered with unpainted shingles which gave them a rather drab external appearance. But the gardens of vegetables and fruit bushes were extremely neat, and when we stepped into Alexei's house it was like leaving Canada altogether and entering Tolstoy's Russia. There were the whitewashed mud walls and the massive, plain homemade tables and benches of a typically Caucasian peasant home; everything was simple, almost ascetic in its lack of unessentials, yet the total effect was one of a surprisingly pleasing sufficiency.

Alexei explained, rather than apologised for, the unelaborateness of his home. The Sons of Freedom, he said, set no store by possessions, which they regard as a means of enslavement. People who wished to own many things were tied down by work and material anxieties. He and his friends, on the other hand, went out and did seasonal work, such as fruit-picking and logging, for three or four months of the year; that allowed them to buy everything they could not grow, and the rest of the time they could spend cultivating their land and their spiritual lives.

I was curious to know whether this extremist group had retained any more of the community organisation than their fellow-Doukhobors, and whether their contempt for possessions involved any renunciation of individual ownership. Alexei shook his head sadly. No, even they had not yet returned to the ideal of communal ownership. But there was one thing in which they refused to acknowledge individual possession, and that was the land. It sounded like an echo of Gerrard Winstanley when he went on to say that the land, like the air, was the gift of God, that no man had created it by his effort, and therefore it should be freely available for all men to use.

This, indeed, was not the only occasion when we felt as if time had slipped back and we were talking to a sectarian of the Reformation, for, like the chiliastic radicals of that age, the Doukhobor enthusiasts have a bewildering habit of mingling the most astute and logical criticism of contemporary society with the most apocalyptic conceptions of their own historical role, and our conversations with them were continually thrown out of joint by these abrupt transitions from the rational to the visionary, and vice versa.

To return to the question of the land, I asked Alexei how in practice they managed to avoid recognising possession. He said that it had all been quite simple. About ten years ago they came to Gilpin, squatted on a piece of Government land, and nobody had tried to turn them off. They had put up individual houses, and each family cultivated its own plot of ground, but none of them recognised or claimed any property rights, or paid any rent or taxes, which the authorities had given up trying to collect. Use, in fact, constituted the only title, and if a family left its house, anybody who chose could move into it and use it as long as he wished.

Alexei had just finished this explanation when a slim, dark young man came into the house. This was Mitya, his son, who had just emerged from prison under the amnesty. I asked him how the Doukhobors had been treated, and he answered that they had actually been much better off than they had expected. They lived together in Quonset huts, they were given books and radios, they ate vegetarian food, and they were not required to do work of any kind. It was clear that the authorities, remembering the total failure of coercive methods in the past, had gone out of the way on this occasion to avoid any unnecessary trouble with their prisoners.

But this relatively enlightened treatment had by no means allayed the bitterness which these people still felt over the way in which they had been handled in the past. Alexei's wife, a jolly, broad old woman, brought to mind the time during the 1930's when there were widespread nude parades and several hundred Doukhobors of both sexes were sent for long terms to a prison camp near Vancouver—for Canadian law is so extreme in its Grundyism that a sentence of three years' hard labour is imposed for appearing nude in public, even if this is done within a purely Doukhobor village. While this mass imprisonment of the adults took place, the children—even the small babies—were taken away from their parents and put into reformatories and industrial schools. Some of the younger children died, and many of them were brutally treated; Mitya was among them and recollected the way in which he and his fellows were beaten and kicked by the officials of these institutions. Such incidents of the past are still very vivid in the memories of the Doukhobors, and make them naturally distrustful of any approach, however friendly in appearance, that may be made by the Government and their representatives.

After the excellent evening meal Alexei told us that the Sons of Freedom—there were about two hundred in this particular village —would be gathering for the meeting that had been arranged. He and his son and daughter were to accompany us. About half a mile down the road we stopped at a building which was larger than any of the houses but had the same drab external appearance. Alexei pushed open the door, and we entered a simple wooden hall, with rows of crowded benches down the side, and in the open aisle a table bearing a loaf of bread, a cellar of salt, and a jug of water, the Doukhobor symbols of hospitality and spiritual brotherhood.

Many people had already gathered, the men on one side, the women on the other, and as we entered they rose, bowed and greeted us in Russian. I must add here that this was not a sign of deference to us individually; it is the custom during a meeting to bow whenever a new arrival happens to come in, to show reverence to the God within each man. A thin old man whose eyes glittered amiably through steel-rimmed spectacles came up and led Inge and me to a small seat at the head of the hall, behind the table. The Sons of Freedom had evidently been waiting for us, since as soon as we arrived this elder began to lead them in communal prayer.

Doukhobors have no priests or pastors, and, while one of the elders usually begins the prayers, this is not always the case; I even remember one meeting on Vancouver Island in which the service was led throughout by the children. In any case, once the prayers have been started, they go on in the manner of a Quaker meeting, and anybody can start praying as the spirit moves him, though the form of the prayers is usually traditional.

We now had an opportunity to glance surreptitiously, like boys peeping through their hands in church, at the celebrated Sons of Freedom, whose name had become a symbol of terror and nihilism to every respectable, law-fearing, tax-paying and church-going Canadian citizen. A more inoffensive-looking group it would have been hard to imagine. On the whole, they seemed like any other assembly of sectarian peasants saying their evening prayers, and it was not until the singing began that one realised the full intensity of their zeal. Their hymns, sung by a hundred voices that had been trained since childhood, far surpassed in magnificence and strength

anything we had expected from the records which had been played
to us on the previous day. These were the traditional songs, commemorating the forerunners, and they combined the power and
weight of orthodox Russian religious music with a liberating
passion, which doubtless sprang partly from the tempestuous experiences of the Doukhobors and partly from their long contact
with the wild half-Asiatic mountaineers of the Caucasus.

The voices of these singers had a surprisingly resonant quality,
and their complicated harmonies gave a full and sonorous effect
almost like that of an organ. The psalms seemed to surge in great
waves of rhythm, and I felt myself becoming so moved and elated
that I could well understand how the Doukhobors brought themselves by means of music to the pitch of religious enthusiasm in
which they would perform their sensational acts of defiance and
destruction. Indeed, I expected at any moment to see some of the
exalted old women beginning to throw off their clothes in the
emotion of the moment, but they had evidently been well
schooled by Alexei, and nothing of the kind happened.

The hymns were followed by more prayers, and at the end of
these the whole assembly suddenly fell on their knees and touched
the floor with their foreheads, a startling Orientalism which we
gathered afterwards was a symbolical adoration of the immanent
God. Then they calmly rose, dusted their knees, and sat down on
the benches, while the elder suggested that we might care to ask
them some questions about their beliefs, which they would answer
to the best of their ability.

The Doukhobors seemed to have a refreshing lack of false
reverence; they evidently did not regard their meeting house as in
any way a sacred building, and once the service was over they
settled down to talk to us in the most amiably informal way. They
had none of the pompous intolerance of the typical fanatic, and
showed a rather abundant sense of humour from which they did
not hold themselves immune. I had looked forward with some
apprehension to this meeting, but in fact I enjoyed it a great deal
more than any of the other interviews we conducted on our
travels.

Naturally, we started by asking the reasons for the burnings
and nude parades with which the Sons of Freedom had been
associated for so long in the public mind. They explained that the
idea behind both forms of demonstration had been one of renunciation. A man wanted to protest against something—it might,

15

for instance, be the drifting of the world towards another war, which was the cause of their last manifestation. It seemed unreasonable to expect other people to do something unless one were ready to make a personal sacrifice to demonstrate one's own sincerity. So a Doukhobor would burn his house to the sound of hymns, and while this was going on he would throw away his clothes to show that he was ready to deprive himself literally of everything to achieve the good he desired. It certainly seemed a desperate kind of symbolism, but perhaps no more so than many other forms of renunciation. After all, the Doukhobor who burns his house for the good of humanity is little stranger or more incomprehensible to *l'homme moyen sensuel* than the revolutionary who throws away his life for the same cause or the monk who forsakes the world for a problematical heavenly future.

However, it seemed that all this kind of activity belonged to the past. The Sons of Freedom had received a new leader, named Sorokin, who had come from Europe as a displaced person and whom they, unlike the rest of the Doukhobors, regarded as the inspired successor to Peter Verigin. He had persuaded them that any kind of violence was wrong and that they must achieve their ends by passive means. Those who were released from prison had bound themselves not to indulge in any further manifestation, and they intended to keep to this pledge.

The mention of a new leader opened another perplexing aspect of Doukhobor beliefs. According to their basic ideas, all men are free, all men carry the spirit of God within them, and none should submit to the rule of an earthly leader. It was difficult to see how this fitted in with the succession of leaders who had dominated their movement like petty Popes throughout its historical period. The answers we received did not contribute materially to our enlightenment. The Doukhobors, we were assured, had no leaders in the ordinary sense of the word, that is to say, leaders with temporal power. But they regarded some men as particularly inspired by the spirit of God, just as the man-Jesus was inspired, and these men, while they lived, became spiritual leaders. The Doukhobors were not obliged to follow their guidance, we were told, but it was always for their own good to do so. As for material affairs, these leaders had no authority whatsoever. They merely expressed their opinions as ordinary men and counted for no more than any other member of the sect.

We found such statements hard to reconcile with the undoubted material power which Peter Verigin had wielded for thirty years, or even with the way in which the new leader was evidently influencing the actions of the Sons of Freedom. But when we tried to go further we found ourselves involved in a tangle of philosophical ambiguities which it would have puzzled a mediæval schoolman to unravel, and we soon gave up our attempt to convince these supreme irrationalists of the need for consistency.

Yet, as soon as we came to questions of practical politics, the Sons of Freedom, like many of the other Doukhobors we had met, showed a surprisingly shrewd and realistic grasp of the contemporary situation. They were interested in peace movements abroad, and they put forward a sound line of argument on the causes of war, which they attributed to nationalism and to propertied interests, with selfishness as the motivating force behind it all. Root selfishness out of the human spirit, and peace and brotherhood would follow as naturally as night follows day.

Towards Russia their attitude was certainly clearer than that of the orthodox sectarians. They appeared to realise very thoroughly that the Communist state would be an even worse place for a sect of their kind than Canada, and they had no desire to return there. As one of their spokesmen remarked, they felt that the place where a man lived out his life was unimportant—it was his spiritual attitude that really counted. As for the Communists, the Sons of Freedom had as little use for them as they had for any other governmentalists, and Alexei declared that the Stockholm Peace Petition was merely a political device to gull sincere people into accepting Communist leadership. Yet at the same time they clung to their own Russian tradition, they only learnt English during their inevitable contacts with the outside world, and there was a thoroughly Dostoievskian ring in the remark of one man who said that if the Doukhobors gave up their language they would lose their identity and their faith.

The discussion was all very good-humoured and friendly, for the Sons of Freedom had little of the intolerance one usually encounters in sectarians, though I think this may have been due mostly to their serene confidence in the unassailability of their own beliefs.

Walking back to our host's house, we expressed to Mitya our feeling of the ambiguity of some of the Doukhobor attitudes. He admitted it without any demur. The Doukhobors never claimed to have any logical doctrine. How could they, when every man

must decide according to his own conscience, and when the conscience itself was irrational and illogical? Even the leaders spoke
often in parables, and for these each man must find his own interpretation. We should never accept what any individual Doukhobor said, but we should talk to many of them and then, out of
their varying opinions, we would discover the essential spirit of
their movement. Some went too far ahead, some stayed too far
behind, and this explained their divisions, which were inevitable
where there was freedom, yet the Doukhobors were fundamentally united, and eventually, when they had realised this unity in
practice, they would be enabled to reach the Kingdom of God on
Earth. For, he remarked in a sudden return to earthly considerations, the Second Coming was no fancy business about Christ descending from the clouds. It meant the establishment of real peace
and goodwill among men, and the end of selfishness and strife,
and for that all Doukhobors strove in their own way.

Alexei owned an ancient motor truck and the next morning he
offered to take us into Grand Forks, making what I am sure was
merely a hospitable excuse that he had to pick up his mail at the
post office. So, after a breakfast of Gargantuan proportions—
enormous round loaves of fresh home-baked bread, millet porridge, cherries and huckleberries—we set out along a little dirt road
which the Sons of Freedom had cut through the forest to connect
their village with Grand Forks, more than seven miles away. In
good weather it might have been a safe but bumpy road, but in
the snow it was excessively hazardous, and the light empty truck
skidded and danced around the corners and ran erratically along
the precipitous riverside verges, until we began to think that the
bed of the Kettle River was a more likely destination than Grand
Forks. But our host always turned deftly out of the most dis-
astrous-looking skids, appearing to enjoy every minute of the
hectic progress and all the time talking calmly about Doukhobor
healing methods, for, as he told us, they had their own bone-
setters who were as good as any trained osteopath, and their
people rarely went to doctors, but preferred to cure themselves by
natural means.

We left him on the post office steps; as we shook hands, he said
that if we ever cared to return for a while to study the Doukhobors, they might be able to find an empty house for us in their
village. It was a suggestion I have been tempted to take up more
than once since I left them, for, despite the curious mingling of

simplicity and ambiguity which runs through their whole lives—
at least, to an observer brought up in a more or less rationalist
tradition—I found a fascinating independence and vigour in these
peasants whose fathers had given the most sensational example of
a spontaneous mass resistance to Tsarist oppression and who had
inspired such eminent Russian thinkers as Tolstoy and Kropotkin.
It seemed to me that they had still a great deal to say in criticism
of a world which has gone too far and too long in its pursuit of
material wealth and power. Perhaps, with all their failures to construct an ideal commonwealth, they can offer no more in the way
of enduring practical achievement than Winstanley with his
abortive experiment on St. George's Hill or Owen with his long
series of gallant failures, but it is less the achievement that counts
in such things than the inspiration, and I have yet to see a group of
people who have been more devoted, in and out of season, to the
vital task in modern society of maintaining the status of the individual against the collectivity, of the rebellious minority against
the tyrannical majority.

37.

We were now intent on making our way as quickly as possible
back to Osoyoos and then striking across the Similkameen Valley
to the recently opened mountain highway from Princeton to Hope.
It was bleak travelling that lay before us after we left our Doukhobor friend. Gilpin, in the shelter of the woods and hills, had not
shown the full rigour of the day, but in the open valley at Grand
Forks the wind became bitter and unavoidable, and, warmly
clothed though we were, the piercing cold had chilled us through
before we had even left the town. I am sure we did not do anything
like justice to Grand Forks, which is one of the most pleasant
settlements in the Kootenays, as we trudged dismally through its
outskirts, but even so we were very much impressed by a large
and extremely well-designed school which had just been completed
there. Canadian education is rather shaky in its pedagogic methods,
but the recently built schools which we encountered in British
Columbia certainly displayed surprising architectural ability; I can
think offhand of at least four new schools there which were as well
designed as the best in Europe—and much better than other
Canadian public buildings. They were functionally adequate,
pleasant to look at, light and airy, and imaginative in their use of
the country's native materials.

But such thoughts did not provide much solace as we tramped along the valley road with the wind cutting across from the northern hills. We had missed the early traffic, if there ever had been any, and there was not even a chance of a lift as we walked on past the sawmills on the edge of the residential district and then into the final outlying belt of Doukhobor territory. This time we had a close view of the big square houses, standing in pairs, which had been built in the early days of the community. They had that barracks-like plainness and solidity which so often appears in phalansterian undertakings, where utility is considered more important than design. However, with the disappearance of community discipline a significant change seemed to have taken place in the life of the Doukhobors who remained, and now the brick houses stood out among a rash of small huts and cabins, like castle keeps over a mediæval village. I do not know how many people lived in these conglomerations of meagre dwellings, for the only Doukhobors we saw were a couple of shawled women lolloping and shouting after a herd of cows, but there was certainly an impression of overcrowding, and, since cleanliness as well as godliness seems among Doukhobors to increase rather than diminish among the radicals and extremists, the cabins of these moderates looked far less tidy and pleasing than the scrupulously clean dwellings and neat gardens of the Sons of Freedom.

We toiled on past them into the foothills, and began to climb out of sight of the valley, into a region of thick new snow which bore the marks of very few wheels. Before long the flakes started to fall again, lashing our faces in the scurries of the wind, and, realising that we had now walked six miles and had not seen a single car that could possibly have given us a long-distance lift, even if its driver had been so inclined, we began to discuss whether it would be wiser to return to Grand Forks rather than carry on over the mountain towards Greenwood, which was still nearly thirty miles ahead.

However, as we stood hesitating, opportunity presented itself in the prosaic form of a gasoline truck, whose driver was humane enough to disregard the rules of his particular form of transport. We climbed in; I had never imagined the cabin of a lorry could seem so snug and comfortable. The driver seemed rather taciturn, and I think his first opinion about us was that we were a little demented. To the average western Canadian, who rarely moves more than half a mile without his car, there is something eccentric in the mere act of walking, and for two people to be tramping a mountain road in this weather must have struck this driver as the height of lunacy. However, when we explained ourselves, he became more open and sympathetic, and I could almost read his brain cogitating that a writer must be expected to act a little peculiarly and might even be justified in doing so if he were earning money by it.

He expanded into conversation and began to tell us about his own work of taking "gas" on long hauls through the southern valleys and mountain ranges. Then we came to a road junction and a sign-post, bearing the single word "Phoenix" and pointing leftwards up a little road where the drifting snow was completely unmarked by any traffic.

"Now there's a place you want to see," the driver said.

"Phoenix—what is it?" I asked, pleased by the name.

"It's a big old ghost town."

"We've seen plenty of ghost towns up and down the west," I replied. "I don't know that we want to look at any more."

"Man, I'm telling you, Phoenix is the ghost town of all ghost towns. They left it more than twenty years ago, but everything's there still—a whole dead town, with miles and miles of streets, 4,500 feet up in the mountains! There's just one inhabitant left, an old man who keeps the pumps going in the mine and lives alone in the middle of all those ruins! I wouldn't take his job at any price!"

"What was Phoenix—a gold town?"

"Copper. They struck there about the same time as Greenwood, but Phoenix was the biggest mine of the lot—at one time they were supposed to be turning out half the copper ore in Canada. But it was the old, old story. The ore got too poor for them to make enough profit, so they started another mine way up the coast, at a place called Anyox. They just pulled out of here overnight, as you might say, didn't give a damn what happened to all the little shopkeepers who went bust when the miners left. And then, when they'd got all they wanted out of Anyox, why, they left that too."

"But why do they even trouble to keep the mine clear at Phoenix?"

"There's plenty of ore still there, and one day they hope the price will go up sky-high, and then they can open up again and make a killing. But I don't know if they ever will. Still, it's a place you sure oughter see. Have to go in on foot or take a car, for there ain't any way of getting there otherwise. Used to be two railroads going there in the old days, but they've been tore up long ago."

However, I felt no desire to trudge through the snow to see even the greatest of ghost towns, and Inge confirmed my feeling by remarking, "We'll wait until the Phoenix rises again."

The driver looked at her a little doubtfully. "Ma'am, you may have to wait a darn long time. They'll have to spend a pile getting that old mine into trim, and they ain't going to do that until they're dead sure of getting it back."

He ruminated a little and then went on: "You never know what will happen in these parts. Them old hills round here, they must be full of gold and copper if only a person could strike the right spots. Now they tell me there's a chap up at Greenwood who's hit a tidy pay dirt in a spot where dozens of folk have tried before and never even found colours. He's gotten more than two grand out of the first ton of earth he hauled out. It may be just a fluke. You never know at that game. Personally, I'd sooner go on driving my truck. I shan't get rich at that, but at least I know where I stand."

He dropped us at Greenwood, where gangs of little red-cheeked Japanese children were tobogganing in the hilly streets, and after lunch we walked again for almost an hour down the narrow valley, past mountainsides which were dotted with piles of dirt from old mines, past a deserted village with its schoolhouse and its great sawmill falling into ruin, until we got a ride with a pair of cowboys who were going into the hills to bring some cattle down from the ranges. One of them explained that the open mountain tops in this part of British Columbia were mostly public property, but the ranchers were allowed to graze cattle there from the spring until the late autumn. When winter set in the cattle had to be rounded up and brought within fences on the rancher's own land. From that time until the cold weather ended the open ranges were reserved for the deer, who otherwise might find it hard to survive, and any cows caught there were seized and confiscated by the game wardens. They were starting the first winter round-up.

We left the cowboys at a desolate part of the valley about six miles east of Rock Creek. It was already late in the afternoon, and, with the thick dark clouds overhead, the light was fading into an early dusk. It had been a much slower day's travelling than we had anticipated—less than sixty miles since Grand Forks—and we began to wonder whether we should be able to cross the mountains that night. The bitter cold we experienced farther east had eased a little, but there was a thin, icy drizzle which made walking hardly more pleasant. We passed a new bridge where a line of little fires was sparkling around the green concrete to protect it from the night's frost, and waited at the end of the road diversion to try and catch a vehicle that might be travelling slowly.

It was dark by the time a lorry stopped, and we had already decided to seek a room in the little hotel at Rock Creek. But we changed our minds when the driver said that he would be going as far as Bridesville, a high village half-way over the mountain, and that even if we did not manage to get a lift at that spot, there would be the nightly bus three or four hours later which would take us down into Osoyoos. He had to make some deliveries at a logging camp near Rock Creek, so we got down and waited for him in the café at the hotel. It was full of loggers, who evidently lived in the rooms above; lurching, heavy-shouldered men who tramped about in caulked boots, garnished with floor-destroying spikes which are designed to keep a hold on the slippery tree trunks and which, incidentally, play a gruesome part in the savage fights that sometimes break out in the tougher logging camps.

After a while the lorry-driver returned and we started to climb up the mountain road. Since we had last passed over it several inches more snow had fallen and there was a slippery crust which worried the driver. A little way up the roadside fence was smashed on the edge of the precipice. "The second this week," he commented. "A kid of eighteen went over there yesterday. It was his first driving job."

A little way farther, on the stretch of winding dirt road, a red light was flashed to us from the verge, and we had to edge around a big stationary vehicle. We stopped to see what was happening. It was a logging truck, piled high with thick spruce trunks, and its air-brakes had given out. The driver dared not travel any farther with such a load behind him.

Bridesville, when we had first passed through it a few days previously, had seemed a quiet and unspectacular place which made no demand on the attention or the memory. But what our driver now recounted (the tale was confirmed to us later by a retired Mountie) gave it a very different aspect, for it was a centre of violence and crime during the Prohibition era. A large gang of bootleggers had made it their depot, and thence they would carry the liquor over the mountain trails by pack-horse, or by wagons protected by guards of armed outriders. Most of the villagers had been involved in this trade, and some of them had been killed in the battles on the frontier with the revenue authorities and with the hijackers. The smugglers maintained their own reign of terror in the mountains and they did not hesitate to shoot anyone who stood in their way. One man who had worked as their agent was shot down in public in the hotel because he had asked for a larger pay-off, and other people died less spectacularly. Prohibition ended, Bridesville resumed its old quiet existence as a secluded mountain village, where, if any smuggling is still carried on, it is done on a modest and peaceful scale.

By the time we reached this place of violent history the snow was falling hard and fast, and it lay more than a foot deep in the village road, which ran round in a loop a hundred yards or so back from the highway. Bridesville seemed completely lifeless in the faint, livid reflection which even on that dense night was thrown up by the snow. A few cabins on either side of the road stood out in dull black, with not a light visible, and it was only the hotel and the store that showed any signs of human activity. The lorry-driver stopped at the store. "Better hang around for the bus," he said. "I guess you can wait in the hotel."

So we trudged along a couple of hundred yards to the hotel. A single porch light weakly lit the boarded front, but only one room within seemed to be illuminated. We opened the door and walked in; it was a small parlour with a big black stove, three or four tables and a tiny serving bar on which a few beer bottles were ranged. A fat old woman stood in the middle of the room and stared at us hostilely. "What do you want?" she said abruptly, and suspicion mingled with enmity in her manner. I asked her at what time the bus left for Osoyoos. "I don't keep any bus stop," she squawked nasally. "You can't wait here. You'll have to wait out in the road." That we were potential customers did not influence her in the least; she seemed to be impregnated with a gall that overcame calculation and humanity alike, and the zest with which she spoke precluded any parleying. When we were outside she actually turned off all the lights at the front of the hotel—this at six in the evening—to discourage us from trying again.

We wandered back to the store. There our experience was more or less repeated. The girl behind the counter was perhaps less actively unpleasant, but in her own stolid way she looked at us just as hostilely as the old woman had done. Still, she did sell us a packet of cigarettes and melted sufficiently to tell us that when the bus came, in about three hours, it would pass along the main road and not through the village street. But when we asked if there were any place in which we could shelter, since we had been refused at the hotel, the shut look of animosity came over her face again, and she merely answered a laconic "No!"

Outside the snow was still falling, and to wait out of doors for the hours until the bus came seemed impossible. There was nothing for it but to try the difficult feat of hitching a lift in the dark on a deserted mountain road. We stamped out of Bridesville, relieving our feelings at the same time by uttering ineffectual but satisfying curses.

I can only explain the animosity of these people as a heritage from the violence of the past, an ingrained suspicion which still makes the villagers see every strange person as a potential danger whom they must hustle from their doors as quickly as possible. If this is the case, it is certainly an interesting example of mental attitudes surviving and affecting people's actions long after the physical cause has vanished.

As we had expected, there was almost no traffic over the mountain on such a night; only two cars passed within the next three-quarters of an hour and neither of them stopped. The snow fell steadily, and we could feel our legs and feet growing numb in spite of the fact that we tramped up and down all the time. At last a half-ton truck drew to a halt fifty yards ahead. There were two men in the cab; they could find room for Inge, but I should have to ride in the back. On these terms they would be glad to take us —every extra person would help to keep the truck from skidding off the road.

This journey was the most uncomfortable ride I ever had. The back of the truck had been filled with boulders to weight it down, and though I managed to clear myself a tiny spot where I could squat on the rucksack with my back to the cab, I was very cramped and had to keep watching the rocks which, whenever the truck took a corner, lurched and rolled thunderously across the steel floor. Added to that, it was impossible to hide completely from the wind, while, as we began to descend, the snow changed into heavy rain which lashed across my head and shoulders. After an interminable hour we at last arrived in Osoyoos. I was drenched and stiff when we alighted at the hotel, but the prospect of a meal and a hot bath seemed to make up for everything else.

Inge, I noticed when we got into our room, was in a state of great amusement. "Do you know what one of the men said when you got on the back?" she laughed. I shook my head, thinking that perhaps he had uttered some kind of rustic gallantry. "He asked me, 'Is he your Dad?'"

"He must have meant it as a flattery to you," I explained without conviction. "A clumsy one, don't you think? Besides, it was very dark, and he couldn't see me properly," I went on, trying to convince myself that my thirty-eight years did not hang upon me with quite such crushing and evident weight.

"Of course, how could he?" Inge replied, but I was not at all pleased by the quizzical look in her eyes. So I changed the subject. "Did they tell you anything interesting?"

"Why, yes. The young one was rather nice, and he was talking all the time about one thing or another. Apparently he started as a cowboy, and then he got tired of working for other people and went out to cut logs. He said that he had two dollars in his pocket when he started off, and in five years he'd built himself up so that he now has 30,000 dollars' worth of equipment. Why can't we do something like that?"

We talked airily around the subject for a while with, of course, no real intention at all of going out into the woods with a power saw to find our fortune. Nevertheless we were really impressed by the quickness with which relatively large profits are made in logging. The ex-cowboy was even a minor example, for in our own village on Vancouver Island I knew two different men who had each started out from scratch at the end of the war and were now worth nearly 100,000 dollars each. Such a situation, where the working man can rise so easily into the middle class of employers and small capitalists, does a great deal to perpetuate the intense democracy and individualism of Canadian society, for when social divisions are fluid and élites have little opportunity to crystallise, class discrimination does not thrive, and the rich pattern of snobberies which exists between classes in England is hardly to be found in western Canada at all.

38.

Down in the valley the air was mild and relaxing after the rigours of the mountains, and there was not a speck of snow to be seen. The next morning, indeed, our departure was delayed by a really phenomenal cloudburst, which kept us cooped in a drug-store for nearly an hour while the road outside steamed with spray and the druggist called down maledictions on the Provincial Government for the lake which formed across the road and threatened to enter his shop. "The only time they did anything to improve these roads," he wailed, "was before the last election. And now we shall have to wait two years until the next." "Get up a petition," said an old man who was sheltering beside us. "A good strong petition is almost as good as an election, for they think that all the signers will vote against them next time if they don't do anything to placate them. I should try it on—I've known it work at times."

With that fragment of rustic political cynicism echoing in our ears we walked out and began to make our way up the valley to the junction with the Princeton road, forty miles north. Here again the highway was almost completely flooded for long stretches of sometimes half a mile at a time, and there were places in which we could keep our feet dry only by edging along the little ridges of tussock grass which had grown under the wayside fences.

Our first driver that morning was another logger in another little half-ton truck, out for a weekend spree, and he showed the usual uninhibited Canadian inclination to talk about himself with only the minimum encouragement. Like so many of the people we met, he had gone through a whole gamut of jobs—for in western Canada adaptability is considered a virtue, and the rolling stone is a man who has gathered useful experience, so that a carpenter will turn up next month as a logger, and six months after that go prospecting, and in another year will get himself a gill-netter and start fishing, and nobody will think him any the worse, provided he has money to spend and, in some form at least, that minimum attribute of human dignity, a car.

This man's last work had been on a fruit farm, but he had soon found that there was no money in this business for the hired man, so he had taken to logging. Now he was skidding spruce logs out of the woods to the point at which they were loaded on to the trailer trucks. It was work that needed a great deal of presence of mind and agility to avoid the danger that always accompanies highly mechanised logging operations.

With the zest which such people show in revealing the utmost details of their private affairs to complete strangers, he went on to tell us that he was paid piece rates for his work and, after deducting taxes and two dollars a day for his keep in the camp where he lived, he received an average of 300 dollars a month. He had not yet been given his pay cheque for the last month, but he had 80 dollars in his pocket (nearly £30), and he intended to spend that on a good binge for the two days he would be away from work.

This, indeed, was a good example of the way in which the British Columbian loggers earn and spend their money. The better-paid grades of this industry are the aristocracy of western labour, and in the forests of the coast, where the Douglas firs and cedars run often to more than six feet in diameter and 200 feet in height, it is not uncommon to encounter fallers whose pay checks reach as high as 750 dollars a month. And as befits an aristocracy, the loggers spend on a lavish scale the money they earn so amply. The danger of their work—for it has a phenomenally high death rate —makes them reckless, and most of their money is spent, not on permanent things like houses, but on articles of prestige, like expensive cars, or on heavy drinking and other money-burning amusements, so that even a short period of unemployment will find most of the loggers and their families living on the storekeeper's credit. The few who are careful with their large earnings are the ambitious men who become master loggers and ascend rapidly into the capitalist class.

Our communicative logger dropped us at the junction of the Princeton road, and then we walked westward towards the mountains and a little way on secured a perch on a pile of ropes which covered the deck of a large co-operative lorry. Keremeos, the town towards which we were now travelling, was about twenty miles on from the Okanagan Valley, and the first half of the road wound high up among the rocky crags, until it ran into snow once again. Though the sun was very brilliant, the air became intensely brittle and cold; in travelling over the whole of British Columbia one soon gets used to these rapid transitions of climate. The mountains here were very bare, with only a few twisted trees growing on the clefts of the piled Cyclopean rocks; a deep black tarn which ran, long and narrow, for a fair distance beside us showed no sign of animal life on its forbidding surface.

Downward from the head of the pass the rock walls receded and we came into a valley which was at first stony pasture and scrubby woodland, and then gave way gradually to dairy farms and deep brown tilth and finally to apple orchards. When at last we reached Keremeos, greeted by a big grinning Indian who waved from the sidewalk, the sun shone richly over the broad flat land which stretched far out on either side of the town to the mountain chains that cupped this fertile upland valley in their insulating embrace and held the warmth to ripen its fields and orchards.

Keremeos itself was a small, clean and amiable town, with no great pretensions and only a fluttering premonition, as the last of the season's apples were packed away in the co-operative warehouses, of the event that in a very few weeks would bring its name into all the newspapers up and down North America.

"Eat what you can while the going is good," cracked a fat, plum-eyed Latin-looking man in the little white restaurant where we ate our lunch. "Why, ain't you heard?" he went on, when we looked puzzled. "There's an Adventist woman here, one of the farmer's wives, and she's been goin' around telling folks that Judgment Day is coming some time next month."

"Well, she's not the first."

"No, I guess she ain't, but folks don't learn from that. You know what the Adventists have been doing round here? Selling their farms and everything else at knockdown prices, and paying off their debts as fast as they can so that they'll have nothing on their minds when the judging starts. Boy, I could kick myself when I think of the bargains I've missed this week, but somehow I didn't feel like taking advantage of folks like that. After all, what if they're right? I'd be among the goats on the great day sure enough then." He went off into a shout of knee-slapping laughter.

"But what do they intend to do now?" Inge asked.

"They're just quietly settling up their business and then they're going to shut themselves up in their old meeting hall and pray till the Good Lord comes to fetch 'em away in a chariot of fire. Boy, what a selfish lot those Adventists are! They don't care a damn for you and me so long as they're well in on the bandwagon when Gabriel blows his horn."

The fat man dissolved into laughter once again. "Boy," he gurgled, with a final bout of knee-slapping, "I wouldn't be that prophetess for a thousand bucks on the day after Judgment Day don't dawn!"

After we had left him, we debated whether we should seek out some of the Adventists and see what they had to say. Inge shook her head. "No, they'll only resent us. In any case, we know how those people talk. Remember Mr. X." Mr. X. was an acquaintance on Vancouver Island who had sold his business and settled down to live on the proceeds with a calm confidence that it would last him until the end of the world. So we left the Adventists to their preparations and struck along the valley.

It was a perfect late autumn day, the first time for weeks that we had been able to take off our jackets and enjoy the sunshine, and we idled on past the orchards where tiny rejected apples still hung on the trees like big opaque garnets. Then, when we felt it was time to be going on, we hitched a lift from yet another logger, in yet another small truck, who took us all the forty miles along the Similkameen River to Princeton.

The Similkameen was very little different from the other rivers of these high valleys—shallow and fast, with a rocky bed which spread out well on either side of the present stream to show the breadth of the spring torrents. The valley narrowed off and rose once again into a snowy and rocky region. There was only one town, at Hedley, where a big copper mine thrust into the mountains; for the rest, this end was barren, deserted and different in every way from the broad, fertile and populous alluvial area around Keremeos.

Princeton was a largish town lying under the mass of the main Coast mountains. Our approach to it was dominated by the towering sludge-heaps which came from the concentrator of the big Copper Mountain mine a few miles to the south—the industry which gives the town its principal economic basis. The streets were a morass of melting slush, and we quickly decided that the best thing would be to leave it immediately and climb on to the firmer snow which we could certainly expect on the high mountain road towards Hope. So we went up the hill to the west, with the grimy buildings and sidings of the copper works lying below in the hollow, and came at last on to a small plateau where the woods started and the snow bore our weight without collapsing into a squelching, sucking pool with every step we took.

Our hopes of traffic were not very high, for the snow was deepening and nobody would take this eighty-mile mountain road in such weather if he could possibly avoid it. We stamped around on the hilltop for what seemed a really interminable period, with the rare cars hurrying by, until we finally decided that if the next vehicle did not stop we would abandon the celebrated new highway and go down into the town to catch the night train into the Fraser Valley.

A large military lorry came lumbering up, and, since army drivers are not usually allowed to carry passengers, we hailed it in a very feeble and defeatist manner. The driver stopped immediately, and he and his companion scrambled out to help us climb into the back. They were going thirty miles to an engineers' camp in the bush, and they would gladly take us on our way, so long as we did not make ourselves too obvious. There was a bench on which we could sit, and there were three or four enormous oil drums on the floor.

The lorry was slow, particularly on the steep hills, but at least it held the road solidly, and the drums, which we watched apprehensively, remained as firm as rocks. We did not have the best of views from our unobtrusive positions, but we saw enough to tell us that we were climbing all the time into a thickly forested mountain country, with great falling slopes beside the road and further ranges rising in succession beyond, patterned with the broken black and white of the snow-covered trees. It was the most deserted piece of country we had yet encountered; farming and mining had not penetrated, even logging seemed to be done on a slight and patchy scale, and there were no habitations of any kind for the first forty miles—only occasional tiny log cabins by the roadside which were clearly used for the most temporary purposes.

The soldiers showed the greatest possible consideration; we had hardly started off when the truck stopped and the driver came hurrying back to lend Inge his sheepskin jacket. And then they went nearly ten miles beyond the turning for their depot in order to take us to the only café on that eighty miles of road, where we should stand a much better chance of a lift and in any case could wait more comfortably for it.

The café was a large, low log house with spreading eaves, flanked on each side by a row of rustic tourist cabins which seemed, from the cars parked before two or three of them, to be inhabited by hunters even in this bleak weather. Inside it was cosy and inviting. A great log fire burnt in the wide fireplace, a commercial traveller was wolfing a teabone steak, and a well-built and amiable blonde stood behind the glittering chrome bar and served us with coffee and excellent home-made pie, the *pièce de résistance* of the Canadian snack-bar, whose quality covers a surprising range between the usual execrability and the occasional delectability.

16

The soldiers were evidently in no hurry to return to their unit, where discipline seemed to be slack and genial, and they stayed and talked with us for the best part of half an hour. They were both men from the east, Bluenoses as the westerners call them, and a perceptible difference of manner as well as of accent distinguished them from the British Columbians. They lacked that hail-fellow-well-met expansiveness, with its big talk and grand ambitions, which is so often noticeable among people bred west of the Rockies, and which is an inevitable characteristic of a land only just emerging from the frontier era of high-blown individualism. The eastern Canadians have a longer record of settlement, and they have retained more of the European reserve.

They were very cynical about their present assignment—building bridges across the mountain rivers which could only be used, in any foreseeable future, by the tourist interests who organised trips on horseback among the mountains. They regarded it as an obvious instance of political interest. Whether their assumption was true I am in no position to judge, but their remarks led me to reflect on the completely cynical attitude which the average Canadian adopts towards public life. He takes it almost for granted that graft and chicanery are an essential part of politics, and yet, with what seems a massive inconsistency, he still goes out to vote for a party which, if it is returned to power, he will criticise and condemn, usually with every justification, until the next election day. I suppose this ambivalence is a sign of a pervading feeling of insecurity which makes the average man hang on to a familiar though unsatisfactory makeshift rather than set out on the chancy seas of social experimentation.

The soldiers left and we hung around for a while, drawn back towards the warmth whenever we looked on the cold scene outside. It began to grow dark, and few drivers stopped at the café. There was a pair of hunters, but when we went out to look at their car we discovered a headless elk strapped on the side, whose gory neck so disconcerted us that we left them alone. Then a cowboy —chaps and spurs all complete—shepherded in a giggling, drunken fat man; they seemed a most unprepossessing pair with whom to travel a slippery road. Finally, a long-distance lorry drew up outside, a huge silver-painted vehicle with an equally large trailer. The driver came in, we got into conversation with him and found that he was going to Vancouver, and he agreed to take us the seventy miles to Chilliwack, where we proposed to spend the night before going on to the Mennonite settlements.

The drive up over the 4,500-foot Allison Pass and then down to Hope was an anxious rather than a frightening experience. It was too dark for us to see much of the precipices, the road was wide and well-made, one of the best in British Columbia, and though the snow was thick and slippery, the heavy truck in which we travelled was better fitted to remain stable than any ordinary car, while it was equipped with every possible device to make winter travelling safe, including a hopper which spread sand before the wheels wherever the road became unduly slippery. It was the falling snow rather than that on the road which was the principal threat, for when we began to go down the western slopes it fell so thickly that we could only see a few yards ahead of us, and the driver had to stop every other mile to clear the clogged windscreen. He accepted it all with great equanimity. "This is nothing to what happens in the middle of winter," he said. Then he pointed out some thin red poles, more than ten feet high, which stood by the roadside at one point. "They're put up to warn the snowplough men not to run into the fences, and sometimes the drifts get so deep that only a little bit at the top is left showing."

Nevertheless, we were all glad when, as we ran down the last stretch of straight highway towards Hope, the snow changed into rain and in the woods we saw once again the frondlike boughs of the cedars drooping like melancholy Edwardian whiskers.

At Hope we stopped for a while at an all-night café; there were several of the great trailer trucks drawn up, and inside a line of youths and girls sat at the coffee-bar, waiting for long-distance rides into the interior. Thirty miles on, at Chilliwack, we left the truck and went to a musty hotel where aged dogs slept on the stairs and dusty heads of moose and mountain sheep decorated the brown-stained walls of the corridors, and where the proprietor, eyeing our rucksack with disfavour, promptly demanded his payment in advance.

39.

The centre of Mennonite settlement in British Columbia is a small town called Yarrow, a few miles south-west of Chilliwack. The next morning we walked along the road through the meadows towards a range of low, tree-covered hills which mark the southern

edge of the Fraser Valley. Here we encountered our first Mennonite, a fat little German, who stopped his car to give us a lift
and barked, "No smoking, please!" when I began to get in with
a cigarette which I had forgotten to throw away. It was not a very
good start, and he proved a rather sulky and uncommunicative
companion as he drove us the rest of the way to the alluvial
meadows where Yarrow stands.

We were disappointed by what we saw. In our minds we had
associated the Mennonites with such movements as the Brueder-
hof, and we had expected to encounter a series of great community
farms. Instead, we came into a wide road which ran dead straight
for nearly two miles over the level land, and on each side of it
were little white clap-boarded houses, with green roofs and geo-
metrically regular patches of bush fruits and strawberries, and
often, behind them, white and green Mansard-roofed barns, all
very spick and span and as soulless as a painted toy farm village.
Indeed, it was only this superlatively neat orderliness that made
Yarrow look like anything more than a typical fairly prosperous
Canadian farming settlement.

A few months before we had come across some numbers of a
Mennonite newspaper, so we thought of searching out the editor
in order to learn something about the community. His office was
a little workshop on the edge of the town where odd printing jobs
were carried out; there was no answer to our knocking, and we
were about to leave when a young man came out of the garden
behind and asked if he could help us. The editor of the paper
was away, and in any case the paper no longer existed, but if
we cared to step into the office he would be glad to talk to us.
So we went in and sat among the stacks of paper and the racks
of type.

He himself had only been in Yarrow for a short time, and we
should be better informed on its particular history by other people
whom we could meet when we went farther into the town. But he
could tell us about the movement in general, and as we were
anxious to clarify our ideas on who the Mennonites were and what
they actually stood for, we encouraged him to do so.

The Mennonites, he said, were the direct descendants of the
Anabaptists of the Reformation, and to this day they maintained
the principal tenets of the old Anabaptist faith—the idea of justification through faith, the belief in adult as distinct from infant
baptism, and the literal interpretation of the commandment

"Thou shalt not kill" as an injunction not to take human life under any circumstances.

But beyond these general beliefs there emerged very wide divergences of practice between the groups which claim common descent from the Anabaptists. Both the Hutterites and the Amish Brethren, who broke away centuries ago, developed communist ideas of village organisation, and subjected their settlements to a very strict regulation of almost every detail of secular and religious conduct. The more orthodox Mennonites avoided these extreme social conclusions. In their original villages they drew a middle course between individual proprietorship and common ownership; each family had its own piece of land for individual cultivation, but there was always a large area held in common for grazing and for filling the village granary which provided for hard times.

Their whole history was one of persecutions and emigrations. They moved out of Holland and Switzerland and Moravia into Prussia, and then, persecuted in Germany, some went to America in the seventeenth century to found the first of the Pennsylvania Dutch settlements, and many others emigrated to Russia, at the invitation of Catherine the Great, who recognised them as good farmers and gave them the land on which they established their villages in the Ukraine.

For nearly a hundred years the Mennonites lived successfully and peacefully in Russia; then, like their neighbours and fellow-pacifists the Doukhobors, they came up against Tsarist introduction of compulsory military service. From 1874 onwards they began to leave Russia in large numbers for the United States and Canada. The emigration continued after the Russian Revolution, for, though many of the Mennonites at first regarded this event as a welcome end to Tsarist persecution, they soon found themselves victimised by the religious intolerance of the Bolsheviks, and in many cases whole villages abandoned their possessions and their farms and fled to Canada.

In the prairie provinces, such as Manitoba and Saskatchewan, they re-established the semi-communal form of their Russian villages, and Kropotkin, who travelled through this country in the 1890's, found much to admire in the mutual aid which they displayed. It was in Saskatchewan that they found themselves living once again side by side with their old and turbulent neighbours the Doukhobors, and there is one story of this period which illustrates admirably the differences between the two sects, and, since I have already departed once in this paragraph from the strict details of the young Mennonite's account, I may as well re-count it. At that time the fields were being ravaged by gophers, and the Doukhobors, who extended their rejection of killing into their relationships with the animal world, were faced with the problem of how to rid themselves of the little rodents without destroying them. Eventually they solved it, at least to their own satisfaction, by catching the gophers alive in cages and at night taking them over the river and releasing them in the neighbour-ing Mennonite settlement. The Mennonites, who were not vege-tarians, killed off the gophers with German thoroughness, but the Doukhobor consciences were salved, since they had not directly caused this massacre of their little brothers.

To return to Yarrow and our conversation, we gathered that the tendency among the sect had been for their social organisation to weaken with every remove farther away from their original home. In British Columbia there was only individual ownership, and, while the people had started their farmers' co-operatives, they had very little in the way of community institutions which were not paralleled in ordinary Canadian settlements. Even their religion was concerning itself more with purely theological matters and less with the daily lives of its members.

Our informant ended by saying that he himself stood rather out-side the Mennonite community, because he had been converted to the Pentecostal Church and believed that his fellow-Menno-nites were lacking in consciousness of the terrible events which, in his opinion, certainly presaged the end of the present world. We were rather surprised to find Adventism lifting its head even here, but it seemed as though the general ebbing of the dynamism of the original Anabaptist faith had left a vacuum in which other revivalist creeds could readily enter. We expected an eloquent attempt at conversion, but the young man merely presented us with a copy of a German-language revivalist magazine. It was en-titled *The Midnight Call*, and when we read it afterwards, we found gloating prophecies of cosmic catastrophes in the near future— the faithful would naturally be exempt—and gruesome clinical descriptions of the sicknesses which had overtaken those who scoffed at the Pentecostal faith healers.

We left the printing shop and went down to the little town. It did not take long to tell that the Mennonites, at least in this district, had made little effort to maintain their traditional character. The names over their shops were German, but the goods in the windows were the same as those in any other small-town store, and the notices and advertisements were all in English. There was no sectarian uniform like that of the Hutterites, and most of the people looked and spoke like ordinary Fraser Valley farmers. There were a few old women in black shawls, a few elderly men in formal clothes which carried a reminiscence of a Europe of the past, and it was the people of this generation who still spoke German among themselves. The rest conversed in English, and so also did the children whom we met coming out of school, though they had a perceptible German accent. There was a small restaurant down the street, and here we hoped that we might at least find a reasonably cooked German meal. But although it was kept by Mennonites, this establishment had surrendered in every respect to the Canadian spirit, and we had to be content with sausage and mash cooked with the standard indifference.

The man in the printing office had told us that the people most likely to help were the pastor and the local councillor, and we walked through the village in search of them, past the big white church and the collegiate institution which provides higher education for the Mennonite children in the Fraser Valley. There was nobody at home in the pastor's house, and when we sought the councillor in the office of the transport agency which he ran, we found that he was away in Vancouver. We were rather at a loss now as to where we could get our information on the history of the settlement, but we remembered having seen a bookshop and decided to return there.

The presence of this bookshop was one of the few respects in which Yarrow really did differ from most western Canadian towns. In that country bookshops—as distinct from the drugstore where a few volumes are sold as a side-line—are usually found only in the largest towns. Outside Victoria, Vancouver and Calgary, indeed, Yarrow was the only town on our travels in which I can actually remember encountering a bookshop. It was a curious place, with many volumes, both in German and English, on Mennonite history and doctrine, and with a good variety of standard literature. The proprietor, a typical elderly South German intellectual, in appearance at least, was the author of some of the books there—reminiscences of life in Russia thirty years ago. He had left the country as recently as 1930, after having tried to work with the Communists for many patient years as the

commissar of his own village. Then, when the religious persecutions began and the Mennonites started to disappear in large
numbers to Siberia, he realised that there was no chance of freedom
under the Bolsheviks, and he finally fled, at the end of the last
wave of Mennonite migrations.

From him, and from an insurance agent, a much younger and
more Canadianised man who gave us a lift on to the main Vancouver high-way, we learnt the history of the Mennonite migration to the Fraser Valley. All the Yarrow people had left Russia
between 1924 and 1930. They arrived in Canada penniless, even
their steamship passages having been advanced to them by the
Canadian Pacific Railway, and they were only enabled to start
farming in British Columbia because of the solidarity of the older
Mennonite communities in North America.

They began to settle at Yarrow in 1928. Then it was a waterlogged marsh which nobody else had tried to cultivate; there
were no ditches and the land was flooded whenever there was
heavy rain. But this did not deter the Mennonites, who were experienced farmers and who realised that the land was good. Ten
families moved in to start the settlement. They built rough houses
of boards and barns of packing cases, with roofs of flattened oil
cans. One farmer even sheltered his cow and calf in the hollow
stump of a cottonwood tree. During the first summer, with a
strange inconsistency for such opponents of alcohol, they worked
in the neighbouring hopfields to enable them to live while they
cultivated their own farms and began to drain the land. From that
beginning Yarrow grew rapidly, and it became the nucleus of a
whole spreading area of Mennonite settlement which in recent
years must have added nearly 10,000 people to the population of
the Fraser Valley. But, as our first informant had told us, they had
never tried to re-establish their old communal economic organisation; it had already been broken up when they left Russia, and for
this reason it was all the more easy to adapt themselves to Canadian
forms of living, a process which has been increasing rapidly in
recent years. Indeed, it has now reached the stage when the Mennonites themselves insist that they are good Canadians and
nothing else. There is very little struggle among them to keep their
German identity, and in this, as in most other respects, they have
proved very much different from their former neighbours in
Russia, the Doukhobors.

The only point on which the Mennonites still practise any important defiance of Canadian normality seems, indeed, to be their objection to taking part in war. We discussed this with the insurance official as he was driving us down the main road towards Vancouver. There was no real Mennonite line, he said, on the question of participation in war. The basic objection was to taking human life, but it was a matter of individual conscience how far that objection was carried. Some rejected only actual combatant duties, others found it necessary to make a completer withdrawal from war. But it seemed always a matter of negative protest, and we saw no evidence that the Mennonites, in Canada at least, had been impelled by any kind of militant zeal to demonstrate against the social tendencies they condemned.

Indeed, as we later walked along the highway we agreed that this visit had been a most dispiriting experience. It had shown us the North American melting-pot at work with a vengeance, breaking down by a kind of environmental digestion the independence of a people who had maintained their identity with the greatest tenacity over four centuries of persecutions. There are many things about traditional Mennonite ideas and ways of living which I do not personally like, but I doubt if they have been replaced by anything better. And, if diversity and character and oddity have any value in the world, as I am sure they have, it is saddening to have witnessed them in such signal subjection to the forces of social unity.

40.

The last stretch of the road down the Fraser Valley to Vancouver was like a recapitulation of the very first afternoon of all our travels, past the farms and the smallholdings, the wayside fruit stands and the little towns, the suburban streets and the used-car lots. There was the bathetic sense of a journey ending, like the feeling one had as a child returning from the summer holidays. The drivers who gave us short lifts lodged in the mind for single flashes of oddity. There was the amiable serenity of one man in the late fifties who had taken a farm which he intended to give a five years' trial before he made up his mind to stay in the valley. There was the solemn old Dutchman who alone had an original theory of our intentions and asked us if we were travelling the country as missionaries. And there was the man in a prosperous car who described himself as a beachcomber. When we looked sceptical, he explained that as the logging booms were being towed down the coast to the sawmills they sometimes encountered rough weather which broke them up and usually detached at least a few isolated logs; he made a very profitable living cruising up and down the coast with his motor boat and salvaging any valuable-looking logs which he saw washed up on the isolated beaches.

As if to remind us once again of the living presence of violence and evil in the world through which we had travelled, a new notice stood beside one of the farmhouses, bearing the unadorned words CUSTOM KILLING, and our last driver took us to Vancouver by way of the prison farm where the guards stood with their rifles in the wooden watch-towers.

The next day we boarded the boat back to Victoria. This time it was one of the luxury ships, with its cinema and its abundant lounges, and we reclined with the easy insolence of travellers who feel they have really earned their rest, as the boat threaded through the narrow rocky passages of the Gulf Islands and finally sailed into Victoria Harbour.

Victoria is one of the pleasantest towns I know at which to arrive. Instead of the ragged slums or the fish-strewn wharves which greet one at so many seaports, there is a neat, square basin, with slopes of bright turf coming down towards the water, and usually a cluster of white yachts and ketches on which the gulls perch and quarrel. Lawns and trees and shrubberies spread back beyond the roads on either side of the basin, and, if one can ignore the granite mock-Gothicism of the Parliament Building behind, there is a feeling of neatness and freshness which one rarely finds anywhere else in Canada. The shopping streets, with their flat sky-lines, are dull and unexciting, but push out into the tree-lined residential streets and into the hilly suburbs, and you will see hundreds of beautifully tended flower gardens, unfenced and open for every passer to enjoy, which in this mild climate bloom far into the winter and some years never cease to bloom. You will discover—among a great deal of neo-Tudor rubbish—bright and simple functional houses which are as well designed as anything on the Pacific coast. You will find beautifully landscaped parks, and fine sandy bays looking out to the hazy islands and the great white mountains of Washington, and corners of woodland, saved from the primeval forest, where wild scillas and little purple cyclamen-like flowers, white lilies and blue lupins and vermilion columbines grow in spring on the close turf, where the arbutus spreads its red, dappled branches and the dogwood opens its big green-white stars and the alien broom rampages in golden thickets to a height unknown on its native hillsides. Even in winter there is something of this neat and fresh and floral look about Victoria which strikes the eye upon returning.

But like so many decorative towns, Victoria has a central stagnation, a core of emptiness which becomes evident upon very short acquaintance. I suppose this is partly because it is to a great extent an unproductive city—an administrative capital full of politicians and bureaucrats; a tourist centre for American innocents which masquerades under the fraudulent title of "A Little Bit of Old England" and teems with Antique Shops and Harris Tweed Shops and Scotch Wool Shops and Staffordshire China Shops and Olde Devonshire Tea Shoppes selling indigestible crumpets; a haven, brutally referred to by rival cities as "the graveyard of Canada", which attracts a most amazing collection of superannuated snobs and fogeys from every remote corner of the Empire. There are streets in the suburbs where you will see hardly a single young person, but only the lame and deaf and the feeble; there are schools where third-generation Canadians still send their children to learn Cheltenham accents and upper middle-class affectations which died in England round about 1939.

There were three hours to fill before we could catch the daily bus to our village, and we thought that some of the time might well be spent looking at some of the Indian exhibits in the museum. They might have more relevance now we had seen the places from which they originated and the descendants of the people who made them. In a way they had, since we knew more about the function of each object in the pattern of the old coastal life. Yet, as we examined the poles and the great six-foot feast dishes and peered into the cases of elaborate dance masks and intricately woven ritual garments, the age to which they belonged seemed as distant as ever; beside these achievements of the past, there was something very pathetic and doomed about the attempts to cling to an old tradition which we had found among the survivors.

In another way this collection was symbolic not only of the Indians it represented but also of the city in which it was gathered. For these magnificent examples of the only great art that has appeared in Canada either before or since the white man came were crammed away in a gloomy, constricted basement where one saw nothing to its full advantage. At the same time, two spacious and well-lit floors up above were filled with faded and moth-eaten stuffed animals. It was typical of the spirit which animates this petty capital, to thrust the bold living creations of the human imagination well underground, and to elevate above them these miserable examples of taxidermy, from which every semblance of animal vitality had long disappeared. The instinct to play safe, to preserve the respectabilities—perhaps Victoria was a Bit of Old England after all, of all the generations of English middle-class caution crystallising incongruously in a land of restless growth and movement.